Kirkpatrick William

A Vocabulary Persian Arabic and English

containing such words as have been adopted from the two former of those

languages, and incorporated into the Hindoui, together with some hundred of

compound verbs... Being the seventh Part of the new Hindi Grammar and

Dictionary.

Kirkpatrick William

A Vocabulary Persian Arabic and English
containing such words as have been adopted from the two former of those languages, and incorporated into the Hindoui, together with some hundred of compound verbs... Being the seventh Part of the new Hindi Grammar and Dictionary.

ISBN/EAN: 9783337299538

Printed in Europe, USA, Canada, Australia, Japan

Cover: Foto ©Andreas Hilbeck / pixelio.de

More available books at **www.hansebooks.com**

A

VOCABULARY,

PERSIAN, ARABIC, [AND ENGLISH;

CONTAINING SUCH WORDS

AS HAVE BEEN ADOPTED FROM THE TWO FORMER OF THOSE LANGUAGES,

AND INCORPORATED INTO THE HINDVI:

TOGETHER WITH SOME HUNDREDS OF COMPOUND VERBS

FORMED FROM

PERSIAN OR ARABIC NOUNS,

AND IN UNIVERSAL USE:

BEING THE

SEVENTH PART

OF THE

NEW HINDVI GRAMMAR AND DICTIONARY.

By WILLIAM KIRKPATRICK,

CAPTAIN IN THE SERVICE OF THE HONOURABLE THE EAST-INDIA COMPANY,
AND PERSIAN SECRETARY TO THE COMMANDER IN CHIEF IN INDIA.

LONDON:
PRINTED BY JOSEPH COOPER, DRURY-LANE.
M.DCC.LXXXV.

TO

LAURENCE SULIVAN, Esq:

THE FOLLOWING

DIVISION OF A WORK,

LIBERALLY PATRONIZED,

THROUGH HIS RECOMMENDATION,

BY THE HONOURABLE

THE COURT OF DIRECTORS OF THE EAST-INDIA COMPANY,

AND INTENDED TO BE COMPLETED IN INDIA,

IS MOST RESPECTFULLY INSCRIBED,

AS A TESTIMONY OF THE ESTEEM AND GRATITUDE

OF HIS MOST OBLIGED

AND MOST FAITHFUL SERVANT,

THE AUTHOR.

LONDON,
JANUARY, 1785.

INTRODUCTION.

THE following Vocabulary, when joined to the fifth and sixth parts of the work described at the end of this volume, (and which parts, though ready for the press, depend necessarily for publication on the preparation of the Nagri type) will, I trust, be found to form a very copious, if not a compleat, dictionary of that idiom or dialect of Hindostan generally, though erroneously, called the *Moors* by Europeans, but properly denominated by the natives, the *Hindvi, Hindi,* or *Hindooi.*

With a view to contracting the size of the present volume or division of the work as much as possible, I have purposely omitted many derivatives that are in use, as well abstract and personal nouns, as compound verbs. Thus under جان *Ján* (the soul or life), I have given the compound verb *Ján-déna,* to die, to yield one's life, but have not inserted *Ján-léna,* to kill or slay (literally, to take away life, as the other

b   phrase

phrafe ftrictly fignifies, to give up life) : and fo under *Jida*
(feparate) I have omitted the abftract noun *Júdái* (abfence,
feparation, diftance). In like manner I have omitted feveral
privatives formed by the prefixion of the particle ـے *bé*
(without) : but a little experience in the language will enable
the learner to fupply thefe deficiencies ; fince, with very few
exceptions, compound verbs may be formed at pleafure from
the Perfian and Arabic nouns in ufe, by the addition of one
or other of the Hindvi infinitives, employed as auxiliaries in
the formation of the compounds included in the fubfequent
pages. To add more at prefent on this head would be to
anticipate what properly belongs to the grammatical divifion
of the work.

    Some of my readers, converfant with the Hindvi, may
think that I have inferted words in the following vocabulary
which are unknown to that tongue ; and, indeed, although
it has been my aim to exclude all fuch as neither occur in the
Hindvi poets, nor are in ufe among the politer and fuperior
claffes of people, yet I will not fo far truft to my own attention, or to my experience in the language, as to affirm pofi-
tively that the charge might not, in a few inftances, be juft.
— But as, at the utmoft, the bulk of the vocabulary cannot
have derived an increafe of more than three or four pages
from this fource, and as it is better that a few unauthorized
words fhould be admitted than that the omiffion of any in
ufe fhould be hazarded, I am hopeful that the error (if I
have really fallen into it) will be confidered as an error on
the

the right fide; efpecially, as it may be fafely afferted that
there is no abfolute rule whereby to regulate the adoption of
Perfian and Arabic words into the Hindvi, the learned in
thofe two languages being always at liberty to introduce, as
well in converfation as in writing, fuch words (for the moft
part fubftantives and adjectives) as they judge proper: and,
in fact, without exercifing this privilege very unrefervedly,
it muft be owned that they would frequently be at a lofs to
exprefs themfelves in a dialect that certainly does not
abound in original abftract terms.

It is neceffary I fhould acknowledge that Mr. Richardfon's
excellent dictionary of the Perfian and Arabic has been of
confiderable ufe to me in compiling the fubfequent vocabulary, by enabling me to difcover and arrange with facility
and readinefs, fuch words as I deemed proper to infert in it.
—I have not always, however, followed either the pronunciation or the explanation of that author, or given the various meanings which he has inferted; becaufe in the practical Perfian the found of the fhort vowel is fometimes different from that which he has adopted; and becaufe many
Perfian and Arabic words are (ufed in the Hindvi,), in fome
fenfes omitted not only by him but all other lexicographers,
and, on the other hand, are perhaps employed in that dialect, only in one of many fignifications properly affigned to
them in his work.

The following table exhibits the founds which the learner is to give to the Englifh letters employed in expreffing the words contained in the vocabulary; in order to his pronouncing them correctly and intelligibly.

To *a*, the found of *a* in *and*.

    á, the found of *a* in *all*.

    c, the hard found of *c* in *care*.

    ch, the found of *ch* in *child*.

    e, the found of *e* in *end*.

    é, the found of the French *é* in *Beauté*, excepting when followed by *h* in the termination of a word or fyllable when it is not to be dwelt on as in *bé* (without), but to be founded fomething like *ú* or *a*: as in *purdéh* (a curtain), which might alfo be written *purdúh* or, *purdah*.

    g, the hard found of *g* in *game*.

    gh, in Perfian or Arabic words a guttural found, and in Hindvi words the found of *gh* in *ghoft*.

    h, (terminating a word or fyllable) the faint found of *h* in *Noah*.

    h, (initial) the found of *h* in *holy*.

    i, (initial) the found of *i* in *Indus*.

    ï, the found of *i* in *idle*, or *dire*.

    i, (terminating a word or fyllable) the found of *i* in *animal*, or of *y* in *daily*, or of initial *e* in *emerge*, or nearly of *ee* in *deem*: though where the *ee* occurs it is invariably expreffive either of the long ی

of

of the Perſian, or the *dhirzoon* of the Hindvi, and is to be dwelt upon rather more than in the word *deem*.

kb, in Perſian or Arabic words the guttural ſound of *cb* in the Scotch word *lcch*; but in Hindvi words, inſtead of this guttural ſound, it muſt be pronounced ſomething like *cb* in *chaos*, the *kb* of the Hindvi being compounded of *k* and an aſpirate both of which muſt be ſounded diſtinctly.

o, or *ó* when forming a ſyllable of itſelf, or terminating one, the ſound of *o* in *holy*. When a conſonant follows in the ſame ſyllable, I have uſed the diphthong *oa* to expreſs the ſame ſound.

u, the ſound of *u* in *tun*.

ú, the ſound of *u* in *bull, cruel,* and *ruby,* the long ‚ of the Perſic being expreſſed by *oo*, which is to be ſounded as in *doom,* or *room*.

ú, (which, except when it comes before *b,* always terminates a ſyllable), the ſound of *u* in *cumin, ducat,* or, *puniſh*.

y, the ſound *y* in *my, by, wry, fy,* &c.; excepting in the begining of a ſyllable or word, when it has the ſound of *y* in *yore*.

Of the other conſonants I think it unneceſſary to ſay any thing, as the ſound of none of them can be vague or equivocal.

Some

Some few deviations from the mode here fixed on for regulating the orthography of Perfian and Arabic words, expreffed in Englifh characters, have crept into the following vocabulary; but none, I truft, that will be found to be of much importance, the principal variation being in the inftance of *ee* (final) which has now and then been ufed to convey the found of *i* (final): as in page 4, under the word اسامی which according to the preceding fcheme, ought to have been written *afámi* inftead of *afúmee*.

For the ufe of fuch as may wifh to read the words contained in the following vocabulary, in the character proper to them, the Perfian alphabet is here fubjoined.

Names of the Letters.	Finals. Connect.	Finals. Unconnect.	Medials. Connect.	Initials. Connect.	Powers, as expressed in English Characters.
Alif	ـا	ا	ـا	ا	*a, á, u, i, e (o followed*
Bé	ـب	ب	ـبـ	بـ	*b. [by* و, *and ee by* ي*).*
Pé	ـپ	پ	ـپـ	پـ	*p.*
Té	ـت	ت	ـتـ	تـ	*t.*
Sé, or Thé	ـث	ث	ـثـ	ثـ	*s (or th, pronounced ac-*
Jeem	ـج	ج	ـجـ	جـ	*j. [cording to the Ara-*
Ché	ـچ	چ	ـچـ	چـ	*ch. [bic method).*
Hé or Hay major	ـح	ح	ـحـ	حـ	*h.*
Khé	ـخ	خ	ـخـ	خـ	*kh.*
Dawl	ـد	د	ـد	د	*d.*
Zawl	ـذ	ذ	ـذ	ذ	*z.*
Ré	ـر	ر	ـر	ر	*r.*
Zé	ـز	ز	ـز	ز	*z.*
Zjé	ـژ	ژ	ـژ	ژ	*zj.*
Seen	ـس	س	ـسـ	سـ	*s.*
Sheen	ـش	ش	ـشـ	شـ	*sh.*
Sawd or Swád	ـص	ص	ـصـ	صـ	*s.*
Zawd or Zwád	ـض	ض	ـضـ	ضـ	*z.*
To	ـط	ط	ـطـ	طـ	*t.*
Zo	ـظ	ظ	ـظـ	ظـ	*z.*
Ine	ـع	ع	ـعـ	عـ	*u, i, á, a.*
Ghine	ـغ	غ	ـغـ	غـ	*gh.*
Fé	ـف	ف	ـفـ	فـ	*f.*
Kaaf or Káif	ـق	ق	ـقـ	قـ	*k.*
Kawf	ـک	ک	ـکـ	کـ	*k.*
Gawf	ـگ	گ	ـگـ	گـ	*g (hard).*
Lawm	ـل	ل	ـلـ	لـ	*l.*
Meem	ـم	م	ـمـ	مـ	*m.*
Noon	ـن	ن	ـنـ	نـ	*n.*
Wa or Wau	ـو	و	ـو	و	*w, oo, ú, ow.*
Hé or Hay minor	ـه	ه	ـهـ	هـ	*h.*
Yé	ـي	ى	ـيـ	يـ	*y, ee, i.*

The

The ſhort vowels, which are called *zubr*, *zair*, and *paiſh* (from their ſituation), being rarely made uſe of in writing, are omitted in this work. The *zubr* is expreſſed in Engliſh characters by *u* (in *up*), the *zair* by *i* (in *ill*), or ſometimes by *e* (in *ell*); and the *paiſh* by *ú*, or *u* (in *ru-by*), or ſometimes by *o*.——Thus ؋ or *meem* if underſtood to have *zubr* is equivalent to *mu*, if *zair*, to *mi*, or *me*, and if *paiſh*, to *mú*, or *mo*.——— In reading, the ſhort vowels are to be ſupplied only by experience or knowledge in the language: the ſenſe of a word often depending on them; as in ﮒﻞ which with *zair* (gil) ſignifies clay, and with *paiſh* (gúl) ſignifies a roſe.

VOCABULARY,

PART VII

A VOCABULARY,

PERSIAN AND ARABIC;

CONTAINING SUCH WORDS AS ARE INCORPORATED INTO

THE HINDVI.

آ

آب *(awb)* Water.

آبدار *(awb-daur)* A water-cooler.

آبحیوان *(awb-hywaun)* ⎫
آبحیات *(awb-byaut)* ⎬ The water of life or immortality.

آباد *(awbaud)* Populous, thriving; *Awbaud-kurna,* to make populous, to colonize.

آبادي *(awbaudi)* Populoufnefs, a town.

ابر *(ubbúr)* A cloud.

ابر مژگان *(ubbúr-mizhgaun)* The eye-lafh (Souda.)

ابرنیسان *(ubbúr-nyfaun)* The pearl-cloud. (Souda.)

ابرو *(ubroo)* The eye-brow.

آبرو *(awbroo)* Character, reputation, honour; *Awbroo-léna,* to difhonour.

آبهوا *(awb-howa)* Air, temperature, climate.

ابتداي *(ibtudáee)* Beginning: *Ibtudáee-mé;* at firft, in the beginning.

آبخورد *(awb-khórd)* Means of fubfiftence.

ابلق *(ubluk)* Pye-balled, black and white.

آبله *(ábileh)* A pimple, puftule, bile.

ابلاغ *(iblaugh)* Conveying, fending.

B

آتش

آتش (*awtush*) Fire.

اتفاق (*ittuffauk*) Incident, chance: *Ituffauk-kurna*; to happen, to unite: *Ituffauk-hona*; to happen, to be agreed: *Ituffauk-fé*; accidentally, it happened, jointly, conjointly.

اثر (*uffer*) Impreffion, effect: *Uffer-kurna*; to affect: *Uffer-hona*; to make an impreffion: *Uffer-léna*; to take or have effect.

اجازت (*ijázet*) Permiffion, leave to depart: *Ijazet-déna*; to permit, to let go, or difmifs.

اجراي (*ijráee*) Accomplishing, performing: *Ijráee-déna*; to perform.

اجراي كار (*ijráee-kaur*) Doing bufinefs.

أجل (*ujjul*) Death: *Ujjul-poanchna*; to be on the point of death.

احسان (*éhfaun*) A favour, kindnefs: *Ehfaun-kurna*; to oblige, favour, &c.

احسانمند (*éhfaun-mund*) Kind, benevolent.

احتياج (*ehtiauje*) Neceffity, neceffary: *Ebtiauje-hona*; to be requifite, to want.

احوال (*ihwaul*) State, condition, account: *Ihwaul-butlaouna*; to ftate one's condition.

احاطه (*eháteh*) Surrounding, an inclofure: *Eháteh-déna*; to furround, inclofe.

احمق (*ihmuk*) A fool, an ideot: *Ihmuk-ka*; ideotical, foolifh.

احتياط (*ehtiaut*) Care, caution: *Ehtiaut-fé*; carefully: *Ehtiaut-léna*; to be cautious: *Ehtiaut-fé-rukhna*; to take care of.

احرام (*éhraum*) Sacred places.

احتمال (*éhtúmaul*) Probable, probability: *Ehtúmaul-hóna*; to be probable.

احد (*éhad*) One.

احدي (*éhdi*) An office under the Moghul empire.

احشام (*éhfhaum*) Followers, retinue, houfehold troops.

احقر (*ihkur*) Moft contemptible. (A felf-humiliatory expreffion.)

احكام (*éhkaum*) Decrees, ordinances, rule.

احيانا (*ihyanun*) In the event, in cafe, fhould.

لختيار

اختیار (ekhtyaur) Will, choice, election, power : Ekhtyaur-me-bona, or ruhna ; to be dependant on.

اخبار (ukhbár) News, intelligence.

آخر (ákhir) Laſt, poſterior, final, in the end, after all : Akhir-bona ; to be at an end, to be finiſhed.

اخری (ákhiri) The end, concluſion.

اختراع (ekhturrái) Invention : Ekhturrdi-kurna ; to invent.

اختصار (ekhtuſſaur) Contraction, abridgment, ſelection.

اختہ (ákhteh) A gelding : Akhteh-kurna ; to geld.

اخراج (ekhrauje) Tributes, expences.

اخلاص (ekhlauſe) Friendſhip, affection, love : Ekhlauſe-rukhna ; to love, eſteem, &c.

اختلاف (ekhtilauf) Difference, diſcord, oppoſition : Ekhtilauf-purrbna ; to differ, diſagree.

ادا (údá) Performance, execution, manner : Udá-kurna ; to perform, to liquidate, pay.

ادب (údub) Reſpect, politeneſs, good manners : Udub-kurna ; to reſpect, to behave politely.

آداب (awdaub) Reſpects, ſalutation ; Awdaub-bújá-laouna ; to pay one's reſpects.

آدمی (audmi) A man.

ادراک (udrauk) Comprehenſion, underſtanding.

ادنا (udna) Mean, low.

اذا (iza) Trouble, injury, oppreſſion.

اذان (azán) The ſignal for ſummoning to prayers by the prieſts from the minarets of the moſques.

ارادہ (irádeh) Deſign, plan, intention : Irádeh-rukhna ; to intend, deſign.

آراسته (draufteh) Adorned, fitted out, trimmed, put in order, prepared.

آراستگی (áraufligi) Decoration, adorning, &c.

آرام (úraum) Eaſe, quiet, health, ſleep, repoſe : draum-léna ; to reſt, to repoſe.

آرامی (áraumí) Peace, tranquility.

آرایش

آرایش (*áráish*) Ornament, embellishment.

اربع (*urbai*) Four.

ارتباط (*irtubaut*) Friendship.

آرد (*árud*) Flour, meal.

اردو (*oordú*) A camp, a court.

ارزان (*urzaun*) Cheap.

آرزو (*árzoo*) Desire, wish, inclination.

آرزومند (*árzoo-mund*) Desirous, longing.

ارشاد (*irshaud*) Direction, command: *Irshaud-déna*, or *kurna*; to direct, command.

ارفاه (*irfáh*) Enjoyment of peace.

ارقام (*irkaum*) Writing, written.

اركان (*urkaun*) Nobles.

اركان دولت (*urkaun e dowlut*) The nobility.

ارمني (*urmunni*) An Armenian.

آره (*awreh*) A saw.

آری (*ári, awri*) Yes.

آزاد (*ázaud*) Free, unconfined, noble.

آزار (*ázaur*) Trouble, sickness, affliction, outrage, injury: *Azaur-déna*; to vex, afflict, trouble, pain.

آزاري (*ázauri*) A sick person.

آزمایش (*ázmáish*) Trial, proof, temptation: *Azmáish-léna*; to prove, to try, to tempt.

آزمای (*ázmái*) Experience.

آزرده (*ázoordeh*) Afflicted, displeased.

آزرده خاطر (*ázoordeh-khátir*) Offended, disgusted.

ازار (*izaur*) Drawers.

ازار بند (*izaur-bund*) The string by which the drawers are tied.

ازل (*ázel*) Eternity.

آسامي (*ásámee*) A renter, a tenant.

آسان (*ásaun*) Easy, facile.

آستان

آستان (*áſtaun*)
آستانه (*áſtauneh*) } A threſhold.

اِستاد (*óſtaud*) A tutor, a maſter.

اسیر (*áſeer*) A priſoner.

اسم (*iſm*) A name.

آسمان (*áſmaun*) The ſky.

استعداد (*iſtáedaud*) Ability, means, capacity.

اسباب (*uſbaub*) Goods, baggage.

اسلام (*iſlaum*) The Mahommedan faith.

استقبال (*iſtukbaul*) The ceremony of meeting a viſitor: the future.

استفسار (*iſtuſſaur*) Enquiry, interrogation: *Iſtuſſaur-kurna*; to enquire, interrogate.

اسپ (*uſp*) A horſe.

آستین (*áſteen*) A ſleeve.

آسایش (*áſauiſh*) Eaſe, repoſe, quiet.

استر (*uſtur*) A lining.

استحکام (*iſtehkaum*) Firmneſs, firm.

استدعا (*iſtudwa*) Supplication.

استره (*uſtooreh*) A razor.

استعانت (*iſtianut*) Aſking aſſiſtance.

استعفا (*iſtafa*) Aſking pardon, deprecating.

استقامت (*iſtukaumut*) Reſidence.

استغفار للہ (*uſtuzghfur-oollah*) God pardon! Heaven avert!

استماع (*iſtúmáe*) Hearing, that which is heard, a report or rumour.

استوار (*ooſtuwaur*) Firm, ſtrong, ſolid.

استواری (*ooſtawauri*) Strength, ſtability, firmneſs.

استیفا (*iſtyfa*) Renouncing, relinquiſhing.

اسرار (*iſraur*) Secrets.

اسطبل (*uſtubbul*) A ſtable.

اسطرلاب (*uſturlaub*) An aſtrolobe.

اسلوب (*uſloob*) Order, method, arrangement.

اسوار (*uſwaur*) A horſeman.

آسودگي

آسودگي (*ásoodigi*) Quiet, peace, content.

آسیا (*ásya*) A mill.

آسیانه (*ásyaneh*) A whet-ftone.

آسیب (*áseib*) Trouble, calamity, damage.

اشنا (*ásbna*) A friend.

اشنای (*ásbnái*) Friendfhip: *Afbnái-lugna*; to be united in friendfhip.

اشراف (*ufbrauf*) Noble or illuftrious perfons.

اشرفی (*úfburfi*) A gold mohr.

اشاره (*ifbáreh*) A fign, token, fignal: *Ifbáreh-déna*; to make figns; to give or make a fignal.

آشیانه (*ásbián*, or *ásbiáneh*) A neft.

اشک (*ufbk*) Tears.

اشتباه (*ifhtúbáh*) Ambiguity, doubt, refemblance.

اشتهار (*ifbtehaur*) Fame, renown, rumour.

آشتی (*awfbti*) Peace, pacification: *Awfbti-kurna*; to make peace.

اشتیاق (*ifbtiauk*) Defire, longing: *Ifbtiauk-rukbna*; to long, to defire.

اشعار (*ufbaar*) Poems, verfes.

اشفاق (*ufbfauk*) Compaffion, tendernefs.

آشفته (*ásbúfteh*) Difturbed, uneafy.

آشکاره (*ásbkáreh*) Known, revealed.

آشوب (*ásboob*) Difturbance, tumult.

اشیا (*ásbya*) Goods, effects, things.

اصیل (*ufbeel*) Genuine, noble.

اصل (*ufbul*) Root, origin, original.

اصحاب (*ufbaub*) Mafters, friends, companions.

اصطبل (*ufbúbul*) A ftable.

اصطلاح (*ifbullaub*) An idiom, a figure in rhetorick.

اصطلاحات (*ifbullahaut*) Idioms, figures.

اصلی (*ufbli*) Effential, radical, noble.

اصول (*ufbool*) Caufes, roots, a mufical mode or tone.

اضافت (*izáfut*) Addition, adjunct.

اضافه (*izúfeh*) Addition, increafe.

اضطراب

اضطراب (*izturaub*) Perturbation, trouble, chagrin.

اضطرار (*izturaur*) Violence, conſtraint.

اضعف (*azaaf*) Weak, very helpleſs.

اطاعت (*itáut*) Obedience, ſubmiſſion.

اطراف (*etrauf*) Environs, ſkirts, diſtricts.

اطفال (*itfaul*) Family, children.

اطلاع (*itulláï*) Knowledge, information: *Itulláï-déna*; to inform, apprize.

اطمينان (*itminaun*) Reſt, quiet, ſecurity.

اطمينان خاطر (*itminauni-khátir*) Peace of mind.

اضهار (*izbaur*) Revealed, diſcovered: *Izbaur-kurna*; to reveal, make known.

اضهر من الشمس (*uzbur-min-ülſhumſe*) As clear as day.

اعزاز (*ïdzaux*) Reſpects, attentions.

اعانت (*éánut*) Help, aid, ſuccour.

اعتبار (*tátubaur*) Veneration, eſteem, reſpect, credit, belief: *Edtu-baur-rukhna*; to give credit to, to believe.

اعتدال (*tátudaul*) Temperature, moderation.

اعتراض (*táturauz*) Diſpleaſure, oppoſition.

اعتراف (*táturauf*) Confeſſion, acknowledgment.

اعتقاد (*tátukaud*) Faith, confidence, belief.

اعتماد (*tátumaud*) Confidence, truſt.

آغاز (*ógbaux*) Beginning.

اغلب (*ugblub*) Moſt probable.

اغوا (*ugbwá*) Seduction, temptation: *Ugbwá-déna*; or *kurna*; to ſeduce, tempt.

اغيار (*ugbyaur*) A rival.

آفت (*áfut*) Calamity, misfortune: *Afut-purrhna*, or *poanchbna*; to miſchance, to happen. (A misfortune.)

آفاق (*áfauk*) The world.

آفتاب (*áftaub*) The ſun.

آفتابه (*áftaubéb*) An ewer.

آفرين

آفرین (*afreen*) Praife! All laud!

افزون (*ufzoon*) Increafing, increafer.

افزونی (*ufzooni*) Increafe, fuperfluity.

افسانه (*uffauneh*) A tale, fable, romance.

افسر (*uffur*) A crown.

افسوس (*uffoufe*) Sorrow, concern, alas! *Uffoufe-kurna*; to grieve, lament.

افسون (*uffoon*) Sorcery.

افسونگر (*uffoon-gur*) A forcerer.

افلاق (*iflauk*) All men and creatures.

افلاک (*uflauk*) The heavens, heavenly bodies.

افواج (*ufwauj*) Troops, armies.

افیون (*ufyoon*) Opium.

انواه (*ufwaub*) Rumour.

آقا (*áka*) A mafter.

اقلیم (*ukleem*) Climate, region, country.

اقسام (*ekfaum*)   ⎱

قسم اقسام (*kifm-ekfaum*) ⎰ Various kinds, of every fort.

اقامت (*ekámut*) Refting, ftaying, abode.

اقربا (*ókurba*) Relations, kindred.

اقبال (*ukbaul*) Good fortune, profperity.

اقتدار (*iktúdaur*) Power, authority, force.

اقتسام (*iktúfaum*) Divifion, partition.

اقدام (*ekdaum*) Care, attention, diligence, effort, endeavour.

اقرار (*ekrár*) Confirmation, agreement, engagement: *Ekrár-déna*, or *kurna*; to promife, engage.

اکابر (*ukaubir*) The rich or great.

آگاه (*ágah*) Acquainted, notice, news.

آگاهی (*ágahi*) Knowledge, notice, care.

اکتفا (*iktifa*) Sufficiency, contentment.

اکثر (*ukfur*) Many, for the moft part.

اگر (*uzgur*) If.

اکرام

اکرام (*ekraum*) Honour, refpect.

اکراه (*ekraub*) Horror, averfion, abhorrence.

اگرچہ (*uggurcheb*) Although.

اکمال (*ekmaul*) Perfections, perfection.

ال (*il, aul,* or *awl*) Offspring, family, race, dynasty.

البت (*albett,* or *albettab*) Certainly.

الا (*illa*)

والا (*willa*) } If not, otherwife, or elfe.

الت (*álut*) A tool.

الات (*álaut*) Tools, implements.

الم (*ulm*) Grief, trouble, anguifh.

اللمان (*allamaun*) A German.

الله (*allab*) God.

اللہی (*illábi*)

الہی (*ilbi*) } Divine ; Oh God !

الجا (*ilnija*) Refuge, afylum.

التزام (*iltúzaum*) Neceffary, expedient.

التفات (*iltúfaut*) Refpect, courtefy, kindnefs.

التماس (*iltúmaufs*) Petition, prayer, requeft : *Iltúmaufs-kurna,* or *rukbna* ; to requeft, petition.

التمغا (*áltumgha*) A tax ; (alfo a royal grant.)

الچی (*ilcbee*) An envoy or ambaffador.

الحال (*ulhaul*) Now, at prefent.

الحمدللہ (*ulbumdúlillab*) Praife be to God !

الخالق (*ulkhalik*) A garment.

الفاظ (*ulfauz*) Words, vocables, terms.

الفت (*oolfut*) Friendfhip, attachment.

القاب (*ulkaub*) Titles, appellations ; the addrefs of a letter.

الہام (*ilhaum*) Infpiration, revelation.

امام (*imaum*) Chief, patriarch, prelate, prieft.

اما (*ummá*) But, however, neverthelefs.

اماکن (*imáken*) Habitations, manfions.

C

آمان

آمان (*ámaun*) Security, fafety, protection.

امانت (*ámánut*) A deposit, truft: *Amánut-rukhna*; to keep, or lodge, as a deposit.

آماني (*úmáni*) Security.

امتحان (*imtihaun*) Trial, proof, experiment, temptation.

امتیاز (*imtiauz*) Diftinction, difcrimination, pre-eminence: *Imtiauz-kurna*; to difcriminate, to treat with diftinction.

امداد (*imdaud*) Affiftance, help, fuccours.

آمدني (*ámdunni*) Income, revenue.

امرا (*omra, oamra*) Nobles, grandees; a noble.

امیر (*ummeer, emir*) A noble, prince, emir.

امرود (*umrood*) A pear.

امروز (*imroze*) To-day.

امساک (*imfauk*) Scarcity, parfimony.

امسال (*imfaul*) This year.

امکان (*imkaun*) Poffibility.

املاک (*umlauk*) Goods, poffeffions.

امن (*ummun, umn*) Security, fafety.

اموال (*umwaul*) Effects, wealth, riches.

امور (*ummoor*) Things, affairs, actions.

امید (*omaid*) Hope, expectation: *Omaid-hona*; to be pregnant: *omaid-fe*; pregnant.

امیدوار (*omaidwár*) Hopeful, hoping, expecting.

امیدواری (*omaidwári*) Hope, confidence.

آمد آمد (*ámud ámud*) Approach.

آنار (*ánaur*) A pomegranate.

انبار (*umbaur*) Magazines, heaps.

انامل (*únamul*) Reckoning by the tips of the fingers.

انبساط (*imbiffaut*) Gladnefs, joy, delight.

انبوه (*umbóh*) Crowd, multitude, concourfe.

انتخاب (*intukhaub*) Election, felection, choice, abftract.

انتظاری (*intúzauri*) Expectation, waiting, anxiety.

انتظام

انتظام (*intizaum*) Order, regularity.

انتقام (*intukaum*) Revenge, vengeance: *Intukaum-léna*; to take vengeance, to revenge.

انتها (*intiha*) The end, extremity.

انجام (*unjaum*) Termination, conclusion, issue.

انجمن (*unjumun*) A company, banquet.

اندازه (*undauzeh*) Measure, dimension.

اندام (*undaam*) Stature, figure, the body.

اندر (*undur*) Within, inside.

اندرون (*unduroon*) Within, inner apartments.

اندک (*unduk*) A little, few.

اندرز (*endoorz*) Last will, last advice, precept.

اندوه (*undóh*) Grief, anxiety, trouble.

انديش (*undaish*) ⎫ Consideration, reflection, suspicion, fear: *Un-*
انديشه (*undaisheh*) ⎬   *daisheh-kurna*; to reflect, to fear.

انس (*oonse*) Society, companionship.

انسان (*insaun*) Mankind.

انشا (*insha*) The belles-lettres, elegance of style.

انصاف (*insauf*) Justice, equity, candour; *Insauf-kurna*; to do justice, to judge.

انعام (*inaam*) A present, gift, donation; *Inaam-dena*; to present, bestow.

انفصال (*infisaul*) Settling, determining: *Infisaul-kurna*; to settle, decide.

انقضا (*inkyza*) Expired, elapsed, ended.

انقلاب (*inkylaub*) Revolution, change.

انقياد (*inkyaud*) Submission, fidelity.

انکار (*inkaur*) Denial, disavowal: *Inkaur-kurna*; to deny, disavow.

انگور (*unggoor*) A grape.

انگریز (*ungraize*) An Englishman.

انشاالله or انشاالله تعالي (*inshaillah, or inshallah-taala*) Please God!

انهدام (*inhidaum*) Destruction, ruin, perdition.

انداز (*undauz*) Meaſure, quantity; air, note.

انواع (*unwaa*) Sorts, kinds.

آواره (*áwareh*) Wandering, diſtreſſed, miſerable.

آواز (*áwauz*) Sound, voice, report, tone.

آوازه (*áwauzeh*) A whiſper; judgement or ſentence.

اوقات (*oukaut*) Times, circumſtances.

اوج (*oaje*) Top, ſummit, eminence.

اوراق (*ourauk*) Leaves (of a book.)

اول (*auwul*) At firſt, firſt, the beginning.

اُوردو (*oordoo*) A camp, the royal camp.

اورنگ (*órung*) A throne, a manufacturing village.

اوزار (*ouzaur*) Sins, offences; aſylums; loads; weapons.

اوصاف (*ouſauſ*) Praiſes, qualities, endowments.

اولا (*ouwúlá*) In the firſt place, firſt of all.

اولیتر (*owlaitur*) Better, beſt.

اولاد (*owlaud*) Poſterity, deſcendants, offspring.

اولیا (*owliá*) The ſaints, the holy.

آوند (*áwind*) A pan, a veſſel.

آه (*awh, ah*) A ſigh, a moan; Alas! Oh!

اهانت (*ehanut*) Diſdain, contempt, enmity.

اهتمام (*ehtumaum*) Diligence, care.

آهِستَ (*áhiſteh*) Softly, ſlowly, tenderly.

آهِستگی (*áhiſtigi*) Slowneſs, ſoftneſs, gentleneſs.

اهل (*ihl, ihle*) People; a term denoting poſſeſſion, profeſſion, occupation, &c.

اهلیت (*ihliyut*) Skill, experience.

اهمال (*ehmaul*) Negligence, careleſſneſs, delay.

آهنگ (*áhungg*) Deſign, purpoſe; ſound, melody.

آهو (*áhoo*) A deer; a vice, defect, fault.

اهلیه (*ihliyeh*) A wife.

اي (*i, ai*) The interjection O! Oh!

ایا (*iyá*) O! Ho!

آیات

آبات (*ayaut*) Verſes of the Koran ; ſigns.

ایاس (*iyauſe*) Deſpair.

ایالت (*iyalut*) Dominion ; rule, ſway.

ایام (*iyaum*) Days, times, ſeaſon ; weather.

آیت (*ait, awit*) A ſign ; a verſe of the Koran.

اینحاد (*itihaud*) Union, friendſhip.

ایتلاف (*itilauſ*) Familiarity, ſociety, friendſhip.

ابجاب (*ijaub*) Neceſſary ; any good or bad action, deſerving of
heaven or hell.

البجاد (*ijaud*) Invention, diſcovery.

ایران (*Iraun, Eeraun*) Perſia.

ابرانی (*Irauni*) A Perſian.

ایزد (*Izid, izd*) God.

ایضا (*rzun*) Alſo, likewiſe, another.

ایفا (*ifa, eefa*) Performing or fulfilling an engagement ; paying, ſa-
tisfying.

ایلجی (*eelchi*) An ambaſſador.

ایما (*eemá*) A ſign, nod, ſignal.

ایمان (*eemaun*) Faith, belief, conſcience.

ایمر (*imab*) Charity land.

ایمر دار (*imab-daur*) One holding charity land.

آبنده (*iindeb*) In future, the future.

آینه (*iineh*) A mirrour.

ایوان (*iwán*) A palace.

آیین (*ieen*) Inſtitute, regulation, cuſtom.

باب

ب

باب (*bawb*) A chapter or division of a book ; an affair or matter.

بابت (*bábut*) Affair, matter, account ; on account of.

باج (*bawj*) Tribute, tax : *Bawj-déna* ; to pay tribute.

باجدار (*bawj-dár*) A tax-gatherer or collector of tributes.

باد (*bawd*) The wind or air : *Bawdé-mokhálif* ; a contrary wind.

بادام (*bádam*) An almond.

بادخایر (*bád-kháeh*) The rupture.

بادشاه (*bádsháh*) A king, prince, sovereign, or monarch : *Bádsháhi* ; empire, kingdom ; reign.

باده (*bádeh*) Wine.

بادیه (*bádiyeh*) A desert.

بار (*bawr*) A burden or load ; fruit, flowers, blossoms ; a time, once.

بارانی (*báráni*) A cloak, particularly one worn as a defence against rain.

بارگاه (*bárgáh*) The place of audience ; *Bárgáh-aam* ; The public hall of audience.

بارکبر (*bárgeer*) A beast of burden ; those cavalry or horsemen who are supplied with horses by the state.

باری (*báree*) At length, at last : *Báree-taala* ; the most high God ! *Báree-shookur* ; God be thanked !

باریک (*báreek*) Fine, slender, subtle.

باز (*bawz*) A hawk ; a player, as *Shetrunj-bawz*, a chefs-player.

بازی (*bázee*) Play, sport : *Koomár-bázee* ; dice (the game).

بازار (*bázár*) A market.

بازو (*bázoo*) The arm : *Bázoo-bund* ; a bracelet.

باضی (*bázee*) Some, certain : (Persons or things.)

باطل (*bátil*) False, vain, futile ; abolished.

باطن (*bátin*) The inward part ; the heart ; hidden, concealed.

باعث (*báis*) Cause, occasion, reason.

باغ (*bawgh*) A garden.

باغبان (*bawgh-ban*) A gardener; also *Bawgh-wan*.

باغچه (*bawgbcheh*) A little garden: corruptedly called *Bugicheh*.

باقی (*bakee*) The remainder; left, remaining; lasting, permanent.

باک (*bawk*) Fear: *Bé-bawk-bóna*; to be fearless, or without apprehension.

بالا (*bálá*) Above, upwards: *Bálá-kháneb*; an upper chamber.

بالغ (*báligh*) An adult; perfect: *Báligh-bóna*; to be of age, to be perfect.

بالفعل (*bilfiál*) In fact, actually; at this moment, now, for the present.

بالله (*billah*) By God!

بام (*bawm*) A terrace; a vault or arch.

بامداد (*bawmdád*) The morning.

بانگ (*bawngg*) A voice or sound; a cry: *Bawngg-marna*; to cry or call.

بانو (*bánoo*) A lady.

بانی (*bánee*) A founder, a builder.

باور (*báwur*) True, creditable; truth, credit; *Báwur-bona*; to deserve credit.

باوجود (*bá-wújood*) Notwithstanding.

باورچی (*báwurchee*) A cook: *Báwurchee-kháneb*; A kitchen.

بایع (*báyee*) Buying and selling: *Bye*; A ledger.

ببر (*bubur*) A tiger: *Sheer-bubur*; A lion.

بت (*boot*) An idol or image: figuratively, a beautiful woman.

بجا (*bú-já*) Proper, fit, right: *Bújá-laowna*; to perform, execute, accomplish.

بچه (*búcheh*) A boy, a child, a son; the young of any creature.

بحث (*búbus*) Controversy, dispute, debate.

بحر (*buhr*) The sea, a river; metre, verse; *Bubri*; marine.

بخار (*bókhár*) A vapour or exhalation: *Bókhár-nikulna*; to break out (as a rash or any eruption of the skin).

بخت

بخت‍ (*bukht*) Fortune, profperity: *Bukhtáwur*; fortunate, happy, profperous: *Kum-bukht*, and *bud-bukht*; miferable, wretched, worthlefs: *Naik-bukht*; amiable, virtuous, happy.

بخش (*bukhfh*) Giving; a gift: *Bukhfhifh*; a prefent, gift, or donation: *Bukhfhifh-déna*; to make a prefent.

بخشی (*bukhfhee*) A giver, a paymafter, a commiffary.

بخور (*búkboor*) Perfume, odour (of Frankincenfe, &c.)

بخیل (*búkheel*) Avaricious, parfimonious, penurious; a mifer.

بر (*bud*) Bad, wicked, vile: *Búdee*; badnefs, vilenefs: — This epithet is compounded with a great variety of nouns.

بدر (*búdur*) The full moon.

بدعت (*bidut*) Violence, injuftice, innovation: *Bidut-kurna*; to opprefs, to commit violence, to wrong.

بدل (*búdul*) Change, exchange: *Búdul-kurna*; to change, exchange, alter: *Búdulee*; exchange, relief (of a guard).

بدن (*búdun*) The body.

بدیع (*búdia*) Rare, ftrange: a curiofity.

بدیہت (*búdihut*) An extempore or impromptu.

بذل (*búzl*) Expence; a gift.

برابر (*búrabur*) Even, equal, alike: *Búrabúree*; Equality.

برادر (*búradur*) A brother, a relation: *Búraduree*; confanguinity.

برج (*boorj*) A baftion; a conftellation; a fign of the Zodiac.

برخ (*birkh*) A little, few: *Birkht*; a fmall quantity.

برخوردار (*burkhoardár*) Enjoying or deriving happinefs; a fon.

بردار (*burdár*) A bearer; bearing: — This word is ufed in forming a great variety of perfonal nouns. — See the Grammar.

برطرف (*bur-turf*) Afide, apart: *Bur-turf-kurna*; to difmifs.

برف (*burf*) Snow.

برق انداز (*burk-undáz*) Literally, a thrower of lightning; a matchlock man.

برقرار (*bur-kúrár*) Firm, immoveable; confirmed.

برکات (*burkát*) Bleffings, benedictious; profperity: *Burkut*; a bleffing.

برهان

برهان *(boorhán)* Demonstration, proof.

برم *(bur-hum)* Confused, embroiled, displeased: *Burhum-kurna*; to confuse, entangle, embroil, displease.

برهنه *(búrúhnéh)* Naked.

بریان *(bireeán)* Roasted, toasted, broiled, parched: *Bireea-kurna*; to parch, broil, grill.

بزاز *(bizáz)* A dealer in cloths or linens.

بزرک *(buzoorg)* Great, grand, powerful; elder: *Búzoorgee*; greatness, grandeur: *Búzoorgán*; elders, seniors, philosophers, sages, nobles, grandees, ancestors: *Búzoorgwár*; great, noble, illustrious.

بزم *(buzm)* A banquet, entertainment, convivial meeting, assembly.

بزله *(buzleh)* A jest.

بس *(bufs)* Enough; it is sufficient: a great many; many.

بساط *(bissát)* A bed, carpet, &c.; any thing spread; extensive, wide (a country): Extent.

بستان *(bostán)* A garden.

بستر *(bistur)* A pillow, cushion.

بسم الله *(bismillah)* In the name of God: *Bismil*; sacrificed: *Bismil-kurna*; to sacrifice (in the name of God).

بسیار *(bisiár)* Many, much, abundance.

بشارط *(búshárut)* Joyful tidings.

بشر *(búshur)* Man, mankind, mortals: *Búshriut*; human nature.

بصر *(busr)* Seeing, discerning: *Busárut*; seeing, sight: *Búseerut*; sight, circumspection, prudence.

بط *(but)* A goose: *Buttuk*; (the diminutive) a duck.

بطریق *(bútúreek)* In the manner of; by way of.

بعد *(bád)* After, afterwards, subsequent.

بعض *(báz,* or *bázee)* Some, certain.

بعید *(búeed)* Distant, far, absent, remote.

بغض *(bughz)* Hatred.

D

بغل

بغل (*bughl*) The arm-pit, the fide, the bofom : *Búghl-me-léna* ; to take in one's arms, or, to one's bofom : *Búghl-jána* ; to ftep afide or move out of the way.

بغي (*búghee*) A rebel ; revolt, rebellion.

بنا (*búká*) Eternity ; duration ; remainder : *Búkáyá* ; remains.

بقال (*búkál*) A fhopkeeper, a dealer in groceries, &c.

بكر (*bikr*) A maid or virgin : *Búkárut* ; virginity.

بكم (*bigum*) A queen ; — the wives of nawabs, and others of the nobility, are, by courtefy, ftiled *Bigums.*

بلا (*búlá*) Misfortune, calamity, evil.

بلاغت (*búlághut*) Eloquence.

بلبل (*búlbúl*) The nightingale.

بلده (*buldeh*) A city or town.

بلست (*bilift*) A fpan.

بلند (*boolund*) High, fublime, elevated, tall : *Boolundee* ; height, elevation, tallnefs.

بلور (*beloar*) Chryftal.

بلي (*búlee*) Yes, indeed.

بن (*boon*) Bafis, root : ftem.

بند (*bund*) A band, ligature, &c. : *Bundo-buft* ; fettlement, management, government.

بندر (*bundur*) A port or harbour.

بنده (*bundéh*) A flave, a fervant ; applied alfo to one's felf in addrefling an equal, by way of humility : *Bundegán* ; fervants, bondmen, flaves : *Bundegee* ; fervitude ; devotion ; miniftry : *Bundegee-kurna* ; to ferve, to reverence, to worfhip or adore (God).

بنكاه (*boongáh*) Baggage, luggage.

بني (*búnee*) Sons : *Bunee-Adum* ; the fons of Adam ; men, mortals.

بنياد (*boonyád*) Foundation, bafis ; progeny.

بوي or بو (*bóee* or *bo*) Odour, fmell : *Bud-bo* ; a ftink or bad fmell : *Bud-bó* or *bó-kurna* ; to ftink.

بودباش

بودباش (bood-básh) Exiftence; fubfiftence.

بور (boor) Barren (applied to land).

بوریا (booryá) A mat: Booryá-báf; a maker of mats.

بول (boal) Urine.

بہا (behá) Price, value (commonly pronounced Bhá in the Hindvi).

بہادر (behádúr) Literally, in value equal to a pearl: a hero, a champion, a brave man; a title of honour.

بہار (behár) The fpring: Behárifián; the fpring feafon: Behári;
vernal.

بہانہ (búbáneh) An excufe, pretext: Búbáneh-kurna; to pretend, to
make a falfe excufe.

بہبودی (béhboodee) Profperity; well-being.

بہتان (boohtán) A calumny, flander, lie: Boohtán-lúgaowna; to
flander, calumniate, accufe falfely.

بہتر (baihtur) Better; it is better.

بہجت (béhjut) Joy, pleafure, gladnefs.

بہرہ (búbreh) Profit, gain; profperity; a portion: Búbreh-mund; fortunate, profperous; profitable.

بہشت (búbifht) Paradife.

بی (bé or béy) A privative particle, ufed much in compofition, being
equivalent to in, un, im, ir, lefs, &c. in Englifh, and implying wanting or being without. — To infert under this
article all the compounds formed by prefixing this privative
particle to Perfian and Arabic nouns, would be to fwell the
vocabulary unneceffarily: it is fufficient to apprize the learner,
that when he cannot find the word he wants under this article, he muft look for the noun of which it is principally
compofed, which will anfwer his purpofe equally well.

بیابان (bey á bán) A defert.

بیاض (byáz) A blank paper or book.

بیان (byán) Explanation; relation: Byán-kurna; to relate, unfold,
explain.

بیبی

بیبی (*beebi*) A lady.

بیچاره (*bé-chárdh*) A poor, helpless creature.

بیحیا (*bé-byá*) Impudent, shameless.

بیخ (*baikh*) A root.

بیر (*baid*) A reed; a willow.

بیشتر (*baishtur*) More; exceeding.

بیغرض (*bé-ghurz*) Disinterested: *Bé-ghurz-ĕé*; disinterestedly.

بیقرار (*bé-kurár*) Unsettled, variable, inconstant: *Bé-kuráree*; fluctuation, variableness.

بیتصور (*bé-kúsoor*) Without fail; compleatly; entirely.

بیقیاس (*bé-kyáss*) Incomprehensible, immense.

بیکار (*bé-kár*) Out of service; without employ.

بیکانہ (*bé-gáneh*) A stranger; a foreigner; unconnected, unknown : *Bégánigee*; the situation of a stranger, an unprotected, or an unconnected person.

بیل (*beil*) A shovel, spade, or pick-axe: *Beildár*, or *bilddr*; a pioneer; a digger.

بیم (*beem*) Fear, terror, dread, danger.

بیمار (*beemár*) Sick, indisposed: *Beemáree*; sickness, disease.

بیمانند (*bé-mánind*) Incomparable ; without parallel.

بیمجال (*bé-mujál*) Powerless, impotent.

بیمروت (*bé-múrúwut*) Unkind, untender, rude.

بیمعنی (*bé-mánee*) Foolish, idle, vain, unmeaning, absurd.

بیوفا (*bé-wúfá*) Faithless, ungrateful: *Bé-wúfáee*; Perfidy, ingratitude.

بیوقت (*bé-wukt*) Untimely, ill-timed.

بیوقوف (*be-wúkoof*) Ignorant, inexpert.

بیوہ (*béwúh*) A widow.

بیہودہ (*bé-hoodeh*) Vain, fruitless, unprofitable; idle, absurd.

بیہوش (*bé-hoash*) Insane, senseless: *Bé-hoashee*; insanity, fainting.

پاپوش

ب

پاپوش (*pápoaſh*) Slipper, ſhoe: *Pápoaſh* (*ſe*) *márna*; to ſlipper, or beat with a ſlipper.

پاداش (*pádauſh*) Retribution, reward, retaliation.

پارچه (*párcheh*) A piece; a garment; cloth, linen.

پارسا (*párſa*) Pure, chaſte, holy, pious: a Pârſee: *Párſdee*; piety, purity.

پارسی (*párſee*) The Perſian language; Perſian.

پاره (*páreh*) A piece or fragment: *Páreh-páreh*; in pieces.

پاره‌دوز (*páreh-doaz*) A kind of cobler.

پاس (*páſs*) For, on account of; a guard; a watch.

پاسبان (*páſs-bán*) A centinel, a guard, a watchman.

پاک (*pawk*) Pure, chaſte, clean: *Pawk-rúbna*; to be cleanly: *Nápawk*; unclean, impure.

پاکیزه (*pawkeezah*) Pure: *Pawkee*; purity, cleanneſs.

پاندان (*pawndán*) A box for containing *Pawn*.

پایاب (*páyáb*) A ford; fordable: *Páyáb-kurna*; to ford (a river).

پایدار (*páidár*) Firm, ſteady, durable.

پایمال (*páee-mál*) Ruined, deſtroyed, trampled upon: *Páee-mál-kurna*; to deſtroy, lay waſte.

پایه (*páye*) A ſtep, a wheel.

پایین (*páyeen*) The lower part, or bottom.

پخته (*poakhteh*) Ripe, mature; clever, expert, cunning.

پذیره (*pizeerah*) Acceptable.

پر (*poor*) Full, compleat: loaded; charged: *Pur*; feathers; wings: *Poor-kurna*; to fill.

پرتو (*purtúwa*) A ray; light.

پرچم (*purchum*) A lock of hair (flowing from the crown of the head).

پرخاش

پرخاش (*purkh.ifh*) War, battle, conflict, commotion, disturbance.

پردکي (*purdigee*) Confinement (especially the confinement of women).

پرده (*purdéh*) A veil, or curtain : *Purdéh-mé-ruhna* ; to live in retirement.

پرکار (*purgár*) A pair of compasses.

پروا (*purwái*) Care, concern, anxiety : *Purwái-rukhna* ; to be solicitous or anxious about ; to care : *Bé-purwái* ; fearless, careless.

پرواز (*purwáz*) Flying ; flight ; springing.

پروانکي (*purwángee*) Permission ; commands : *Purwángee-déna* ; to permit, license.

پروانه (*purwáneh*) A patent or diploma ; an order or mandate ; a letter-royal ; a moth.

پرور (*purwur*) Nourishing, protecting, patronizing ; frequently used in forming compound epithets : *Purwurifh* ; education, protection, &c. : *Purwurifh-kurna* ; to rear, bring up, educate, protect, patronize.

پروردگر (*purwurdigár*) The nourisher ; the Almighty.

پرهيز (*purhaiz* or *purhaizee*) Abstinence, continence : *Purhaizee-kurna* ; to abstain, to fast : *Purhaiz-gár* ; an abstainer ; sober.

پري (*púree*) A fairy ; a good genius or spirit.

پريشان (*púrefhán*) Afflicted, ruined, distressed, confounded, dispersed, dishevelled : *Púrefhánee* ; Distress, ruin ; dispersion.

پس (*pufs*) Then, therefore ; finally : *Pufs-o-paifh* ; evasion, prevarication : *Pufs o paifh-kurna* ; to prevaricate, evade, trifle.

پست (*pufl*) Low : *Puflee* ; lowness.

پسر (*piffur*) A son, a child, a youth.

پسند (*púfund*) Approbation ; agreeable, grateful ; approving, admiring : *Púfund-kurna* ; to approve, to like : *Púfund-kurna* or *léna* ; to choose, to select : *Púfund-lugna* or *bóna* ; to like, to please, to prefer, to be agreeable : *Púfundeedéh* ; acceptable, agreeable, worthy, laudable : *Ná-púfund* ; disagreeable, offensive, odious, unpleasing.

پشت

پشت (*pooſht*) The back : *Pooſhtee* ; ſupport : *Pooſhtee-kurna* or *déna* ; to ſupport : *Pooſht o púnáh* ; a protector ; an aſylum.

پشتر (*puſhtéh*) A little hill or eminence ; a heap.

پشم (*púſhum*) Wool, down : *Puſhmeen* or *puſhmeenéh* ; Woolen.

پشیمان (*púſhimán*) Penitent, aſhamed : *Púſhimán-bona* ; to be penitent or ſorry ; to be aſhamed : *Púſhimán-kurna* ; to make aſhamed : *Púſhimánee* ; penitence, ſhame.

پلک (*púluk* or *púlik*) The eye-lid.

پلنک (*púlung*) A bed ; properly, a bedſtead made with tape.

پناه (*púnáh*) Protection, refuge ; an aſylum : In compoſition it ſignifies one who harbours, and is ſometimes uſed in a bad ſenſe ; as, *Shureer-púnáh* ; a wicked or roguiſh perſon.

پنجه (*punjéh*) A ſort of link (reſembling the five fingers of the hand) uſed in Hindoſtan.

پنهان (*pinhán*) Concealed, hid.

پنیر (*púneer*) Cheeſe.

پوزش (*pooziſh*) An excuſe, apology ; pretence.

پوش (*poaſh*) A covering (uſed in compoſition) : *Póſhauk* ; garments.

پول (*pool*) A bridge.

پهلو (*públoo*) The ſide.

پهلوان (*pulhwán*) A hero, champion ; a ſtrong athletic man ; a prize-fighter.

پهن (*púbn*) Breadth, width : *Pubná* ; Broad, wide ; breadth.

پیاده (*peeádéh*) A foot-man, a foot-ſoldier ; a pawn at cheſs.

پیاز (*peeáz*) An onion.

پیاله (*peeáléh*) A cup.

پیام or پیغام (*pyám* or *pygbám*) A meſſage : *Pygbámbur* or *Pygbumbur* ; a meſſenger, an envoy ; a prophet : *Pygbám-léjúna* or *poanchína* ; to carry, or deliver, a meſſage.

پیچ (*paich*) Twiſt, fold ; curvature ; a ſcrew : *Paich o táb* ; folds, twiſtings, knots, &c. : *Paich-déna* or *kurna* ; to twiſt, &c. : *Paichiſh* ; Inflexion, contorſion, writhing.

پیرا

پیرا (*pydá*) Invention, difcovery, exhibition, production: *Pydá-kurna*; to difcover, find, produce; get, earn: *Pydá-hona*; to be born; to be found; to be earned or got: *Pydáifh*; earnings, gettings.

پیر (*peer*) An old man; a founder or chief of any religious body or feft: *Peeri*; old age.

پیرامن (*pyrámun*) Environs, circuit; the fkirt of a garment.

پیراہن (*pyráhun*) A fhirt, a fhift, a covering.

پیروی (*pyrúwee*) A train; following; a confequence: *Pyrúwee-kurna*; to follow; to follow the footfteps.

پیشاب (*paifháb*) Urine; *Paifháb-dán*; an urinal: *Paifháb-kurna*; to make water.

پیشانی (*paifhánee*) The forehead.

پیشتر (*paifhtur*) Before, formerly, heretofore.

پیشرو (*paifhró*) A fore-runner, a guide.

پیشکار (*paifhkár*) A manager, or minifter; an agent.

پیشکش (*paifhkufh*) A prefent.

پیشکی (*paifhgee*) Money paid in advance.

پیشنهاد (*paifh-nehád*) Cuftom, habit; regulation.

پیشوا (*paifhwa*) The chief or foremoft; formerly the prime minifter of the Mahrattah empire: — now the Sovereign.

پیشہ (*paifhéh*) A trade or bufinefs; *Paifhéh-wur*; a tradefman.

پیک (*pyke*) A meffenger, carrier, courier.

پیکار (*pykár*) War, battle, conteft.

پیکان (*pykán*) The point of a fpear, arrow, &c.; a fpear.

پیکر (*pykur*) The face, countenance, or form.

پیمان (*pymán*) An agreement, treaty, compact, ftipulation: *Ihud e pymán*; alliance, treaty.

پیمایش (*pymáifh*) Meafure: *Pymáifh-kurna*; to meafure.

پیوند (*pywund*) Connection, conjunction; kindred; faftened; touching.

پیشواز (*paifhwáz*) A female drefs.

تاب

تٔ

تاب (táb or tdo) Heat; light; power: Túbán; luminous, bright: Táb-laouna; to be able to bear.

تابش (tábijh) Heat; splendour.

تابع (tábai) A subject, dependant: Tábai-dár; obeying; a follower or subject; a servant.

تابوت (táboot) A coffin; a bier.

تاج (táj) A crown or diadem: a close cap.

تاخت (tákht) Spoil, plunder; attack, assault: Tákht-táráj; booty, prey, plunder: Tákht-táráj-kurna; to plunder; properly, to assault and plunder.

تاخیر (tikheer) Delay, procrastination.

تادیب (tádeeb) Correction, chastisement.

تار (tár) A thread; the string of a musical instrument.

تاراج (táráj) Plunder, spoil.

تارک (tárúk) The crown of the head.

تاریخ (táreekh) A history; an era; the date of a letter or event; an epitaph.

تاریک (táreek) Dark: Túreeki; darkness.

تازه (tázeh) Fresh; new; tender; raw; recent: Tázégee; freshness.

تازی (tázee) The Arabic language; a breed of horses.

تازیانه (táziáneh) A whip or scourge.

تاس (táfs) A cup, plate or dish; particularly a saucer.

تاسف (taaffuf) Grief, lamentation, regret.

تاکید (tákeed) Injunction, confirmation: Tákeed-kurna; to enjoin strictly.

تالاب (tilaub) From whence Tuld; a sort of lake: a reservoir of water; a tank.

E

تالیف

تالیف *(táleef)* Composition, production (of a book): *Táleef-kurna*; to compose or produce a book.

تامل *(taamul)* Consideration, deliberation; *Taamul-kurna*; to weigh maturely, to consider well, to reflect on.

تانیث *(táneefs)* Of the feminine gender.

تاوان *(táwán)* A mulct; a fine; an imposition; an oppressive tax or fine: *Táwán-léna*; to levy an unjust or oppressive contribution.

تاویل *(táweel)* Explanation, interpretation (especially of dreams).

تاه *(táh)* A plait, fold, &c.

تایید *(táeed)* Assistance, aid, help.

تب or تپ *(tub or tup)* A fever.

تباه *(túbáh)* Ruin; corruption; destroyed; spoiled; injury; mischief.

تبدیل *(tubdeel)* Change, alteration, substitution: *Tubdeel-kurna*; to change, alter, shift.

تبر *(túbr)* An axe or hatchet.

تبرک *(tubruk)* Blessing, benediction; a sort of present.

تبسم *(tubuſſúm)* A smile or simper.

تتبع *(tútúbá)* Imitation: *Tútúbá-kurna*; to imitate, to follow.

تتمہ *(tútimméh)* Continuation; supplement; appendix.

تجارت *(tijárut)* Trade; merchandize: *Tijárut-kurna*; to trade.

تجاوز *(tújáwuz)* Departing or deviating from; *Tújáwuz-kurna*; to deviate from; to offend or err.

تجربہ *(tújurbéh)* Experience; an experiment, trial or proof: *Tújurbéh-kár*; experienced in business: *Tújurbéh-léna*; to try, prove.

تجسس *(tújuſſoos)* Search, inquiry, examination.

تجویز *(tujweez)* Contrivance, device: *Tujweez-kurna*; to contrive, devise, settle, hit upon.

تحریر *(túhreer)* Written; a writing.

تحسین *(túhſeen)* Praise, approbation; *Túhſeen-déna* or *kurna*; to praise, approve, applaud.

تحصیل *(túhſeel)* Collection, acquisition: *Túhſeel-kurna*; to collect (revenues).

تحفز

تحف‍ (*tohféh*) A rarity or curiofity; a prefent; rare, uncommon, excellent, admirable.

تحقیر‍ (*túhkeer*) Contempt, difdain: *Túhkeer-rukhna*; to defpife or hold in contempt.

تحقیق‍ (*túhkeek*) Truth, certainty, confirmation, inveftigation: *Túhkeek-kurna*; to inveftigate, to afcertain.

تحکم‍ (*túbukkúm*) Rule, command.

تحمل‍ (*túbummul*) Patience, forbearance, refignation: *Túhummul-kurna*; to endure, fuffer; to be patient, to fubmit.

تحور‍ (*túhúwur*) Hafte, anger.

تحویل‍ (*túhweel*) Return, renovation, change.

تخاوض‍ (*túkbáwuz*) Difference, diffention.

تخت‍ (*tukht*) A throne; *Tukhtéh*; a plank, a board: *Tukhtgáh*; the royal refidence: *Tukhtéh-nurd*; a dice-table; a backgammon table.

تخفیف‍ (*tukhfeef*) Abridgment; decreafe, diminution.

تخلص‍ (*túkhulloofs*) A proper name; the name affumed by poets.

تخلل‍ (*túkbullul*) Difturbance, difcord, diffention.

تخم‍ (*tokhum*) Seed.

تخمیر‍ (*tukhmeer*) Fermentation; forming into leaven.

تخمین‍ (*tukhmeen*) Conjecture, opinion, guefs.

تدارک‍ (*túdárúk*) Chaftifement; precaution, provifion: *Túdárúk-kurna*; to provide againft; to take the neceffary meafures againft any evil; to oppofe; to chaftife.

تدبیر‍ (*tudbeer*) Council, deliberation; order, regulation, difpofition: *Tudbeer-kurna*; to regulate, order, arrange, manage.

تذکره‍ (*tuzkúréh*) A memoir.

تذکیر‍ (*tuzkeer*) The mafculine.

ترازو‍ (*túrázoo*) A fcale or balance.

تراش‍ (*túráfh*) Shaving, erafing, cutting: — Ufed in forming many compounds, as *Kúlm-túráfh*; (a pen cutter) a penknife, &c.

تراشه‍ (*túráfhéh*) A fhaving, chip, paring, &c.

E 2

ترانه‍

تراز *(túránéh)* Modulation, melody, fymphony ; a trill or fhake.

تربيت *(turbiut)* Education, inftruction : *Turbiut-déna* or *kurna* ; to educate, inftruct, admonifh.

ترتيب *(turteeb)* Order, difpofition, arrangement.

ترجمان *(turjúmán)* An interpreter : *Turjúméh* ; interpretation, tranflation : *Turjúméh-kurna* ; to tranflate, to interpret.

تردد *(túruddúd)* Paffing from one thing to another ; anxious confideration ; clofe application to an end : *Túruddúd-kurna* ; to confider a matter deeply ; to fall upon the means of effecting a bufinefs.

ترش *(toorfh)* Acid, four : *Toorfh-roo* ; an auftere countenance.

ترصد *(túruffúd)* Expectation, hope.

ترفه *(toorféh)* Elegant, beautiful, delicate ; an elegant prefent.

ترقب *(túrukkúb)* Expectation.

ترقي *(túrukky)* Increafe, augmentation, advancement, profperity.

ترک *(turk)* Abandoning, forfaking : *Turk-kurna* ; to abandon, forfake ; leave off, quit.

تركيب *(turkeeb)* Compofition, compound, mixture.

تره *(túréh)* Garden-herbs in general ; called alfo *Turkáree.*

تزوير *(tuzweer)* Impofture, fraud, deceit.

تسبيح *(tufbeeh)* A rofary of beads.

تسخير *(tufkheer)* Subduing, taking, reducing : *Tufkheer-léna* or *kurna* ; to reduce, fubdue, capture.

تسكين *(tufkeen)* Pacifying, quieting : *Tufkeen i khátir* ; peace of mind.

تسلي *(túfulli)* Confolation, comfort : *Túfulli-déna* ; to comfort, confole, give affurances to.

تسليم *(tufleem)* Salutation : *Tufleemát* ; falutations : *Tufleem* or *Tufleemát-bújá-laouna* ; to perform falutation.

تسميه *(tufmeeah)* Giving a name ; appellation : *Tufmeeah-kurna* ; to name, call.

تشبه *(túfhubheh)* Refemblance, fimilitude.

تشبيه *(tufhbeeh)* A comparifon, fimile, allegory.

تشخيص *(tufhkheefs)* Diftinguifhing perfectly.

تشدید (*tushdeed*) The character ˇ which, placed over a letter, denotes that it should be doubled.

تشریف (*tushreef*) Visiting: (ennobling) *Tushreef-laouna*; to visit (spoken of a superiour or person of distinction).

تشویش or تشوش (*tushweesh* or *tushuwush*) Disquietude, alarm, apprehension.

تصدق (*tusudduk*) Alms; devoting; sacrificing: *Tusudduk-kurna*; to devote, to sacrifice to, to offer up.

تصدیع (*tusdeea*) Importunity, troubling: *Tusdeea-dena*; to trouble, pester, importune (literally, to give a head-ache.)

تصرف (*tusurruf*) Possession; *Tusurruf-kurna*; to take possession of: *Tusurruf me leaouna*; to get into one's possession.

تصغیر (*tusgheer*) Diminution; a diminutive noun.

تصفیه (*tusfeeah*) Purifying, clearing up; reconciliation.

تصنیف (*tusneef*) Composition, writing a book: *Tusneef-kurna*; to compose, write (a book).

تصور (*tusuwur*) Imagination, fancy, reflection, supposition: *Tusuwur-kurna*; to imagine, fancy, suppose.

تصوف (*tusuwuf*) Mystery, theology.

تصویر (*tusweer*) A picture or image.

تطاول (*tutawul*) Usurpation, tyranny; conquest.

تطویل (*tutweel*) Extending, prolonging.

تعاقب (*tu-akub*) Pursuit, following: *Tuakub-kurna*; to pursue.

تعالی (*tuala*) The most high: *Khoda-tuala*; the most high God.

تعاون (*tuawun*) Assistance.

تعبیر (*tabeer*) Interpretation (particularly of a dream).

تعجب (*tuajub*) Admiration; wonderful.

تعجیل (*tujeel*) Haste, quickness.

تعراد (*tadad*) Number, amount, account, computation.

تعدی (*tuadi*) Cruelty, violence, tyranny: *Tuadi-kurna*; to oppress, tyrannize.

تعرض (*tu-arruz*) Opposition, obstacle, impediment.

تعریف

تعریف *(táreef)* Defcription, explanation, praife: *Táreef-kurna*; to praife, commend, defcribe.

تعزیر *(tázeeah)* Lamentation: — the effigies borne in the proceffion of the Afhoorah or Dâha.

تعزیر *(tázeer)* Correction, reproof.

تعزیل *(tázeel)* Refigning (an office).

تعظم *(tuazzúm)* Magnificence, greatnefs.

تعظیم *(tázeem)* Reverence, refpect, honour: *Tázeem-kurna*; to honour, refpect, reverence.

تعلق *(túllúk)* Connection, dependence, property, poffeffions, appertaining to: *Túllúk-rukhna*; to refpect, concern, to appertain, belong, to be connected with.

تعلیق *(táleek)* Sufpenfion, fufpended; the name of a Perfian character.

تعلیم *(táleem)* Inftruction, education: *Táleem-kurna*; to educate.

تعمیر *(támeer)* Building, re-building: *Támeer-kurna*; to erect (a building); to eftablifh.

تعویز *(táweez)* An amulet or charm againft forcery.

تعیین *(túïyun)* Appointed, affigned; deputed.

تغافل *(túgháful)* Negligent, carelefs, inadvertent.

تغنی *(túghunni)* Contented; finging.

تغیر *(túgheer)* Change, alteration; removal: *Túgheer-kurna*; to remove (from an office).

تغاوت *(túfáoot)* Difference, diftinction, variation, contradiction, diftance: *Túfáoot-kurna*; to vary, deviate, differ; to remove; to feparate, diftinguifh.

تغحص *(túfuhhús)* Inveftigation, inquiry, fearch.

تفخر *(túfúkhúr)* Proud, vain.

تفرج *(túfurrúj)* Recreation, relaxation of mind.

تفریق *(túfreek)* Separation; diftribution.

تفسیر *(túfseer)* Explanation, commentary.

تفصیل

تفصیل *(tufseel)* Divifion (into chapters); an account or lift of particulars.

تفضل *(túfuzzúl)* Excelling, eminent: *Túfuzzúlát*; favours, kindneffes.

تفویض *(tufweez)* Refigning, committing to another.

تقاضا *(túkázá)* Urgency, importunity, dunning: *Túkázá-kurna* or *déna*; to dun, importune, urge (efpecially the payment of a debt).

تقاوی *(túkáwee)* Vying, contending with.

تقدس *(túkuddús)* Pure, holy; purified: *Tukdees*; fanctity, purity.

تقدیر *(tukdeer)* Fate; inevitable decree.

تقدیم *(tukdeem)* Priority, precedence; performance: *Tukdeem-kurna*; to perform; to put before.

تقرر *(túkurrúr)* Fixed, confirmed.

تقریب *(tukreeb)* Occafion, conjuncture; caufe, pretence, motive.

تقریر *(tukreer)* A narrative, relation, recital, detail.

تقسیم *(tukfeem)* Divifion, diftribution: *Tukfeem-kurna*; to diftribute.

تقصیر *(tukfeer)* Error, fault, crime, offence, failure: *Tukfeer-lugna*; to be in fault, to be to blame: *Tukfeer-kurna*; to offend, err; to commit a crime.

تقلید *(tukleed)* Imitation, counterfeiting; forgery.

تقوی *(tukwá)* The fear of God: *Ibl-tukwá*; thofe who fear God; the pious.

تقویت *(tukwiut)* Confidence, affurance, comfort, reliance, ftrength.

تقویم *(tukweem)* An almanac.

تقید *(túkiyud)* Attention, diligence, application, induftry.

تکبر *(túkubbúr)* Arrogance, pride, haughtinefs.

تکرار *(tukrár)* Repetition; altercation: *Tukrár-kurna*; to altercate, difpute; repeat, dwell on.

تکریر *(tukreer)* Repetition, revifal, renewal, reply.

تکریم *(tukreem)* Honour, refpect, reverence: *Tukreem-kurna*; to refpect, honour, &c.

تکلف

تکلف (*túkullúf*) ⎫ Trouble, inconvenience ;

تکلیف (*tukleef*) ⎭ Ceremony, form :

   Be-túkulhíf ; without trouble or ceremony.

   Tukleef-déna ; to trouble, to put to an inconvenience.

تکیہ (*túkiéh*) A place of repofe ; any thing upon which one leans ; a pillow ; a place of retreat for perfons dedicating themfelves to God ; a hermitage ; figuratively, fupport, afylum : *Túkiéh-núfbeen* ; recluſe ; a hermit, a dervife.

تلخ (*tulkh*) Bitter : *Tulkhee* ; bitternefs.

تلف (*túluf*) Confumption, expence ; prodigality, ruin, deftruction : *Túluf-kurna* ; to expend, confume, wafte.

تماشا (*tumáfhá*) An entertainment, a fhow, a play ; a difturbance : *Túmáfhá-kurna* ; to divert, to entertain, to play ; to make a difturbance.

تمام (*túmám*) Entire, compleat ; the whole, the end, conclufion.

تمثیل (*tumfeel*) An example ; a comparifon, fimilitude, &c.: *Tumfeel-laouna* ; to bring or produce an example.

تمجید (*tumjeed*) The glorification of God.

تمرد (*túmurrúd*) Refractory, ftubborn, obftinate, difobedient.

تمسک (*túmuffúk*) A bond, an obligation (in writing).

تمکین (*tumkeen*) Dignity, majefty, authority ; affiftance, fupport.

تمنا (*túmúná*) Wifh, prayer, defire, fupplication.

تمہید (*tumheed*) Arrangement, fettlement, management, confirmation.

تن (*tun*) The body, perfon, ftature ; an individual.

تناول (*túnáwul*) Eating.

تنبیہ (*tumbeeh*) Punifhment, admonition : *Tumbeeh-déna* or *kurna* ; to punifh.

تنخواہ (*tunkhwáh* or *tunkhá*) An affignment (on the revenues).

تند (*toond*) Swift, fharp, fevere, rapid.

تندرست (*tun-doorúft*) Healthy, vigorous : *Tun-doorúftee* ; health.

تندور (*tundoor*) An oven ; alfo *Tunnoor*.

تنک

تنگ (*tungg*) Narrow, ſtrait; a belt or girth. — This word is uſed in forming many compounds; as, *Tungg-duſt,* wretched; *Tungg-dil,* narrow-hearted, &c.; *Tungndee,* a ſtrait or difficulty; *Tungzee,* narrowneſs, poverty, diſtreſs.

تنها (*tunhá*) Alone, ſolitary; only, ſingly; private, ſecret.

توارخ (*túwáreekh*) Hiſtories, annals.

تواضع (*túwáza*) Attention, kindneſs, civility; treating, entertaining: *Túwáza-kurna;* to treat kindly or civilly; to entertain.

توانكر (*túwángur* or *túwungur*) Rich, opulent: *Túwungurree;* richneſs.

توبه (*tóbéh*) Repentance, vowing to ſin no more: *Tóbéh-kurna;* to cry out for mercy.

توت (*toot*) A mulberry.

توتیا (*tootiá*) Tutty.

توجه (*túwujjéh*) Turning towards, regarding, attending to; kindneſs, favour, attention: *Túwujjéh-kurna;* to be kind to.

توحید (*towhaid*) Unity; the unity of God.

توده (*tódéh*) A mound or heap.

توشه (*tóſhéh*) Proviſions, means of ſubſiſtence.

توصیف (*towſeef*) Deſcription, commendation.

توفیق (*towfeek*) The guidance, grace or favour of God.

توقر (*túwukkúr*) Reſpected, honoured.

توقع (*túwukka*) Hope, expectation: *Túwukka-rukhna;* to hope.

توقف (*túwukkúf*) Delay, heſitation, tedlouſneſs: *Túwukkúf-kurna;* to delay, poſtpone.

توکل (*túwukkúl*) Reſignation, confidence, truſt, reliance.

تولد (*túwullúd*) Born, generated.

ته (*túh* or *tyh*) A fold or plait; empty; the bottom, beneath: *Túh-khánéh;* an apartment below ground.

تهدید (*tuhdeed*) Threat, menace.

تهمت (*tóhmut*) Accuſation, charge, ſuſpicion of guilt: *Tóhmut-lugaowna;* to accuſe, charge, to render ſuſpected.

F

تھی

تهي *(tehee)* Emptinefs; empty, vain.

تيار *(tydr)* Ready, prepared: *Tyáree*; readinefs, preparation: *Ty.ir-kurna*; to prepare, make ready.

تیر *(teer)* An arrow: *Teer-undáz*; an archer: *Teer-undázee*; archery.

تیره *(teeréh)* Dark, obfcure.

تیز *(taiz)* Sharp, acute, pointed, fwift.

تیغ *(taigh)* A fword, a faulchion, a fcymitar.

ﺚ

ثابت *(fábit)* Proved, confirmed, eftablifhed; fixed: *Sábit-kurna*; to prove, eftablifh (particularly by witneffes).

ثاني *(fánee)* The fecond: *Sánee-ul-hál*; another time.

ثبت *(fubt)* Firmnefs: *Subt-kurna*; to infcribe, fubfcribe.

ثقال *(fukál)* Heavy, loaded; alfo, *fukeel*.

ثليث *(fuleefs)* Eafy, fimple, plain.

ثمر *(fúmur)* Fruit; advantage.

ثواب *(firwáb)* A premium, reward; any good work.

جا

ج

جاى or جا (*jd* or *jáe*) Place: *Bé-já*; improper, unfit.

جاده (*jádéh*) Manner, practice; the right road.

جادو (*jádoo*) } A magician or enchanter.
جادوكر (*jádoo-gur*) }

جارى (*járee*) Running, flowing, proceeding; current, circulating: *Járee-bona*; to be current or in circulation; to pass, flow, &c.

جاسوس (*jásoofs*) A spy: *Jásoofee*; spying.

جام (*jám*) A cup, a goblet.

جامع (*jámai*) A great mosque.

جامه (*jáméh*) A garment, vest, gown.

جان (*ján*) The soul, spirit, mind: *Ján-déua*; to give up the ghost, to die: *Jánee*; my soul! my love!

جانب (*jánib*) Part, side.

جانشين (*já-núsheen*) A deputy, a successor.

جانوار or جانور (*jánwár* or *jánwur*) An animal.

جاودان (*jáwidán*) } Eternal.
جاويد (*jáweid*) }

جاه (*jáh*) Dignity, grandeur, rank.

جاهل (*jáhil*) An ideot or fool.

جايز (*jáiz*) Permitted, allowable; passing.

جايداد (*jáedád*) An assignment in land for the maintenance of any establishment, as a body of troops, or the like.

جايكير or جاكير (*jáegeer* or *jágeer*) A pension in land: *Jágéer-dár*; a pensioner.

جبه (*júbéh*) A tassel, the knot of a spear.

جبر (*jubr*) Violence, force, power: *Jubr-sé*; by force.

جد (*Judd*) A grandfather, an anceftor: *Jidd*; endeavour, effort, labour: *Jidd o jébd*; labour, effort, &c.

جرا (*joodá*) Separate, diftinct, divided: *Joodá-joodú*; one by one: *Joodá-kurna*; to feparate, divide, difunite.

جدل or جرال (*júdál*) Altercation, conteft: *Jung o júdaul*; battling, fighting.

جروال (*judwul*) A line or rule; the lines drawn on the margin of a book.

جدید (*júdeed*) New.

جرات (*júrát*) Boldnefs, audacity, prefumption.

جراح (*jurráb*) A furgeon.

جرم (*joorm*) A crime, a fault: *Lá-joorm*; faultlefs.

جری (*júree*) Bold, brave, intrepid.

جریده (*júridéh*) Single, unattended (travelling).

جز (*júz*) Befides, except; a fheet, of paper, or of a book.

جزا (*júzá*) Compenfation, reward, retribution.

جزوی (*júzwi*) A part, a little, a few.

جزیه (*jiziéh*) Tribute, capitation-tax (levied on infidels).

جسارت (*júsúrut*) Boldnefs, prefumption.

جست و جوی (*jooft o jooe*) Search, diligent enquiry.

جسم (*jifm*) A body: *Jifmáni*; corporeal.

جشن (*jufbn*) Joy, pleafure; profperity; a feaft; a feftival.

جفا (*júfá*) Oppreffion, injuftice, violence, injury: *Júfá-kurna*; to opprefs, injure, &c.

جفت (*jooft*) A pair: *Ták-jooft* or *Ták kee jooft*: the game of odd or even.

جگر (*jigur*) The liver, the heart.

جل (*Jull*) ⎫ Majefty, glory, fplendour, power: *Jul-júlálébá*
جلال (*júlál*) ⎬ and *julfbánéhú*; epithets or attributes of the
جلالت (*júlálut*) ⎭ Divinity.

جلاب (*jooláb*) Any purgative; jalap.

جلادت (*júládut*) Agility, activity; ftrength.

جلا

جلاه (*joolláh*) A weaver.

جلد (*juld*) Quick, brisk, speedily: *Juldee*; quickness, speed; hastiness (of temper): *Jild*; a volume or book; the cover or
binding of a book: *Jild-bund*; a book-binder.

جلوه (*jilwéh*) Splendour; the bridal ornaments.

جلوس (*joolúss*) Accession to the throne; beginning of a reign.

جليل (*júleel*) Great, glorious, illustrious: *Júleel-ul-kudr*; high or
glorious in dignity or rank.

جماع (*júmaa*) ⎫ A collection, a crowd, a troop, a body.
جماعت (*júmáut*) ⎬ An assembly, meeting, society.
جميت (*júmiyut*) ⎭ Recollection; collected in one's self.

جمال (*júmál*) ⎫
جميل (*júmeel*) ⎬ Beauty, elegance.
جميلت (*júmeelut*) ⎭

جمد (*jumd*) Congelation, concretion.

جمع (*júmá*) Collection, accumulation; assembly; conjunction; the
plural number; a multitude: *Júmá-kurna*; to collect, accu-
mulate; to assemble.

جمعه (*goomáh*) Friday.

جمله (*joomléh*) The whole, the aggregate, the sum or total: *Min-
joomléh*; from, or out of, the whole: *Fil-joomléh*; upon the
whole.

جمهور (*joombúr*) All, universal; grandees; high heaps of sand.

جن (*jin*) A demon, genius, spirit.

جناب (*júnáb*) Majesty, highness: power, dignity; presence.

جنازه (*júnázéh*) A bier; a funeral.

جنت (*junnut*) Paradise.

جنس (*jinss*) A genus, species, kind, sort; goods, effects, moveables.

جنک (*jung*) War, battle; a combat, fight.

جنکل (*junggul* or *jungle*) A wood, a forest; a desert.

جنون (*joonoon*) A demoniac, an insane person; insanity.

جو (*jow*) Barley.

جواب

جواب (*júwáb*) An anfwer, reply: *Júwáb-déna*; to anfwer or reply; to refute or confute; to difmifs or difcharge.

جواد (*júwdd*) Liberal, beneficent.

جوار (*jiwár* or *júwár*) Neighbourhood, propinquity.

جواز (*júwáz*) Allowed, permitted, lawful.

جوان (*júwán*) A young man, a youth: *Júwán-murd*; a brave, noble, generous man: *Júwán-murdee*; bravery, generofity: *Júwánee*; youth.

جواہر (*júwáhir*) Jewels, gems; of *Jóhur*; a jewel: *Jóhurri*; a jeweller.

جود (*jood*) Liberality.

جور (*jowr*) Injuftice, violence, tyranny, oppreffion.

جوش (*joafh*) Ebullition, agitation; boiling, fermentation.

جوشن (*jowfhun*) A cuirafs.

جولان (*jowlán*) Moving, fpringing, wandering.

جهاز (*júház*) Paraphernalia.

جهان (*jéhán*) The world.

جهت (*jeht*) Form, fafhion, manner, mode, caufe, reafon, regard.

جهد (*júhd*) Endeavour, effort, labour, diligence.

جهل (*juhl*) Ignorance.

جهنم (*júhunnum*) Hell.

جیب (*jeib*) A pocket.

ﺝ

چابک (*chábúk*) A whip; active, fwift; beautiful: *Chábúk-márna*; to whip, to beat: *Chábúkee*; celerity, agility: *Chábúk-fúwár*; an expert or active rider; a riding-mafter, or one who breaks in horfes.

چاپلوس (*chápúloofi*) A flatterer, a deceiver: *Chápúloofee*; flattery.

چادر

چادر (*chádur*) A cloth, a sheet.

چار (*chár*, contracted from چهار *chéhár*) Four.

چاره (*chárch*) A remedy, cure, help, aid: *Béchárch* and *Náchárch*; poor, miserable, helpless, incurable.

چاشنی (*cháshnee*) Taste, trial.

چاك (*chák*) A fissure, rent: *Chák-kurna*; to tear, to rend.

چاكر (*chákur*) A servant: *Chákúree*; service, servitude.

چالاك (*chálák*) Quick, nimble; ingenious.

چتر (*chutr*) An umbrella, a tent, a pavilion.

چخماج (*chukhmaj*)
چكماك (*chukmák*) } A fire-steel and tinder-box.

چراغ (*chirágh*) A light, a lamp: *Chirágh-dán*; any case or vessel for a lamp.

چراكاه (*chúrágáh*) A pasture, a meadow.

چرب (*churb*) Fat, greasy; vicious: *Churbee*; fat, grease: *Churb-zoobán*; smooth-tongued.

چرخ (*churkh*) The sphere, the celestial globe: *Churkhéh*; a wheel of any kind; a reel.

چست (*choost*) Quick, brisk, ingenious: *Choostee*; agility.

چشم (*chushm*) The eyes; figuratively, hope.

چشمه (*chushméh*) A fountain; a source, a spring.

چمچه (*chumchéh*) A spoon, ladle, spatula; the diminutive of *chúmuch*.

چمن (*chúmun*) A garden, a meadow, a parterre.

چنگ (*chungg*) A harp.

چنگال (*chunggál* or *chunggul*) The claws, talons, &c.

چوب (*choab*) A staff, rod, baton: *Choab-dár*; a footman who carries a sort of staff or baton made of silver.

چوبان (*chowbán*) A shepherd, a pastor.

چهره (*chéréh*) Face, countenance, visage, air, mien.

چیت (*cheet* or *cheent*) Painted muslins, &c.; chintz.

چیز (*cheez*) A thing, any thing: *Ná-cheez*; nothing, good for nothing.

چین (*Cheen*) China; a wrinkle: *Cheeni*, Chinese; powdered sugar-candy.
حاجات

ح

حاجات (*háját*) Wants, neceſſities.

حاجت (*hájut*) Want, neceſſity, poverty: *Hájut-mund*; indigent, neceſſitous.

حاجب (*hájib*) A porter or door-keeper.

حاجي (*hájee*) One who has performed the pilgrimage to Mecca; a pilgrim.

حارث (*hádis*) New, happening recently.

حادث (*hádiſth*) An event or occurrence, an accident, a novelty.

حاسد (*háſid*) Envious, an envious perſon; an enemy.

حاشا (*h.iſhá*) God forbid! let it not be!

حاشيه (*háſhiéh*) Margin (of a book); hem (of a garment); border, brink.

حاصل (*háſil*) Produce, profit, advantage: *Háſil-kurna*; to get, obtain, gain, acquire: *Háſil-hona*: to produce, yield, &c.; to be got, acquired, received: *Háſilúl-kúlim*; upon the whole; the reſult, or, the ſhort of the matter is.

حاضر (*házir*) Preſent, ready, at hand, in waiting: *Házir-kurna*; to produce, make appear, bring before (a perſon or thing): *Házir-hóna*; to be preſent, ready: *Házir-rúhna*; to ſtay or remain at hand, or in waiting: *Háziree*; preſence; breakfaſt; deſert; repaſt.

حافظ (*háfiz*) One who has the whole Koran by heart; a guardian.

حاكم (*hákum*) A commander, a governor, a ſovereign, a ruler.

حال (*hál*) State, condition, ſituation: the time preſent: *Hálí*; now, at preſent: *Hálát* (plural of *hál*) circumſtances, condition.

حالت (*hálut*) Condition, poſture of one's affairs; circumſtances.

حامد (*hámid*) A praiſer (of God).

حامل

حامل (*bámil*) ⟩ Carrying; a porter; a carrier; a bearer.

حامله (*bámiléb*) ⟨ Pregnant; a pregnant woman: *Hámiléb-bona*; to be with child.

حامي (*bámee*) A protector, defender.

حب (*boob*) Love, affection, friendship.

حباب (*búbáb*) A bubble of water.

حبس (*bubfs*) Imprifonment; detention.

حبشي (*hubfbee*) An Ethiopian.

حبيب (*búbeeb*) A friend, a favourite.

حج (*buj* or *budge*) A pilgrimage to Mecca.

حجاب (*bijáb*) Modefty, fhame: *Hijáb-kurna* or *bóna*; to be afhamed, to appear bafhful or afhamed, to be referved through modefty.

حجار (*bujjár*) A lapidary.

حجام (*bújám*) Properly, a phlebotomift or bleeder; but ufually, a barber.

حجامت (*bújámut*) Shaving: *Hújámut-kurna*; to fhave.

حجت (*boojut*) A pretence; an argument, proof, or reafon: *Hoojut-kurna* or *lćowna*; to pretend, to adduce as a reafon.

حجره (*boojréb*) A clofet or chamber.

حد (*bud*) ⟩ Boundary, limit,

حدود (*budood*) ⟨ Frontiers, confines.

حديث (*búdeefs*) A novelty, hiftory, tradition; for the moft part applied to the fayings of Mahomet.

حذر (*búzur*) Caution, prudence, timidity.

حذف (*buzf*) Taking away, rejecting, cutting off (a letter or fyllable of a word): *Huzf-kurna*; to reject, omit, contract.

حرارت (*búrárut*) Warmth, heat, ardour, fervour; fever.

حراست (*biráfut*) Care, watching, guarding: *Hiráfut-kurna*; to watch, guard, take care of.

حرام (*búrám*) Unlawful, forbidden, prohibited: *Húrám-zádéh*; illegitimate, a baftard; but for the moft part ufed to fignify a rogue or wicked fellow: *Húrám-zádgee*; roguery, wickednefs:

G   *Húram-*

Húrám-zádgee-kurna ; to play the rogue, to commit a wicked trick or prank.

حرب (*hurb*) War, battle, hostility.

حرس (*hirse* or *hirfs*) Care, watching, guarding : See *Hirásut*.

حرص (*hirse* or *hirfs*) Avidity, covetousness, ambition : *Húreefs* ; covetous.

حرف (*hurf*) A letter (of the alphabet) ; a word, a particle.

حرکت (*hurkut*) Motion, action, procedure ; for the most part used in a bad sense : *Hurkut-kurna* ; to commit an improper action.

حرم (*húrum* or *hurm*) The haram, seraglio, or women's apartment.

حرمت (*hoormut*) Honour, reputation, character ; reverence, dignity : *Bé-hoormut-kurna* ; to dishonour, disgrace.

حریب (*húreef*) An enemy, an adversary, a rival ; also, a friend or associate.

حرین (*húzeen*) Sad, melancholy, afflicted.

حساب (*hisáb*) Computation, calculation, reckoning, account : *Hisáb-kurna* : to count, reckon, compute, &c. : *Hisáb-déna* ; to render an account : *Hisáb-monggna or léna* ; to call to an account, to take account.

حسب (*husb*) According, according to, in the manner, agreeably to, in conformity.

حسد (*húsud*) Envy, malevolence.

حسرت (*husrut*) Grief, regret : *Husrut-lugna* ; to grieve, to regret, to be afflicted.

حسن (*hoosn*) Beauty, goodness ; well, good, excellent : *Húsúnát* ; good works.

حشر (*hushr*) Concourse ; resurrection.

حشمت (*hushmut*) Pomp, equipage, magnificence ; a great train or retinue.

حصار (*hisár*) A fortified place ; siege : *Hisár-kurna* ; to besiege.

حصب (*hisséb*) A portion, share, lot, part : *Hisséb-kurna* ; to divide into shares, lots, &c.

حصن

حصن (*hoofn*) Chaſtity, female reſerve, privacy : *Hiſn* ; a caſtle or fortreſs.

حضرت (*huzrut*) An epithet often joined to the names of the Deity, of the prophets, patriarchs, &c. ; alſo a title by which kings, princes, and great men are addreſſed, equivalent to majeſty, highneſs, &c. ; literally, preſence, vicinity, area (of a moſque or palace).

حضور (*hůzoor*) Preſence ; the preſence (of a king, prince, or any ſuperiour perſon) ; quiet, repoſe.

حظ (*huzz*) Pleaſure, delight.

حفاظت (*bifſizut*) Care, preſervation, cuſtody ; protection, ſecurity.

حفظ (*hifz*) Memory ; protection, care : *Hifz-ilhy* ; heavenly care or protection.

حق (*huk*) Right, due ; truth, juſtice ; God : *Ná-huk* ; unjuſt, unjuſtly : *Huk-ni-huk* ; right or wrong (corruptedly *hoc-noc*).

حقارت (*hůkůrut*) Vileneſs, baſeneſs ; contemptibleneſs, contempt : *Húkůrut-kurna* ; to treat with contempt, to deſpiſe.

حقوق (*hůkook*) Rights, duties, laws ; juſt claims.

حقه (*hookéh*) A ſort of Indian pipe : *Hookéh-peena* ; to ſmoke : *Hookéh-burdår* ; the ſervant who prepares the pipe.

حقیر (*hůkeer*) Baſe, mean, contemptible : *Húkeer-rukhna* or *ginna* ; to hold in contempt.

حقیقت (*hůkeekut*) Truth, fact, ſincerity ; news, account ; true ſtatement of a matter : *Húkeeki* ; true, real, own (as one's own brother).

حکام (*hukkám*) Princes, governors, judges.

حکایت (*hikáiet*) A tale, ſtory, hiſtory.

حکم (*hookum*) Command, order, direction ; licence, permiſſion ; power, authority, dominion : *Hookum-déna* or *kurna* ; to order, command, &c. : *Hookum-léna* ; to get leave or permiſſion : *Hookum-monggna* ; to apply for or demand inſtructions ; to ſo-

licit

licit leave : *Hookum-bújá-laowna* ; to obey orders : *Bé-hookum* ; without orders, without leave : *Hookum-fé* ; by order.

حکما (*hookmá*) Sages, philofophers.

حکمت (*hikmut*) Skill, knowledge : cunning, art ; trick, myftery.

حکومت (*húkoomut*) Dominion, jurifdiction, government : *Húkoomut-kurna* ; to rule, govern, &c.

حکیم (*húkeem*) A doctor, phyfician ; philofopher.

طل (*hull*) Solution (of a queftion or difficulty) ; loofing (a knot) : *Hull-kurna* ; to folve or refolve ; to untie or unravel.

حلال (*húlál*) Legal, a lawful thing : *Húlál-kurna* ; to flay according to the forms prefcribed by religion (as fheep, fowls, &c.) ; generally, to murder.

حلاوت (*húláwut*) Sweetnefs : *Hulwáe* or *Hulwye* ; fweet meats, fweet cakes, confectionary.

حلق (*húluk*) The throat, the windpipe : alfo *Hulkoom*.

حلقہ (*hulkéh*) A ring, a circle.

حمال (*hummál*) A porter, a carrier of burdens.

حمام (*hummám*) A bath, a bagnio.

حمایت (*himáet*) Protection, defence : *Himáet-kurna* ; to protect, defend, fupport, countenance, abet.

حمد (*humd*) Praife : *Ulhumd-lillah* ; Praife be to God !

حمل (*huml*) A load or burden ; fruit (of the womb, or of a tree).

حملہ (*humléh*) An attack, charge, affault, ftorm : *Humléh-kurna* ; to charge, ftorm, &c.

حوا (*Húwá*) Eve.

حواس (*húwáfs*) Senfe, the fenfes.

حوال (*húwáléh*) Charge ; care, cuftody : *Húwáléh-kurna* ; to make over, refign ; to put in charge, to commit to the care.

حوالی (*húwáilee*) Environs : *Húwailee* ; a houfe.

حوری or حور (*boor* or *booree*) A virgin of Paradife ; a black-eyed nymph.

حوض (*howz*) A bafon or refervoir of water ; a fountain.

حیا

حيا (*hyá*) Shame, bashfulness, modesty : *Bé-hyá* ; shameless, impudent.

حيات (*byát*) Life.

حيران (*byrán*) Astonished, confounded.

حيرت (*byrut*) Amazement, stupor.

حيض (*hyz* or *byze*) Menses.

حيف (*hyfe*) Alas ! — tyranny, oppression.

حيلـ (*beeléh*) Fraud, stratagem, finesse ; art, cunning : *Heeléh-báz* ; a rogue, cheat, knave : *Heeléh-kurna* ; to deceive, to act with art, cunning, &c.

حين (*heen*) Time ; interval (of time) : *Heen-e-hyát* ; life-time.

حيوان (*hywán*) An animal or brute.

<h1 style="text-align:center">خ</h1>

خاتم (*khátim*) A seal, a ring.

خادم (*khádim*) A servant.

خار (*khár*) A thorn : *Khár-khár* ; disquietude.

خارج (*khárij*) External, without : *Khárij-kurna* ; to expel.

خارش (*khárish*) The itch.

خاشاك (*kháshák*) Chips, leaves, shavings, &c.

خاص (*kháfs*) ⎤ Pure, fine ; particular, peculiar, private, special :
خاصه (*kháséh*) ⎦ *Kháffoaam* ; the particular and the common ; all, every body.

خاصيت (*kháfiut*) Property, quality, virtue.

خاطر (*khátir*) The mind, soul ; for the sake or love of : *Khátir-jumma* ; a collected mind, ease of mind, confidence, reliance : *Khátir-jumma-kurna* or *déna* ; to assure, encourage, hearten, animate.

خاك

خاک (khák) Earth, duſt.

خاکستر (khákiſtur) Aſhes.

خال (khál) A mole.

خالو (kháloo) An uncle (by the mother).

خالـﻪ (kháléh) An aunt (by the mother).

خالي (kháli) Empty, vacant, unoccupied, hollow: *Khali-kurna*; to empty, to evacuate, to make hollow.

خام (khám) Raw, unripe; vain.

خاموش (khámoaſh) Silent: *Khámoaſhee*; ſilence, taciturnity.

خان (khán) A title among Mahommedans; but not always a patent dignity, being very commonly aſſumed by perſons of low condition, and eſpecially by Patans.

خاندان (khándán) Family, houſehold.

خانمان (khánm.in) Property, houſehold goods, furniture.

خانـﻪ (khánéh) A houſe; uſed in forming many nouns of place, as *Kitaub* or *Kootub-khánéh*; a library: *Tope-khánéh*; a park or train of artillery, &c.

خاين (kháin) A deceiver, a cheat, a diſhoneſt perſon: ſee *Khiánut*.

خايـﻪ (kháié) A teſticle.

خبر (khubr) News, intelligence, advice, information, apprizal: *Khubr-déna*; to adviſe, apprize, inform: *Khubr-léna*; to look after, enquire into: *Kbubr-dár*; take care! beware! alſo, an intelligencer: *Khubr-dáree*; care, caution: *Khubr-dáree-kurna*; to take care of, to attend to: *Bé-khubr*; unacquainted, ignorant, unapprized.

ختم (khutm) The concluſion, end, termination: *Khutm-kurna*; to conclude.

خجل (khújul)   ⎱
خجلت (khajlut)   ⎰ Shame, baſhfulneſs.

خدا (khodá) God; alſo *Khódái* or *Khôdye*.

خداوند (khodáwund, contractedly *Kbáwind*) Lord, maſter: Sir! my lord! a maſter, a huſband.

خدمت

خدمت *(khidmut)* Service, employment, office; kindnefs, friendly office: *Khidmut-gár*; a fervant.

خراب *(khúráb)* Vile, bafe; fpoiled, ruined, deftroyed: *Khúrábee*; vilenefs, badnefs, bafenefs; ruin, deftruction; *Khúráb-kurna*; to fpoil, ruin, &c.: *Khúrábát*; taverns, brothels.

خراج *(khiráj)* Tribute, tax: *Khiráj-déna*; to pay tribute.

خراط *(khurrát,* corruptedly *Khurrádee)* A turner.

خربوزه *(khurboozéh)* A mufk-melon.

خرج *(khurch* or *khurj)* Expence, expenditure: *Khurch-kurna*; to fpend, expend, difburfe, lay out: *Khurch-burdár*; a fort of fteward or fuperintendant of difburfements; a marketer.

خرخشه *(hurkhúfhéh)* A tumult, difturbance, riot.

خرد *(khird)* Underftanding, wifdom: *Khirdmund*; wife, fenfible, intelligent: *Khoord*; little, fmall, young: *Khoord-fál* or *Khoord-fáléh*; a youth, one of tender years.

خرکوش *(khurgofh)* A hare; literally, afs-ear'd.

خرم *(khoorm)* Chearful, pleafant, delightful: *Khoormee*; gladnefs, delight.

خرما *(khoorma)* A date.

خرمن *(khirmun)* The harveft.

خرمهره *(khurmúhréh)* A cowri.

خروش *(khúroafh)* A loud cry, an exclamation.

خریدار *(khúreedár)* A buyer, a purchafer.

خریطه *(khúreetéh)* A bag, a purfe (in which they inclofe letters); figuratively, a letter.

خریف *(khúreef)* The autumnal harveft.

خزان *(khizán)* The autumn, the falling of the leaves.

خزانه *(khúzánéh)* Treafure, a treafury, a magazine: *Khúzinchee*; a treafurer.

خس *(khufs)* Straw, a weed: *Khufs-khufs*; the root of the Jungle grafs, of which they make a fort of fcreen that, being watered, has the effect of changing the hot wind which paffes
through

through it, to a cool and refreshing air: those screens (which are called *Tutties*) are also made of a green briar named *Júwi-séh*: when made to roll up they are called *purdèhs* or curtains.

خسارت *(khúsárut)* Loss, damage.

خسر *(khoosúr)* A father-in-law.

خسوف *(khúsoof)* An eclipse of the moon.

خشک *(khooshk)* Dry, withered, stale: *Khooshki*; by land (in oppo-sition to water).

خشم *(khushm)* Anger, rage, fury.

خشنود *(khushnood)* Content, satisfied: *Khushnoodi*; satisfaction, plea-sure.

خصال *(khisál)* Good qualities, virtues.

خصلت *(khuslut)* Disposition, nature.

خصم *(khusm)* An enemy, antagonist; also master, lord, husband.

خصوص *(khúsoofs)* A particular or special matter; particularly: *Khú-soofun*; particularly, especially, chiefly, above all.

خصومت *(khúsoomut)* Enmity.

خصی *(khúsy)* An eunuch, a he-goat.

خط *(khutt)* A letter; hand-writing; a line; the beard.

خطا *(khútá)* Error, crime, fault: *Khútá-kurna*; to err, mistake, fail, to commit a fault.

خطاب *(khitaub)* A title.

خطبه *(khootbéh)* An oration in which the titles of the king are pro-claimed.

خطره *(khutréh)* Fear; danger: *Khutr-nák*; dangerous: *Bé-khutr* or *Be-khutréh*; without danger, safe.

خطوط *(khútoot)* Letters, epistles.

خفه *(khúféh)* Properly, strangling or suffocating; but more generally, angry; and thence *khufgi*, anger, displeasure, and *khúféh-kurna*; to make angry, to enrage, to displease.

خفیه *(khoofyéh)* Concealed, disguised: *Khoofyun*; secretly, disguisedly.

خلاب *(khiláb)* Mire, clay, filth.

خلاص

خلاص (*khuláfs*) Free, liberated, releafed : *Khulási-kurna* ; to free, to liberate : *Khuláfs* ; freedom, releafe.

خلاصت (*khuldfut* or *khuldféb*) The beft part of any thing, the effence.

خلاف (*khiláf*) Contradiction, oppofition ; contrary, oppofite, unfavourable : *Khiláf-kúbna* ; to contradict one's felf, to prevaricate.

خلال (*khilál*) A toothpick : *Khilál-kurna* ; to pick ones teeth.

خلالت (*khúlálut*) Sincere friendfhip ; alfo *Khoolut*.

خلد (*khoold*) Eternity ; paradife : *Khúlud* ; the heart, the mind.

خلعت (*khylaat*) A robe of honour.

خلف (*khúluf*) A fucceffor, an heir ; figuratively, a favourite fon.

خلق (*khulk*) The creation, mankind : *Khulkúlláh* ; God's creatures : *Khoolk* ; nature, difpofition : *Khoolkut* ; creation.

خلل (*khúlul*) Difturbance, diforder, confufion, ruin : *Khúlul-kurna* ; to make a difturbance, &c.

خلوت (*khulwut*) Retirement, folitude, fecret confultation ; a fecret or private place : *Khulwut-khánéb* ; a private or fecret apartment : *Khulwut-kurna* ; to confer or confult in fecret.

خليف (*khúliféb*) A caliph : — Applied now, through corruption or fome allufion not eafily to be difcovered, to tailors and cooks.

خم (*khum*) Crooked, curved : *Khum-kurna* ; to bend, crook, &c.

خمار (*khúmár*) Crop ficknefs after drinking : *Khummár* ; a drunkard.

خمر or خمير (*khumr* or *khúmeer*) Dough, leaven ; what is ufed to ferment.

خنجر (*khunjur*) A dagger or poniard.

خندق (*khunduk*) A ditch.

خنیا (*khúnyá*) Melody, finging : *Khúnyá-gur* ; a mufician or finger.

خو or خوی (*khoo* or *khooe*) Difpofition, nature, habit : *Naik-khoo* ; good, virtuous : *Bud-khoo* ; bad, vicious.

خواب (*khwáb*) A dream, fleep : *Khwáb-daikhna* ; to dream.

خواجه (*khwájéb*) A gentleman, a mafter, a governor ; a title of courtefy.

H

خوجه

خوجه *(khójéh)* An eunuch.

خوار *(khwár)* Wretched, contemptible; ruined: *Khwári*; wretched-ness, ruin; vileness.

خواست *(kháſt or khwáſt)* Desire, request, wish.

خواص *(kháwáſs)* The servant who sits behind his master on the elephant; a valet, a favourite; properties, qualities: *Khúwáſi*; that part of the *Howdah* or canopy of an elephant where the *Khúwáſs* is seated.

خوان *(khwán or khán)* A table, a tray on which victuals are spread or served.

خوانسامان
خانسامان } *khwánſámán* or *khánſámán* or *kháſámá* { A steward of the household; a butler; compounded of *Sámán*, stores, and either *Khán* (a lord, master, chief), or *Khánéh* (a house), or *Khwán* (a table), but most probably of the first.

خواه *(khwáh or kháh)* Wishing; praying for: — Used in forming many compounds; such as *Khyre-khwáh*; a well-wisher, &c.: *Kháh-ná-kháh* or *Khá-mú-kháh*; (literally, wish or not wish) nolens volens.

خوب *(khoob)* Well, fine, good; elegant, beautiful, charming, excellent: *Bhoat-khoob*; very well: *Khoobi*; goodness, fineness, &c.

خوراك *(khorák)* Provisions, meat; literally, eatables.

خورش *(khooriſh)* Eating and drinking.

خوش *(khooſh)* Pleased; pleasant, delightful, sweet, elegant, healthy, mild, lovely, &c.: *Khooſhi*; pleasure, joy, satisfaction, &c.: *Khooſhi-kurna*; to rejoice, &c.: *Khooſh-dmúdi*; flattery: *Khooſh-ámud-kurna*; to flatter:—This word is used in forming a variety of compounds; as, *Khooſh-bo*; fragrant: *Khooſh-kho* or *Khooſh-tubba*; of an amiable temper: *Khooſh-muzzéh*; delicious, agreeable to the palate, &c.

خوشه *(khooſhéh)* A cluster (of grapes, &c.); an ear of corn.

خوف

خوف (*khoaf*) Fear, dread, terror: *Khoaf-purrbna*; to be alarmed.

خونی (*khooni*) A murderer (from *Khoon*, blood): *Khooni-kurna*; to murder.

خیاط (*khyát*) A tailor.

خیال (*khiál*) Fancy, imagination: *Khiál-kurna*; to fancy, imagine, suppose: *Khidlát*; fancies, imaginations: *Khidli*; a fanciful perſon; fantaſtical.

خیانت (*khidnut*) Perfidy, diſhoneſty: *Khiánut-kurna*; to cheat, deceive, impoſe upon.

خیر (*khire*) Good, goodneſs; well, very well: *Khire o áſiut*; good health: *Khyriut*; wellbeing.

خیرات (*khyrát*) Charity, alms: *Khyrát-déna*; to beſtow alms.

خیره (*kheeréh*) Malevolent, malignant, wicked; vain, dark, obſcure.

خیلی (*khylé*) Many, much, very long.

خیمه (*kheeméh*) A tent: *Kkeeméh-doax*; a tent-maker: *Kheeméh korrbá-kurna*; to pitch a tent: *Kheeméh girrá-déna*; to ſtrike a tent.

د

داخل (*dákhil*) Entering, penetrating, arriving: *Dákhil-hona*; to enter, to penetrate; to arrive; to be arrived: *Dákhil-kurna*; to place or fix in.

داد (*dád*) Juſtice, equity.

دار (*dár*) A gallows; a manſion, dwelling, ſeat, country; as *Dár úl Khiláfut*; the ſeat of the empire (Dehli); a poſſeſſor, holder, lord, proprietor; uſed in forming many compounds; as *Zúmeen-dár*, a landholder; *Soobah-dár*, a governor of a province, a native captain of a company of Sepoys.

دارو کبیر

دارو كير (dír o geer) Tumult, conflict.

دارو (diroo) Medicine (in general): alſo, ſpirituous liquor.

داروغه (diroghah) A ſuperintendant.

داستان (dáſtán) A fable, romance, tale, hiſtory.

داعي (dá-éy) One who invites or ſtimulates; an author; a cauſe; one who prays or wiſhes; a claimant.

داعیه (diyéh) Petition, wiſh, deſire; claim.

داغ (dágh) A ſtain, a mark, a ſpot, a freckle: Dágh-lugna; to be ſtained or ſpotted; to get ſpoiled: Dágh-déna; to mark, to ſtain.

دام (dám) A net, a trap, a gin, a ſnare:— In prayer, may it endure for ever! May it be eternal or perpetual!

داماد (dámád) A ſon-in-law.

دامن (dámun) The ſkirt of a garment, the train of a gown; the border, the foot or declivity (of a mountain): Dámun-geer; an accuſer: Dámungeeri; accuſation, arraignment.

دان (dán) A particle uſed in compoſition, and ſignifying that which contains: as Kullum-dán, a pen-caſe or ink-ſtand: Piſhaub-dán, an urinal; Shummai-dán, a candleſtick, &c.: being alſo the participle of دانسٹن (dániſtun) to know, it is ſometimes employed in forming a claſs of perſonal nouns; as Kudr-dán, one who knows the merits of a perſon, a diſcerner of the characters of men, &c.

دانا (dáná) A wiſe man, a learned or ſenſible perſon: Dínáee; wiſdom.

دانش (dániſh) Knowledge: Dániſh-mund; wiſe, intelligent, a wiſe man.

دانه (dánéh) Grain (in general); a grain or ſeed; a pimple, a ſpeck.

داه (dáh) Commonly pronounced Díha; the well-known faſt or time of mourning in the month of Mohurrum, inſtituted in commemoration of the death of Huſſan and Hooſain; called alſo Aſhooréh, which, as well as Dáh, ſignifies Ten, the number of days that the faſt or mourning continues.

داي

دایر or داي (*dáii* or *dáih*) A nurse, a female servant: *Dood-peelye-dái*; a wet-nurse: *Junnye-ddi*; a midwife.

دایره (*dáireb*) A circle, circumference, orbit.

دایم (*dáim*) Permanent, perpetual; always, continually.

دبدبه (*dubdubéh*) Pomp, parade, state: *Dubdubéb-sé*; pompously, with great state.

دختر (*doakhter*) A girl, a daughter; a virgin.

دخل (*dukbl*) Intrusion, interference; disturbance, molestation; entrance: *Dukbl-kurna*; to interfere, interpose; enter, penetrate.

دراج (*doorráj*) A woodcock.

دراز (*dúráz*) Long: *Dúrázee*; length, tediousness, prolixity: *Door o dúráz*; diffusedly; a great length.

دربار (*durbár*) A court, a hall of audience.

دربان or دروان (*durbán* or *durwán*) A doorkeeper, a porter.

درجه (*durjéb*) A degree of rank; rank, honour, station.

درخت (*dúrukbt*) A tree (corruptedly pronounced *durkbut*).

درخواست (*durkbwáft*) Desire, request, demand, petition: *Durkbáft* or *Durkbwáft-kurna*; to request, solicit, &c.

درد (*durd*) Pain, grief, affliction; pity, compassion, sympathy: *Durd-lugna* or *kurna*; to pain, ache; to pity, sympathize.

درزي (*durzi*) A tailor; corruptedly called *Durji* or *Durjee*; the Hindostans generally changing z into *j*, and the gutturals خ and غ (*kb* and *gb*) into *k* and *g* as often as these letters occur in the Persian and Arabic words adopted by them; the reason of which is, that the proper Hindvi knows no such sounds, as may be seen in the Nagree alphabet. This impurity of pronunciation, however, is least observable in the superior orders, many of whom understanding the Persian, and others having a constant intercourse with such as do, are thereby enabled to avoid it.

درست (*dúroost*) Right, fit, proper, just, true; well, safe, sound, entire: *Dúroost-kubna*; to speak truly, to observe justly: *Tun-dúroofti*; health.

درشت

درشت (*duroosht*) Harsh, stern, rigid: *Duroshti*; harshnefs, severity.

درگاه (*durgáh*) A large mosque, a court.

درمیان (*dur-mián*) The middle, in the middle.

درنگ (*dirung*) Slow, tedious: *Dirung-kurna*; to delay, protract, &c. *Dirungee*; slownefs, delay.

دروازه (*durwázéh*) A door, a gate.

درویش (*durwaish*) A dervife; poor, indigent; a beggar.

دروغ (*duroagh*) A lie: *Duroagh-kuhna*; to lie: *Duroagh-go*; a liar.

دریا (*duryá*) The fea, a river.

دریغ (*diraigh*) Sorrow; repugnance; difinclination, backwardnefs: *Diraigh-kurna*; to withhold, to refufe, deny, to be backward or difinclined, to feel a repugnance.

دست (*duft*) The hand: *Duft-khut*; fignature: *Duft-khut-kurna*; to fign, to fubfcribe: *Duft-dweix*; a written engagement to contract: *Duft-rufs*; power, capacity; that which is attainable: *Duft* (from *Duft* or *Dufht*, a defert) a ftool or evacuation.

دستار (*duftár*) A turban.

دستانه (*duftánéh*) A glove or gauntlet.

دستک (*duftuk*) A pafs, a grant, a mandate.

دستگاه (*duftgáh*) Power, ftrength.

دستگیر (*duftgeer*) An affiftant, patron, protector: *Duftgeeri*; protection, patronage, aid.

دستور (*duftoor*) Cuftom, ufage, mode; premium, profit, commiffion; what is claimed from tradefmen by fervants purchafing commodities for their mafters.

دسته (*duftéh*) A handle; a handful: *Duftéh-kágbis*; a quire of paper.

دشمن (*dooshmun*) An enemy: *Dooshmúni*; enmity: *Dooshmúni-kurna* or *rukhna*; to hate, to entertain a hatred, to fall out, to be at enmity.

دشوار (*dooshwár*) Difficult, troublefome: *Dooshwári*; difficulty, trouble.

دعا (*dua* or *dooá*) A prayer, wifh: *Bud-dooá*; a curfe.

دعوت (*dáwut*) Invitation (to dinner, &c.); fummons; pretenfion.

دعوی

دعوی (*dáwé* or *dáwá*) Claim, pretenſion; a lawſuit: *Dáwé-bird-búri-kurna*; to pretend to an equality.

دغا (*dúgba*) Treachery, deceit, impoſture: *Dúgba-kurna* or *déna*; to deceive, circumvent, betray: *Dúgba-báz*; a traitor, impoſtor, rogue.

دفتر (*duftur*) A regiſter, roll, journal, record: *Duftur-khánéb*; an office for writing: *Dufturi*; the head clerk of an office.

دفع (*dúfa*) One time, once: *Ky-dúfa*; how often? *Dúfa*; repulſion: *Dúfa-kurna*; to repulſe, remove, drive away, avert.

دفن (*dufn*) Interred, entered: *Dufn-kurna*; to enter, inter, bury; conceal.

دقت (*dikkut* or *dikb*) Trouble, uneaſineſs; diligence, cloſe application, pains: *Dikb-kurna* or *déna*; to give trouble, to teaze, to vex, to plague.

دقیق (*dukeek*) Subtle, minute, fine.

دل (*dil*) The heart, mind, ſoul: *Dil-déna*; to encourage, to apply heartily.

دلاسا (*dil-áfa*) Conſolation, comfort: *Dil-áfa-déna* or *kurna*; to comfort, conſole, &c.

دلال (*dúlál*) A broker.

دلالت (*dúlálut*) Argument, demonſtration; ſign, indication, mark.

دلاور (*dil-áwur*) Intrepid, brave; *Dikáwúri*; bravery, courage.

دلبر (*dil-bur*) A ſweetheart, a lovely woman.

دلخواه (*dil-kháb*) Deſire; a beloved object, a fine woman.

دلخوش (*dil-khoofb*) Glad, contented: *Dil-khoofbi*; joy, content.

دلدار (*dil-dár*) A lover, a miſtreſs.

دلگیر (*dil-geer* or *dulgeer*) Afflicted: *Dilgeeri*; affliction.

دلیر (*dilair*) Brave, intrepid; impudent, bold, inſolent: *Dilairi*; boldneſs, bravery; impudence, aſſurance, confidence.

دلیل (*dúleel*) An argument, demonſtration, proof.

دم (*dum*) The breath; a moment: *Dum-léna*; to reſt, pauſe, to take breath: *Hur-dum*; every moment: *Doom*; the tail, end, extremity.

دما

دما (*dúmá*) Aſthma.

دماغ (*dimágh*) Haughtineſs, pride.

دمبال (*dúmbal* or *doombul*) A tail.

دمل (*doommul*) A bile; a felon; a ſwelling; alſo *Doombul*.

دمہ (*dúméh*) A pair of bellows.

دنیا (*doonyá*) The world: *Doonyá-dár*; a worldly perſon: *Doonyáwi*; worldly, relating to this world.

دوتا (*dootá*) Double, doubled.

دوا (*dúwá* or *dúwái*) Medicine; a remedy: *Dúwái-khánéh*; a medicine ſhop.

دواب (*doáb*) The country lying between the Ganges and the Jumna.

دوات (*dúwát*) An ink-holder or pen-caſe: *Dúwát-kullum*; pen and ink, an ink-ſtandiſh.

دور (*dowr*) An age, revolution, circuit, circle: *Door*; far, diſtant, remote: *Doori*; diſtance, remoteneſs.

دربین (*doorbeen*) A teleſcope.

دوزخ (*dozukh*) Hell.

دوست (*doaſt*) A friend: *Doaſtee*; friendſhip: *Doaſtee-rukhna*; to love, eſteem as a friend.

دوستدار (*doaſtdár*) A friend.

دوکان (*dookán*) A ſhop: *Dookán-dár*; A ſhopkeeper.

دولت (*dowlut*) Riches, wealth, fortune, proſperity, happineſs: *Dowlut-mund*; rich, fortunate, happy.

دون (*doon*) Baſe, mean, ignoble.

دباشی (*déh-báſhi* or *Déhbáſh*) Literally, a commander of ten; a perſon having a place of truſt; a valet.

دبر (*dubr*) Fortune, chance.

دہشت (*duhſhut*) Fear, terror, confuſion: *Duhſhut-lugna*; to fear, dread, apprehend, to be in a fright.

دہل (*doohul*) A drum; from whence the Hindvi *Dóbul*.

دیار (*diár*) Country, region.

دیانت (*didnut*) Religiouſneſs, piety.

دیباچہ

ديباچه‌ (*deebáchéh*) A preface, exordium or preamble (to a book).

ديدار (*deedár*) Meeting, feeing one.

ديده‌ (*deedéh*) The eyes.

دير (*dair*) Slow, late, long ago: *Dairee*; flowneſs, latcneſs, &c.: *Dairee-lugna*; to be flow, late, &c.

ديگ (*daig*) A large pot or cauldron: *Daigchéh*; a fmall pot: *Daig-dán*; a trevot or pot-hook.

دين (*deen*) Faith, religion: *Deen-dár*; religious, faithful.

دينار (*deenar*) A dinar; a piece of money.

ديو (*dio* or *deo*) A demon or genius.

ديوار (*diwár*) A wall: *Chár-diwár* or *Chár-diwári*; a garden wall, or the like; an inclofure; a paling (fquare).

ديوان (*diwán*) An accomptant; a collection of odes: *Diwán-khánéh*; a court, a hall of audience, a divan.

ديوانه‌ (*diwánéh*) Mad, furious, foolifh, infane: *Dewángi*; infanity.

ز

ذات (*zát*) Nature, fubftance, effence; fect, tribe: *Zát-léna*; to render a perfon incapable of affociating with the brethren of his religion; to deprive one of his religion; to take away ones caft: — A Hindoo is deprived of his *caft* if an alien to his faith touch his food, or, in many cafes, even his perfon. — The fame rigid notion is entertained by the inferior claffes among the Mahommedans. — *Zát-déna*; to facrifice ones religion, as a woman who enters into criminal engagements with an alien to her faith, or who, to gratify fuch an one, drinks out of the fame cup with him, or the like.

ذايقه‌

ذایق (*záikeb*) Taſte, reliſh.

ذبح (*zúbub*) Slaughter, ſacrifice : *Zúbub-kurna* ; to kill, to ſlaughter, to ſacrifice.

ذخیره (*zákbeerab*) Treaſury, magazine, granary ; ſtores, ſupplies, &c.

ذرہ (*zurréb*) An atom, a particle, a grain, a morſel.

ذکا (*zúká*) Acuteneſs of genius, penetration.

ذکر (*zikr*) Mention, recital, relation ; ſubject, topic, matter (of diſcourſe) : *Zikr-kurna* ; to talk of, to mention.

ذلالت (*zálálut*) Abjectneſs, meanneſs.

ذلیل (*záleel*) Abject, mean ; wretched, baſe.

ذم (*zumm*) Reproach, accuſation, detraction.

ذوق (*zowk*) Taſte, delight, joy, pleaſure, voluptuouſneſs.

ذیل (*zile*) Following, that which follows or is annexed ; as, to a letter on buſineſs, a liſt of particulars referred to, &c.

ر

راتب (*rátib*) Proviſion, any ones lot or portion of the neceſſaries of life : *Rátibéb* ; a ſalary, ſtipend, pay.

راحت (*rábut*) Quiet, repoſe, tranquillity.

راز (*ráz*) A ſecret or myſtery ; a bricklayer.

راس (*rás*) A ſtring or head of cattle.

راست (*ráſt*) Right, true, juſt : *Ráſti* ; rectitude, truth.

راسخ (*ráſikb*) Firm, durable, conſtant, rooted.

راضی (*rázi*) Content, ſatisfied : *Rázi-bona* ; to be content, to conſent or acquieſce : *Rázi-kurna* ; to ſatisfy, to cauſe to agree, to pleaſe.

راقب (*rákib*) A rival.

راقم

راقم *(rakim)* A writer, a writing.

رام *(rám)* Tame, obedient: *Rám-kurna*; to tame.

ران *(rán)* The thigh.

راوند *(ráwund)* Rhubarb; called, also, *Ráwundé Cheeni*.

راویان *(ráwián)* Hiftorians (plural of *Ráwi*).

راب *(ráb*, or, contractedly, *rúb)* Way, road, path: *Ráb-bur*; a road-guide: *Ráb-zun*; a robber: *Ráb-díree*; a paffport.

رای *(rái)* Opinion, thought, counfel; a Rajah.

رایات *(ráyát)* Standards, banners; efpecially the banners or colours of an army in motion; figuratively, a camp.

رب *(rubb)* God: *Yá-rubb!* My God! Oh God! *Rubbáni*; divine.

ریاعی *(rúbái)* A quatrain or verfe of four hemiftichs.

رباه بازی *(rúbáb-bazee)* Knavery, cunning; compounded of *rúbab*, a fox, and *bazee*, play or trick.

ربط *(rubt)* Union, friendfhip, attachment.

ربیع *(rúbi)* The fpring, the fpring harveft: *Rúbi ul owwul* (the third month of the Mahommedan year) and *Rúbi úl ákbir* (the fourth month); two fpring months.

رجا *(rújá)* Hope, also fear.

رجب *(rújub)* The feventh month of the Mahommedan year.

رجوع *(rújoo)* Return, turning towards: *Rújoo-laowna* or *lowna*; to turn towards, to fide with, to fubmit, to yield.

رحلت *(réhlut)* Travelling, departure; figuratively, death: *Réhlut-kurna*; to die.

رحم *(rúhim)* Compaffion, mercy; the uterus or womb: *Rúhim-kurna*; to pity, to compaffionate: *Rúhim-luggna*; to be moved, to be affected or touched with pity.

رحمان *(rúhmán)* God, the merciful or compaffionate.

رحمت *(rúhmut)* Pity, tendernefs.

رحیم *(rúheem)* Merciful, compaffionate; one of the Divine attributes.

رخ *(rúkh)* The cheek; fide, quarter, point; the caftle at chefs.

رخت *(rúkht)* Apparatus, furniture.

I 2

رخسار

رخسار *(rúkhfár* or *rúkhfáréh)* The cheek, the face, the mien, the air.

رخصت *(rúkhfut)* Licenfe, permiffion, efpecially to depart: *Rúkhfut!*
Depart! or, you have leave to go: *Rúkhfut-monggna*; to afk
leave to depart: *Rúkhfut-kurna*; to difmifs, to difcharge from
attendance: *Rúkhfut-déna*; to give leave to go: *Rúkhfut-léna*;
to obtain leave, to take leave (to depart): *Bé-rúkhfut*; without
leave.

رخنه *(rukhnéh)* A fracture, a cleft, a notch, a crack; figuratively, a
difturbance, a breach or *fracas*, mifchief, damage, ruin.

رد *(rudd)* Repulfe, refiftance, refutation: *Ruddé-júwáb*; a reply or
refutation: *Rudd-kurna*; to vomit.

ردیف *(rúdeff)* The letter with which each diftich of a feries of poems
ends. In a dewan or collection of odes there are as many
feries as there are letters of the alphabet, every diftich of each
poem in the firft feries terminating in ا or *alif*, and every diftich of each poem in the laft feries ending in ی or *yé.*

رزال *(rúzál, rúzáléh, or rizáléh)* Mean, worthlefs, bafe: *Rizáléh-
ádmi*; a low, mean fellow.

رز *(ruz)* A vineyard.

رزق *(rizk)* Subfiftance, fupport, daily bread; a penfion or allowance.

رزم *(ruzm)* War, battle: *Ruzm-gáh*; a field of battle.

رساله *(rifáléh)* A body of horfe; a letter, a fmall tract or book; the
prophet (Mahommed): *Rifáléh-dár*; a commander of horfe;
in general, any military commander.

رسل رسایل *(rúfl-rúfáil)* Letters, epiftles, epiftolary correfpondence.

رستخیز *(rúftekhaiz)* The day of refurrection.

رسم *(rúfm)* Manner, cuftom, ufage; a law, precept, rule, regulation.

رسن *(rúfun)* A rope, a cord; from hence, probably, the Hindvi word ·
Ruffi.

رسوا *(rúfwá)* Difgraced, difhonoured: *Rúfwái*; difgrace, difhonour,
infamy, ignominy: *Rúfwá-kurna*; to difgrace, difhonour, &c.

رسوخ *(rúfookh)* Firm, conftant: *Rúfookhiut*; firmnefs, conftancy,
fteady friendfhip.

رسول

رسول (*rúsool*) A prophet, a meffenger, an ambaffador: *Ul-rúsool*; Mahommed (the prophet).

رسوم (*rúsoom*) Cuftoms, laws; duties, taxes; the poftage of letters, &c.

رشته (*rishtéb*) A thread, a line; a feries: *Rishtéb-dár*; a kinfman.

رشد (*rushd*) Rectitude, the right way: *Rúsheed*; a guide or conductor.

رشک (*rushk*) Envy, jealoufy, emulation.

رشوه (*rushwéb* or *rushwut*) A bribe, bribery: *Rushwéb-déna*; to bribe, to corrupt.

رضا (*rúzá*) Confent, acquiefcence, agreement; permiffion, leave (efpecially to depart): *Bé-rúzá*; without leave, confent, &c.: *Rúzá-monggna*; to defire leave.

رطل (*rutl*) A pound of twelve ounces.

رعد or رعار (*raad*) Thunder.

رعایا (*rú-ayá*) Subjects, peafants, the lower order of people; the plural of *Riyut*.

رعنا (*ránа*) Delicate, beautiful, tender, lovely.

رغبت (*rughbut*) Curiofity, ftrong defire, avidity.

رفا (*rúfá*) Mending (as a garment): *Rúfú-kurna*; to mend; figuratively, to make up a breach in friendfhip.

رفاقت (*rúfákut*) Society, companionfhip: *Rúfúkut-kurna*; to affociate with, to join, to adhere to.

رفاییت or رفاه (*rúfáb* or *rúfáhiyut*) Repofe, quiet, tranquillity.

رفتار (*rúftár*) Walking, motion.

رفع (*rúfa*) Repelling, removing: *Rúfa-kurna*; to remove, difpel, repel.

رفعت (*rifát*) Eminence, highnefs, nobility.

رفو (*rúfoo*) Sewing clofe, counterpoint; darning: *Rúfoo-kurna*; to darn, to patch, to mend; *Rúfoo-gur*; a darner, &c.

رفیع (*rúfee*) High, fublime, eminent, exalted.

رفیق (*rúfeek*) A companion, colleague, affociate.

رقت (*rikkut*) Pity, condolence, tendernefs.

رقص (*ruks*) A dance, a ball.

رقعه

رقم (rikab) A letter, a note.

رقم (rukm) A writing: Rukm-kurna; to write; to mark.

رقيب (rúkeeb) A rival; one who watches; a guardian.

رگ (rug) A vein.

ركاب (rikáb) A stirrup: Huzráb-rikáb; attending, accompanying (a superiour): Rikábi; a dish or plate (properly of an octagonal form).

ركن (rúkn) A pillar, prop, &c.; aid, support; a grandee (plural, urkán).

رمز (rumz) A sign, nod, wink: Rummáz; speaking by signs.

رمضان (rumzán) The ninth month of the Mahommedan year, during which strict Mussulmans observe a rigorous fast between sun-rising and sun-setting.

رمل (ruml) Geomancy, or the science of sand.

رنج (ranj) Grief, vexation, pain of body or mind; also, Runjish and Runjish é khátir; offence, disgust, &c.

رنجور (runjoor) Sick, infirm, afflicted.

رند (rind) A drunkard, a debauchee; plural, Rindán.

رنگ (rung) Colour, hue; paint: Rung-raiz; a dyer: Rungeen; co-loured, tinctured; flowery, elegant: Rung-kurna; to colour, paint, tinge: Rung-déna; to dye, paint, &c.: Rung-á-rung; various-coloured, of different sorts.

روي or رو (roo or rooe) The face: Roo-bá-roo; opposite, face to face: Roo-bú-roo-kurna; to confront, to bring face to face, to bring or produce before.

روا (rúwá) Allowable, worthy, proper, fit, just, suitable, becoming, agreeable: Rúwá-hóna; to be fit, proper, &c.: Rúwá-dár; right, allowable, lawful: Rúwá-rukhna; to tolerate, allow, permit (a practice).

رواج (rúwáj) Usage, in use, custom, practice.

روان (rúin) Life, soul: Rúwán; flowing, proceeding; used in forming many compounds: Rúwánéh; a permit: Rúwánéh-kurna;

kurna ; to difpatch : *Ruwánéb-bóna* ; to be difpatched, to depart, to fet out.

روایت (*rúwáis*) A narrative, hiftory.

روپیه (*roopiyéh*) A rupee: *Roopáb* ; filver.

روح (*rooh*) The foul, the fpirit : *Rúbáni* ; fpiritual, holy.

رود (*road*) A river : the ftring of a mufical inftrument.

روز (*roze*) A day : *Roze-roze* ; every day, daily : *Roze-gár* ; fortune,
time, the world, an age : *Roze-náméh* ; a journal, a diary :
Roazi ; fuftenance, daily food, lot, fate, portion ; fervice,
livelihood : *Béroazgír* ; without employ, without the means
of living.

روزه (*roazéh*) Fafting : *Roazéh-rukhna* ; to faft : *Roazéh-dár* ; one
who obferves faft.

روش (*rúwifb*) Mode, manner, habit ; cuftom, rule.

روشن (*rófbun*) Light, fplendid, clear, manifeft ; illuftrious, enlight-
ened : *Roafbnii* ; light, alfo ink.

روشناس (*rúfbúnás*) Knowing the face ; acquainted with ; well
known.

روضه (*rouzéh*) A garden.

روغن (*róghun*) Oil, butter.

روغن زرد (*róghun-zurd*) Ghee, a fort of butter made of buffalo's milk :
Róghun-feeáh ; oil.

روکردان (*roo-gurdán*) Averted, with the face turned away : *Roo-gur-
dán-kurna* ; to turn away the face, to abandon, forfake, &c. :
Roo-gurdáni ; deferting, forfaking, turning away from.

روم (*room*) The Roman empire, Romelia, the Turkifh empire, Greece :
Roomi ; a Grecian.

رومال (*rúmál*) A handkerchief ; compounded of *Roo* (the face), and
Mál (the Perfian participle *rubbing* or *wiping*).

رونق (*rounuk*) Beauty, elegance, fplendour, ornament ; figuratively,
order, regularity, fymmetry.

ره (*réh*) A road, path, track.

رہا (rehá) Liberation, escape: *Rehá-kurna*; to liberate, set free.

رہبر (rúh-bur) A guide; see رہبر, *ráhbur*.

رہزن (rúh-zun) A highwayman, an infester of the roads: *Rúhzunni*; robbing, a highway robbery.

رہین (rúhin) A pledge, a pawn: *Rúhin-déna* or *rukhna*; to pledge, to pawn; to give as a hostage.

رہنما (rúh-númái) A guide, a pilot: *Rúhnúmái*; guidance, direction, conduct: *Rúhnúmái-kurna*; to guide, conduct, &c.

رہوار or رہوال (rúhwár or rúbwál) An ambler, an easy-paced nag.

ریا (reeá) Hipocrisy, dissimulation.

ریاست (riásut) Government, dominion; governing, ruling.

ریاضت (riázut) Abstinence, austerity; mortifying the flesh: *Ihl* or *Sáheb é riázut*; abstemious, austere; a sober, abstemious, or austere person.

ریاضی (riázy) Mathematicks.

ریب (raib) Doubt, suspicion; necessity; bad fortune.

ریبت (reebut) Suspicion, doubt; slander, calumny.

ریحان (reebán) An odoriferous herb; sweet basil, &c.

ریز (raiz) Pouring, scattering, dropping, &c.; participle of *raikhtun*, and used in forming many compound epithets and personal nouns, as *Khoon-raiz*; a murderer, &c.

ریزش (raizush) Pouring, flowing.

ریزہ (raizéh) A small piece or bit; broken in small pieces; a crumb; *Raizéh-raizéh*; in pieces.

ریس (ryis) A chief, a leader, a head, a principal, a commander.

ریسمان (reesmán) A rope, cord, thread.

ریش (reesh) A wound, a sore; the beard.

ریگ (raig) Sand: *Raigistán*; a sandy place, a strand.

ریم (reem) Pus, matter; humours; dregs, drofs, lees.

ز

ز

ز *(ze)* Contracted from از *uz*, from, by, of, &c.

زاج *(záj)* Copperas, vitriol.

زاده or زاد *(zád or zádéh)* Born; a son, a child: In Hindvi rendered feminine by changing the termination to *i* or *ee*: thus *Saheb-zadéh*, a young gentleman; *Sahéb-zádee*, a young lady: This word is used in forming many compounds; as *admi-zád*, born of man; a man: *Purri-zad*; born of an angel or fairy; figuratively, a beautiful woman: *Shah-zádéh*; born of a king, a prince: *Shah-zádee*; a princess.

زار *(zár)* A groan, a plaint, a lamentation; also, a particle denoting place; as, *Gúl-zár*; a garden of roses, or a flower garden.

زاری *(zári)* Crying, lamentation, bewailing.

زاکی *(záki)* Pure, holy, pious.

زاهد *(záhid)* Religious, devout; a religious or holy person.

زاید *(záid)* Redundant, superfluous.

زایل *(záil)* Failing, perishing, vanishing; deficient.

زبان *(zúbán)* The tongue; a language, idiom, or dialect.

زبدت *(zúbdut or zúbdéh)* The best of any thing, the cream of milk.

زبر *(zúbur)* Above; high, superior; superiority; strong, forcible.

زبردست *(zúbur-dust)* A strong man; a man of violence: *Zúbur-dusti*; violence: *Zúbur-dusti-kurna*; to commit violence, to act unjustly, to wrong, to injure, to oppress.

زبور *(zúboor)* The psalms of David.

زبون *(zúboon)* Vile, bad, infamous, worthless, ugly: *Zúbooni*; badness, vileness, &c.

زحمت *(zúhmut or zóhmut)* Disquietude, trouble, molestation, annoyance; pain, indisposition: *Zóhmut-kurna, déna,* or *poanchhina*; to afflict, molest, trouble, &c.

K

زخم

زخم (*zukhm*) A wound, a scar, a cut : *Zukhmi* ; wounded, a wounded person : *Zukhm-lugna* or *khána* ; to receive a wound : *Zukhm-déna* or *kurna* ; to wound.

زر (*zur*) Gold, money : *Zurreen* ; golden.

زراعت (*ziráut*) Agriculture, husbandry ; sown fields : *Ziráut-kurna* ; to cultivate the ground.

زربفت (*zur-buft*) Brocade, cloth of gold.

زرد (*zurd*) Yellow ; pale, livid : *Zurdi* ; yellowness.

زردوز (*zur-doze*) An embroiderer : *Zurdózi* ; embroidery : *Zurdózi-kurna* ; to embroider.

زشت (*zisht*) Ugly, deformed, hideous, vile, filthy, odious : *Zisht-roo* ; ugly-faced, an odious or disagreeable countenance : *Zishti* ; deformity, ugliness.

زعاف (*záif*) A sudden death ; a deadly poison.

زعفران (*záferán*) Saffron : *Záferáni* ; of a saffron colour.

زکا (*zúkká*) Becoming, fitting, adviseable ; purity : *Zúká* ; genius, wit, understanding.

زکات (*zúkát*) Alms.

زکام (*zúkám*) A defluxion, a cold.

زلال (*zúlál*) Pure, limpid.

زلزله (*zulzúléh*) An earthquake.

زلف (*zúlf*) A curling lock, a ringlet.

زمام (*zimám*) A rein, a bridle.

زمانه or زمان (*zúmán* or *zúmáneh*) Time, an age, fortune, chance, fate, destiny : *Zúmáneh-sázi* ; time-serving, accommodating ones self to the time : *Zúmáni* ; temporal, worldly.

زمرد (*zúmrúd*) An emerald.

زمره (*zúmréh*) A multitude, a troop, a body.

زمستان (*zúmistán*) Winter : *Zúmistáni* ; a winter dress.

زمین (*zúmeen*) The earth, ground, soil ; a region, country ; land.

زن (*zun*) A woman, a wife ; also the participle of زدن, to strike, beat, &c. used in forming a variety of compounds ; as *Ráb-zun,*

زن (zun, a robber or highwayman, &c.: Zunkéb; an old woman, a woman.

زنا (zinái) Adultery, fornication; Zinái and Zinákár; an adulterer or fornicator.

زنار (zúnnár) The string worn by Brahmans: Zúnnár-dár; a Brahman.

زنانه (zúnánéh) Womanly, feminine, effeminate; a feraglio; also, the women of the feraglio.

زنبور (zumboor) A wasp, a hornet.

زنجف (zinjuf) Corruptedly Sunjáf: the fringe, border, binding, or other ornament round the edge of a garment.

زنجير (zinjeer) Improperly pronounced Zunjeer, a chain: fetters, irons.

زنخدان or زنخ (zunkb or zunkbdán) The chin, the pit in the chin.

زندان (zindán) A prison.

زندكاني (zindegáni) Life, living, existence.

زندكي (zindegi) Life.

زنكي (zunggi) An Ethiopian, a negro.

زنهار (zinbár) Care, attention, caution; protection; take care! never!

زواجر (zúwájir) Prohibition; forbidden, prohibited.

زوال (zúwál) Misery, wretchedness, decline.

زوج (zouj) A husband: Zowjéh; a wife.

زود (zud or zood) Quick, swift, soon, readily, suddenly: Zoodi; quickness, swiftness, celerity, velocity; hastiness or warmth of temper.

زور (zoor or zoar) Strength, power, force, vigour; violence: Zoar-kurna; to exert ones strength; to force: Zoar-fé-léna; to seize, to usurp.

زوراور (zoar-áwur) A strong, robust, or athletic person: Zoaráwúri; strength, vigour.

زه (zéb or zih) A bow-string.

زهد (zúhd or zóhd) Devotion; renouncing the things of the earth: continence.

زهر (*zúhur*) Poifon, venom : *Zúhur-kátil*; mortal poifon : *Zúhur-khá-na*; to take poifon, to poifon ones felf : *Zúhur-dár*; poifoned, venomous.

زهره (*zúhreh*) The planet Venus : *Zúhreh*; the gall or bile; power, vigour, fpirit.

زیادت (*ziádut*) Increafe, augmentation, furplus : *Ziádti* or *Zyadti*; fuperfluity, abundance.

زیاده (*ziádeh* or *zyadeh*) More, too much : *Zyadigi*; increafe, addition : *Zyadeh-kurna*; to increafe, augment, add : *Zyadeh-kur*; increafe ! — When fpoken at table it is underftood as an order for removing the victuals; but it is, in ftrictnefs, a fort of grace, comprehending a fupplication to God to continue or increafe his bounty.

زیارت (*ziárut*) A vifit, a pilgrimage : *Ziárut-gáh*; a place of devotion or pilgrimage : *Ziárut-kurna*; to vifit (a perfon or place held in reverence); to perform a pilgrimage.

زیان (*zián*) Damage, detriment, injury, lofs, prejudice.

زیب (*zeeb* or *zaib*) An ornament; elegance, beauty; lovely, graceful : *Zeebá*; beautiful, adorned : *Zeebái*; beauty, gracefulnefs.

زیج (*zeej*) Aftronomical tables; a mafon's rule.

زیر (*zair*) Under, below, beneath, at the bottom; the under or lower part : *Zair-o-zubr*; below and above, topfy turvy : *Zair-o-zubr-kurna*; to fubvert, overturn, reverfe, ruin : *Zair-duft* (oppofed to *Zubr-duft*) under command, in the power; a fubject, a vaffal, &c.

زیرا (*zairá* and *zairákeh*) Becaufe, on account of, fince.

زیرک (*zeeruk*) Ingenious, intelligent, fagacious, penetrating.

زین (*zeen* or *zin*) A faddle.

زینت (*zeenut*) Ornament, decoration; beautifulnefs.

زیور (*zaiwur*) Jewels, trinkets or ornaments of gold, filver, or precious ftones.

سـ

سا (*sá*) A particle denoting resemblance, and used in forming a variety of compound epithets; as, *Umbur-sá*; resembling ambergris.

سابق (*sábik*) Formerly, preceding.

ساحر (*sáhir*) An enchanter, a sorcerer.

ساحل (*sáhil*) The shore or sea coast.

سادات (*sádát*) Siyuds, descendants of Mahommed, lords, princes.

سادہ (*sádéh*) Pure, simple, plain, unmixed: *Sádéh-dil*; innocent, simple, harmless.

سار (*sár*) A particle which, added to nouns, denotes place or resemblance.

ساز (*sáz*) A musical instrument: *Sáz-o-sámán*; apparatus, arms: *Sázush*; collusion, connivance: *Sázush-kurna*; to connive at, to screen, to enter into an engagement to betray or deceive, to agree (in a bad sense): *Sázindéh*; a player on musical instruments.

ساعت (*sáut* or *saat*) An hour, a moment; a watch or clock.

ساعي (*sá-y*) Endeavouring, labouring; one who labours or endeavours.

ساغر (*sághur*) A cup, a goblet, a bowl.

سانق (*sák*) The leg.

ساقي (*sáki*) A cup-bearer.

ساکت (*sákit*) Silent, quiet.

ساکن (*sákin*) Fixed, quiescent; an inhabitant.

ساکوت (*sákoot*) A silent man.

سال (*sál*) A year: *Sáli*; aged: *Sáliánéh*; yearly, a yearly stipend or income.

سالار (*sálár*) A leader, a commander, a chief.

سالک (*sálik*) A traveller.

سامان

سامان (*símán*) Meafure, quantity; underftanding; opulence; materials, furniture, apparatus.

سامع (*síma*) Hearing; a hearer.

سامي (*sími*) Sublime, exalted.

سان (*sán*) Caufe, reafon, manner: added to nouns, it fometimes denotes fimilitude.

سايبان (*sáebán*) A canopy, a pavilion, a tent, a parafole or paraplui; of *Sáéh* or *Sáyéh*, a fhade or fhadow.

ساير (*sáir*) The whole; taxes or duties on commodities; excife.

سايس (*sáis*) A groom, an equerry.

سايه (*sáéh* or *sáyéh*) A fhade, a fhadow: *Sáyéh-dár*; fhady: figuratively, protection, afylum, &c.

سپارش (*fipárifh* or *fifúrifh*) A recommendation, a character: *Sipárifh* or *Sifúrifh-kurna*; to recommend, to fpeak of a perfon in terms of commendation: *Sifúrifh-déna*; to give a perfon (as a fervant) a character.

سپاس (*fipafs*) Prayer, praife (efpecially to God).

سپاه (*fipáh*) Generally written and pronounced *Sepoy* in India; a foldier: *Sipáhi*; military, belonging to a foldier; a foldier: *Sipáh-fálár*; the general of an army, a great officer or commander: — This is the fame word as the Turkifh *Spahi*, which occurs fo often in the Englifh prints.

سبب (*fubub*) A caufe, reafon, motive, argument, mean, medium, inftrument: *Bé-fubub*; caufelefsly, without reafon: *Subub-déna*; to account for.

سبحان (*fubbán*) Praifing, glorifying (God): *Subbán-alláh*; O great God! (ufed to exprefs amazement): *Huk Subbáno tálá*; God the moft holy and omnipotent.

سبد (*fubud*) Hair-cloth.

سپر (*fipur*) A fhield, a buckler, a target.

سبز (*fubz*) Green: *Subz-rung*; of a green colour.

سبزه (*súbzéh*) Green, a green herb, a pot-herb: *Subzi*; verdure, greenness.

سبع (*súba*) Seven : the seventh part ; also *Súbút*.

سبق (*súbuk*) A lecture, a lesson ; reading.

سبك (*súbúk*) Light (opposed to *heavy*): weak, facile, unsteady, of a contemptible character: *Súbúk-nidyéh*; cheap, of little value, in low esteem: *Subúki* or *Subki*; lightness; despicableness, disesteem : *Subki-luggna* ; to incur contempt, to let ones self down, to fall into disrepute or disesteem.

سبو (*súboo*) A cup, an ewer, a jar.

سپہر (*spuhr*) The sphere, the celestial globe ; fortune, time, the world.

سپید (*súpaid*) White : *Súpaida*; white lead : *Súpaidi*; whiteness, paleness.

سپیده (*súpaidéh*) Whiteness, the white of an egg ; a white paint used by women.

سبیل (*súbeel*) A way, road, path ; a mode, a manner.

ستاره (*sitáréh*) A star.

ستایش (*sitáish*) Praise, returning thanks.

ستم (*situm*) Tyranny, oppression, violence, injustice, injury : *Situm-kurna* ; to oppress, tyrannize, &c.: *Situm-gár* ; a tyrant, oppressor, &c.

ستور (*sútoor*) An animal, a quadruped, a beast of burden ; cattle.

ستون (*sútoon*) A pillar, a column, a prop.

ستوه (*sútooh* or *sútóh*) Distress, affliction, uneasiness, indigence.

ستیز (*sútaiz*) Competition, contention ; a battle, conflict.

سجاد (*sujjúd*) Adoring, bowing the body in adoration: *Sujjidéh*; a carpet on which the Mahommedans prostrate themselves when at prayer : *Sujdéh*; an act of adoration : *Sujdéh-kurna*; to worship, adore, &c.: *Sujdéh-gáh*; a place of worship, a mosque, &c.

سجر

سحر *(sŭhur)* The dawn, the crepuscle, the morning: *Sybr*; magic, sorcery, necromancy.

لخی *(sŭkhi)* Liberal, generous, munificent: *Sŭkhawut*; liberality, munificence, generofity: *Sŭkhi*; a liberal or generous man.

سخت *(sukht)* Hard, ſtrong, firm, ſolid, violent, intenſe, unfortunate, auſtere, rigid, ſevere: *Sukhti*; hardneſs, aſperity, vehemence, indigence, adverſity: *Sukht-kŭhna*; to ſpeak harſhly or ſeverely.

سخن *(sŭkhún or sŭkhun or sókhun)* Speech, talk, diſcourſe; a word, a vocable, a ſaying; a thing, matter, buſineſs, affair: *Sŭkhun-kŭhna*; to ſpeak: *Bud-sókhun*; improper or immodeſt words, ſpeech or diſcourſe.

سد *(sudd)* An obſtruction, impediment: *Sudd-kurna*; to impede, obſtruct, block up the way: *Sud*; a hundred.

سر *(sur)* The head, top, end, point, extremity, ſummit: (from hence, probably, the Hindvi *Sir* or *Seer*)—*Sirr*; a ſecret or myſtery: *Sur or Sir-káttna*; to behead: *Sur-o-kar*; buſineſs, affair, concern.

سرای or سرا *(sŭrá or sŭrái)* A palace, a houſe, an inn; a public building in a town or village where travellers are accommodated gratuitouſly.

سراپا *(sŭrápá)* From head to foot, totally.

سراج *(siráj)* The ſun, a lamp, lantern, light; plural, *Soorúj*, which is the ſame as the common Hindvi term for the Sun.

سراسیمه *(sŭrásiméh)* Amazed, confounded, ſtupified, aſtoniſhed.

سراغ *(sŭrágh)* A ſign, a mark, a trace: *Sŭrágh-powna*; to diſcover traces of, to find out.

سرافراز *(sur-ufráz)* Eminent, diſtinguiſhed, exalted: *Sur-ufráz-hóna*; to be honoured or exalted: *Sur-ufráz-kurna*; to honour, promote, exalt, dignify: *Sur-ufrázi*; elevation, promotion to titles or honours.

سرامد

سرامد (*surámud*) Perfect, compleat, accomplished ; master of any art, profession, or excellence.

سرانجام (*sur-unjám*) Materials, ingredients, apparatus ; conclusion, end, accomplishment : *Sur-unjám-kurna* ; to prepare, to finish, to accomplish, to equip, to furnish the means.

سرباز (*sur-báz*) Brave, intrepid : *Surbázi* ; courage, boldness.

سربلند (*sur-búlund*) Eminent, glorious : *Sur-búlundi* ; eminence, aggrandizement, exaltation.

سرپوش (*sur-poash*) Covering the head ; a lid ; that part of the *Hookah* which covers the *Chillum* or tobacco and *Gúl* : it is in common made of copper.

سرپیش (*sur-paish* or *sur-paich*) An ornament worn in the front of the turban, and generally made of jewels.

سرتاپا (*sur-tá-pá*) From head to foot.

سرتیز (*surtaiz*) Sharp-pointed.

سرچشمه (*sur-chushmeh*) A fountain.

سرحد (*surhudd*) Frontier, confine, boundary.

سرخ (*súrkh*) Red : *Súrkhi* ; redness, a red tincture, red ink ; brick-bats or brickdust ; a grey horse.

سرخوش (*sur-khoosh*) Chearful, gay (especially from liquor).

سرد (*surd*) Cold : *Surdi* ; coldness, a cold : *Surdi-purrhna* or *luggna* ; to feel cold, to catch cold.

سردار (*surdár*) A chief, a leader, a head, a general, a commander, a master, a superintendant : *Surdári* ; command, direction, power, authority.

سررا (*sur-é-ráh*) The high road, the higher part of the road.

سررشته (*sur-rishteh*) A rope, thread, cord ; that which unites ; connected ; desire, wish : *Sur-rishtegi* ; connection, as the parts of a discourse, &c.

سرزنش (*sur-zúnish*) Reproach, reproof, chiding, railing at.

سرسام (*sursám*) Stupified ; a tumour of the brain : *Sursámi* ; stupidity, phrenzy.

L.

سرشت

سرشت (*súrſbt*) Nature, temperament, conftitution, complexion, difpofition.

سرف (*súruſ*) Prodigality, exceeding bounds; exercife, ufe, habit.

سرکه or که (*firkd* or *firkéh*) Vinegar.

سرکار (*furkár*) An overfeer, agent, or fuperintendant; generally written
   Sircar, and implying an accomptant or cafh-keeper.

سرکزشت (*fur-gúzuſbt* or *fur-gúduſbt*) Event, accident, tranfaction,
   relation of what has happened.

سرکردان (*fur-gurdán*) Wandering, ftraying; confounded, aftonifhed,
   depreffed, humble, wretched: *Sur-gurdáni*; diftrefs, wonder, &c.

سرکش (*fur-kuſb*) Refractory, difobedient, contumacious, rebellious:
   Sur-kúſbi; contumacy, difobedience.

سرکشته (*fur-guſbtéh*) Aftonifhed; wandering, at a lofs.

سرما (*furmá*) The winter, the cold feafon: *Surmái*; cold.

سرمایه (*furmáyéh*) Capital, ftock in trade, means.

سروم (*foorméh*) Antimony; an ointment with which they tinge the
   eyes.

سرنامه (*furnáméh*) The fuperfcription of a letter.

سرو (*furv* or *fúró*) The cyprefs-tree.

سروان (*furwán*) Properly, a chief or leader, but applied only to a
   camel-driver.

سرود (*fúrood* or *fúroad*) Melody, mufic, finging.

سرور (*furwur*) A chief, leader, prince, lord: *Súroor*; joy, pleafure.

سرنگ (*furhungg*) A general, commander, captain, or chief of any
   kind, an overfeer; hence *Serang* or *Sirung*, a captain of Laf-
   cars (marine or military).

سریش (*fúraiſb*) Corruptedly *Súraiſe*, glue, gum.

سریع (*fúrie*) Quick, fwift, nimble, ready.

سزا (*fúza*) Retribution, reward or punifhment (but generally the latter): *Súzá-powna*; to be requited, to be punifhed: *Súzáwár*;
   worthy, deferving, meriting: *Súzáwári*; merit, worthinefs.

سست

سست (*foost*) Languid, liftlefs, impotent, weak, feeble, idle, lazy, indolent, foft, tender, negligent: *Soost-pymán*; faithlefs, perfidious, unfteady to one's engagements: *Soostí*; languor, debility, indolence.

سطر (*sútir*) A line, a row, a feries, a column.

سعادت (*saádut*) Felicity, happinefs, profperity, good fortune: *Saádut-mund*; happy, fortunate, auguft.

سعد (*sád*) Felicity, happinefs, propitioufnefs.

سعي (*sái* or *sy*) Endeavour, effort, labour, diligence; *Sy-kurna*; to endeavour, exert, try, labour.

سفال (*sufáléh*) Low, mean, vile: *Sufálut*; lownefs, wretchednefs.

سفر (*sufur*) A journey, voyage; travelling: *Sufur-kurna*; to travel, to journey.

سفره (*sufréh*) A table, any thing in which victuals are placed: *Sufrut*; travelling provifions, a traveller's wallet.

سفل (*sufl* or *sufúlut*) Meannefs, an inferior condition: *Sufléh*; ignoble, vile, bafe, contemptible, fordid.

سفيد (*sufaid*) White, grey, hoary: *Sufaidi*; whitenefs, &c.

سقا (*súka*) A carrier or vender of water.

سقف (*sukf*) A roof, ceiling, flooring.

سكات (*sukát*) Silence; filent; alfo, *Sukoot* or *Sukoot*.

سكنه (*suknéh*) A habitation.

سكندر (*Sicundur*) Alexander the Great.

سكونت (*sukoonut*) Refidence, abode, dwelling; tranquillity: *Sukoonut-rukhna* or *kurna*; to refide, dwell, inhabit.

سكه (*sikkéh*) Commonly written *Sicca*; a dye for coining; the impreffion on money: *Sikkéh*; or *Sicca Rupee*; a rupee of full ftandard weight, oppofed to a *Sunwát* (or *Sunat*) rupee, which is a *Sicca* become light through ufe.

سلاح (*siláh*) Arms, armour: *Siláh-kháneh*; an arfenal.

سلاطين (*sulóteen*) Kings, princes: thofe prifoners of ftate at Dehli who are of the royal blood. The fucceffive jealoufy of the

L 2 reigning

reigning monarchs has rendered this clafs of wretched captives
very numerous.

سلام (*sulám*) A falutation; peace be with you! God preferve you!
Sulám-kurna; to falute, to bow to.

سلامت (*sulámut*) Safety, peace, falvation, immunity.

سلب (*sulub*) Furniture, arms, apparatus.

سلخ (*sulkh*) The end, or laft day, of a month.

سلس (*sulis*) Eafy, ductile, docile.

سلطان (*sultán*) A monarch, king, fovereign: *Sultáni* or *Sultúnut*;
empire, dominion: *Sultúnut-kurna*; to reign, rule, govern.

سلف (*suluf*) The paft, former times.

سلک (*silk*) A thread; a feries, order, train.

سلوت (*sulwut*) Content, chearfulnefs, felicity.

سلوک (*sulook*) Mode, manner, rule; treatment, behaviour: *Bud-sú-
looki*; bad treatment: *Súlook-kurna*; to treat well.

سم (*súm* or *soom*) The hoof of a horfe, &c.

سما (*súmá*) The fky, the heavens.

سمات (*simát*) A fign, mark; figns, marks, &c.

سماحت (*súmáhut*) Liberality, beneficence; eafinefs, facility.

سماع (*súmá*) Hearing, liftening; the ear, the hearing.

سمت (*sumt*) Way, path; part, quarter, fide.

سمع (*suma*) Hearing.

سمن (*súmun*) Jafmine, the lily of the valley.

سمند (*súmund*) A horfe of a noble breed.

سموم (*súmoom*) A hot parching wind which deftroys man and beaft.

سن or سنه (*sin* or *sunnh*) Year, age.

سنان (*sinán*) A fpear.

سنبل (*súmbúl*) The hyacinth.

سنت (*súnnut*) Regulation, inftitution, the divine commandments;
circumcifion: *Súnnut-kurna*; to circumcife.

سند (*súnud*) A commiffion, patent, or grant under a feal: *Sind*, the
Indus.

سندان

سنران (*sindán*) An anvil.

سنک (*sungg*) A ſtone: *Sungg-tiráſh*; a ſtone-cutter, a ſtatuary: *Sungg-raizéh*; gravel, a pebble.

سنکرف (*sungurf* or *ſhungurf*) Cinnabar, vermilion.

سنکین (*sunggeen*) Stony, reſembling ſtone, hard, firm; a bayonet.

سنوات (*sunwát*) Years, plural of *sunnh*:—A *Sicca*, or rupee of full weight, becomes a *Sunwát* after a certain number of years.

سنی (*sunni*) Lawful; an orthodox Muſſulman.

سو or سوی (*sú, soo*, or *sui*) Side, part, quarter; towards.

سواد (*súwád*) Blackneſs; black; environs, ſuburbs.

سوار (*súwár*) A horſeman, a cavalier: *Súwár*; a driver: *Súwárin*; cavalry, horſe: *Súwár-hóna*; to be mounted, to mount: *Súwári*; any carriage or travelling equipage; a train or ſuite.

سواف (*súwáf*) Death, a mortal diſeaſe (eſpecially among cattle).

سوال (*súwál*) A queſtion, interrogation, demand, requeſt, propoſition: *Júwáb-súwál*; anſwer and queſtion, converſation, diſpute, diſcuſſion, negociation, treaty: *Júwáb-súwál-kurna*; to negociate, treat of a matter, diſcourſe.

سوانح (*súwáneh*) Incidents, events, occurrences, accidents.

سوختکی (*soakhtigi*) Burning: *Dil-ſoakhtigi*; affliction, heart-burning.

سود (*sood*) Gain, advantage, emolument; intereſt or premium on money lent; uſury.

سودا (*sowdá*) Melancholy, madneſs, love; traffic, trade, commerce; ſtock (market proviſions): *Sowdágur*; a merchant: *Sowdágúri*; trading, commerce, merchandize: *Sowdágúri-kurna*; to trade, traffic, &c.

سوراخ (*soorákh*) A hole, an orifice, a paſſage: *Soorákh-kurna*; to perforate; alſo, *Soolákh*.

سوره (*sooréh*) The firſt ſection or chapter of the Koran.

سوز (*soaz*) Heat, ardour, inflammation; pain, torment; burning, inflaming (uſed in compoſition).

سوزش (*súziſh*) Burning; anxiouſneſs, ſolicitude; pain.

سوغات

سوغات (*sowghát*) A present brought or sent from a distance.

سوک (*soog*) Grief, anguish, misfortune; mourning (for the death of a friend or relation).

سوکند (*sŏgund* or *sowgund*) An oath: *Sogund-léna, kurna,* or *khání*; to swear, to take an oath, or to make oath.

سوہان (*sūbán*) A file.

سہل (*suhl*) Easy, not difficult, soft, easily.

سہو (*súho* or *sohuv*) Error, mistake, blunder, inadvertency, slip, forgetfulness, omission, negligence: *Súbo-kurna*; to mistake, blunder, neglect, forget.

سہولت (*súhoolut*) Facility, ease; smoothness, plainness (ground).

سہی (*súhi*) Straight, erect (cypress).

سہیل (*sóbeil*) The star Canopus.

سیادت (*síádut*) Dominion, rule, reigning, governing.

سیار (*syár*) Wandering, moving, travelling: *Syáréh*; moving stars.

سیاست (*síásut*) Punishment, chastisement: *Siásut-kurna*; to punish, chastise.

سیاق (*siák*) Arithmetic, numeration by the Arabic alphabet.

سیال (*syál*) Flowing rapidly like a torrent: *Syáléh*; a torrent.

سیاہ (*siáb*) Black, dark: *Siáhi*; blackness, darkness; ink: *Siáh-goosh*; the black ear, the name of an Indian quadruped.

سیب (*seeb*) An apple.

سیخ (*seekh*) A spit, a roasting-spit.

سید (*siyud*) A lord, a prince; the principal Mahommedan sect.

سیر (*syre* or *sire*) Walking, moving about: *Syre-kurna*; to walk or ride for the air, or to view a country: *Seer*; full, replete: *Seeri*; satiety, repletion: *Seerab*; moist, succulent.

سیرت (*seerut*) Disposition, nature, character, quality.

سیف (*syfe* or *sife*) A sword, a sabre, a falchion.

سیل (*seel*) Flowing, a torrent: *Seeláb*; an inundation.

سیم (*seem*) Silver: *Seemeen*; of silver, silver, silverized: *Seemáb*; quicksilver, mercury.

سیپا

سيما (seemá) The face, countenance, aspect.

سينه (seenéh) The bosom, the breast.

سيورغال (siyúrghál) A fief, a feudal tenure.

سيه (síeh) The same as Siáh, black.

شس

شاباش (shábásh) Bravo! Excellent! Shábáshi; (usually pronounced Shabasi or Sabasi) applause.

شاخ (shákh) A branch, a shoot; a horn.

شاد (shád) Chearful, exulting, pleased, delighted: Shádi; gladness, joy, rejoicing; a wedding: Shádi-kurna; to make rejoicings, to celebrate a wedding, to marry: Shadmán; joyful: Shádmáni; a rejoicing: Shádkámi; gladness, happiness, content.

شارع (shárai) A highway, a straight road.

شارک (sharik) A species of nightingale.

شاشس (shásh or shúshéh) Urine.

شاعر (sháir) A poet.

شاکر (shákir) Praising, thanking.

شاکرد (shágird) A scholar, a student, an apprentice.

شال (shál) A shawl.

شام (shám) The evening.

شامل (sh.imil) Communicating, comprehending; united, confederated: Shámil-hona; to be united, to be joined together, to be attached to, or engaged in, any cause.

شان (shán) State, condition, dignity, degree.

شانه

شانه (*shánéh*) A comb.

شاه (*sháh*) A king, emperor, prince: *Sháh-zádéh*; a prince: *Sháh-wár*; royal, noble: *Shábi*; royal, kingly; empire.

شاهد (*sháhid*) A witness: *Sháhidi*; testimony, evidence, witness: *Sháhidi-déna*; to bear witness, to give evidence.

شاهراه (*sháh-ráh*) The king's highway, the high road.

شاید (*sháid*) Perhaps, may be; fitting, proper.

شایسته (*sháistéh*) Suitable, proper, worthy, honourable: *Sháistigi*; propriety, fitness, worthiness, aptitude.

شب (*shub*) The night: *Shub o roze*; night and day.

شباب (*shubáb*) Youth.

شبان (*shubán*) A shepherd.

شبخون (*shub-khoon*) A night attack, a surprise, an alert: *Shubkhoon-kurna*; to attack or assault (a camp, &c.) by night.

شبنم (*shub-num*) Dew.

شبیه (*shúbéh*) An image, resemblance, similitude: *Shúbeeh*; alike, resembling.

شبهه (*shúbhéh*) Doubt, ambiguity, suspicion: *Shúbhéh-rukhna*; to entertain doubts.

شتاب (*shitáb*) Haste, speed, dispatch; also, *Shitábi*: *Shitáb-jána*; to go quickly: *Shitábi-kurna*; to make haste.

شتر (*shútúr*) A camel: *Shútúr-súwár*; one who rides on a camel; a courier or messenger mounted on a camel: *Shútúr-bán*; a camel-keeper.

شترنج (*shutrunj*) Chess.

شجاع (*shújá*) Brave, intrepid, magnanimous: *Shújáut*; bravery, valour, intrepidity, fortitude.

شجر (*shujr*) A tree, a plant.

شخص (*shukhs*) A person, individual, body; a man.

شدت (*shiddut*) Vehemence, violence, force; adversity, affliction (plural, *Shúdáid*): *Shiddut-sé*; violently, vehemently, forcibly: *Shúdeed*; vehement, rigorous, severe.

شر

شر *(ſhurr)* Wicked, malignant; wickedneſs, depravity: Hence *Shú-rárut*; wickedneſs, miſchief, roguery.

شراب *(ſhuráb)* Wine, liquor.

شربت *(ſhurbut)* Sherbet, a beverage compoſed of roſe-water and ſugar.

شرح *(ſhúrúh or ſhúréh)* Explanation, interpretation, commentary: *Shúrúh-kurna*; to explain, define, interpret, comment; to ſtate, relate.

شرط *(ſhurt)* A condition, agreement, compact, ſtipulation; a wager; plural, *Shúráit*: *Shurt-kurna*; to engage, ſtipulate, &c.: *Shurt-lúgaowna*; to lay a wager.

شرع *(ſhúra)* Law, juſtice, equity, faith, religion; a ſtraight, high, or public road: *Shúry*; legal, juſt, equitable.

شریف and شرف *(ſhúruf and ſhúreef)* Noble, illuſtrious; dignity, nobility: *Shoorſá*; nobles: *Shurſiyut*; nobility, illuſtrious birth.

شرق *(ſhurk)* The riſing (of the ſun); the Eaſt: *Shurki*; oriental.

شركت *(ſhurkut or ſhirkut)* Society, company, partnerſhip, communication, participation: *Shúreek*; a partner in trade, an aſſociate, an accomplice: *Shúreeki*; a partnerſhip: *Shúreek-hona*; to be united, aſſociated, or confederated.

شرم *(ſhurm)* Baſhfulneſs, modeſty, ſhame: *Shurm-rukhna*; to behave modeſtly: *Shurm-luggna*; to be aſhamed: *Shurmindigi*; ſhame, baſhfulneſs: *Bé-ſhurmi*; impudent, ſhameleſs, immodeſt: *Bé-ſhurmi*; impudence, immodeſty: *Shurm-nák, Shurmſár,* or *Shurmindéh*; aſhamed, baſhful, modeſt, reſerved, confuſed.

شروع *(ſhúroo)* Beginning, commencement: *Shúroo-kurna*: to begin, enter upon.

شرب *(ſhúrúb)* Deſire, appetite, avidity, gluttony.

شریر *(ſhúreer)* Wicked, miſchievous, roguiſh; a wicked or miſchievous perſon: *Shúreer-púnáh*; a wicked or roguiſh fellow: *Shirreer*; a very great raſcal: *Shúreeri*; wickedneſs, roguiſhneſs.

شریعت *(ſhúriut)* Law, juſtice.

M

شریف

شریف (*shúreef*) Noble, eminent.

شست (*shust*) Aim, or the manner of holding the bow when shooting : *Shust-kurna* ; to take aim.

شعار (*shaar*) A sign, mark, symbol.

شعاع (*shaa*) Light, splendour, lustre, rays (of the sun).

شعبان (*shában*) The eighth month of the Mahommedan year.

شعر (*shiar*) Poesy, metre, verse : *Shúara* ; the poets.

شعلہ (*shúléh* or *shúaléh*) Flame, blaze ; light, flash : Hence *Mushaal* ; a flambeau or torch.

شغل (*shúghl* or *shooghl*) Occupation, employment, study, attention, diligence.

شفا (*shifa*) Health ; restoration or re-establishment of health.

شفاعت (*shúfáut*) Deprecation, intercession ; intreaty.

شفتالو (*shuftáloo*) A peach.

شفق (*shúfuk*) The twilight ; pity, condolance.

شفقت (*shufkut*) Compassion, pity, tenderness : *Shufkut-kurna* ; to pity, compassionate, &c. : *Bé-shufkut* ; inhuman, unkind, merciless, unpitying : *Shúfeek* ; merciful, compassionate, benevolent, affectionate.

شقہ (*shúkah*) A letter (especially one from a person of rank).

شک (*shuk*) Doubt, suspicion, jealousy, fear, ambiguity, uncertainty : *Shuk-rukhna* ; to be suspicious or doubtful of : *Shuk-luggna* ; to conceive doubts or suspicions.

شکار (*shikár*) The chace, hunting ; prey : *Shikár-kurna* ; to hunt, pursue : *Muchhi-shikár-kurna* ; to fish, to angle : *Shikári* ; belonging to hunting ; a fowler, a sportsman.

شکاف (*shigaf*) A fissure, crack, crevice, cleft.

شکایت (*shikáit* or *shikayut*) Lamentation, complaint, accusation, impeachment : *Shikáit-kurna* ; to complain, accuse, upbraid, find fault, abuse, revile.

شکر (*shúkur*) Sugar : *Shúkur-kund* ; Sugar-candy : *Gúl-shúkur* ; conserve of roses : *Shúkúr* or *Shookúr* ; thanks, gratitude, praise (of God):

God) : *Shookúr-kurna* ; to return thanks : *Shúkrán* ; gratitude, acknowledgment.

شكرف (*sbigurf*) Great, glorious, excellent, beautiful, good, fine.

شكست (*sbikuft*) Defeat; broken : *Sbikuft-khána* ; to be defeated : *Sbikuftigi* ; defeat, ruin ; bankruptcy : *Dil-sbikuftéh* ; broken-hearted, afflicted : *Sbikuftéh* ; the current Persian hand in which letters, &c. are generally written in India.

شكفت (*sbigift*) Wonder, astonishment, rarity : *Sbigúftéh* or *Shigoaf-téh* ; expanded, blown ; flourishing : *Sbigoaftigi* ; flourishing (state) : *Gul-sbigoofíéh* ; a new or full-blown rose.

شكل (*sbukl*) Figure, form, shape, manner ; image, effigy, picture.

شكم (*sbikum*) The belly.

شكو (*sbulo*) Complaining, upbraiding.

شكوه (*sbúkooh*) Majesty, grandeur, dignity, pomp, power.

شكيب (*sbúkaib* or *sbúkaiba*) Patient ; patience.

شلغم (*sbulgbum*) A turnip.

شمار (*sbúmár*) Number, numeration, computation, reckoning, account: *Bé-sbúmár* ; innumerable : *Roze e sbúmár* ; the last day : *Sbúmár-kurna* ; to count, to number, to calculate.

شمس (*sbumfs*) The sun : *Sbumfi* ; solar.

شمشير (*sbumsbeer*) A scimitar, sabre, sword.

شمع (*sbúma*) A candle : *Sbúma-dán* ; a candlestick.

شم (*sbummeh*) Odour, perfume : *Sbúmeem* ; odour, fragrance.

شناس (*sbinás*) Intelligent, knowing : *Sbinísái* ; knowledge.

شنكرف (*sbungurf*) Cinnabar, vermilion.

شوارع (*sbúwárai*) Highways, public roads.

شوال (*sbúwál*) The tenth month of the Mahommedan year.

شوخ (*sboakh*) Wanton, impudent ; joyous, gay, brisk : *Sboakh-bona* ; to be impudent, saucy, insolent, disrespectful, presumptuous : *Shoakbi* ; impudence, wantonness, joyousness : *Shoakbi-kurna* ; to behave wantonly, impudently, &c.

M 2

شور

شور (*shoor*) Salt, very bitter; salfuginous ground; figuratively, a barren foil; commotion, tumult, noife, difturbance: *Shoor-kurna*; to make a noife, cry out, &c.: *Shoor-bukht*; infamous.

شوربا (*shúrba* or *shúrwa*) Broth, foup.

شوره (*shúreb* or *shoareb*) Saltpetre, nitre; marfhy, unfertile ground.

شوشر (*shúfheb*) A particle or grain; chips.

شوق (*shoak* or *showk*) Love, defire, inclination, affection, longing: *Shoak-lugna*; to be fond of, to long for, to wifh: *Shoakrukhna*; to love, defire.

شوکت (*shókut* or *showkut*) Majefty, pomp, dignity.

شوم (*shoom*) Unlucky, unfortunate, inaufpicious; a mifer; miferly, wretched.

شوهر (*shóhur*) A hufband.

شهاب (*shiháb*) Bright ftars, a flaming fire, a flame.

شهادت (*shuhádut*) Teftimony, atteftation; martyrdom.

شهامت (*shuhámut*) Generofity, bravery.

شهد (*shuhd*) Honey; an evidence, witnefs.

شهر (*shuhur*) A city, a town.

شهرت (*shóhrut*) Renown, fame, report, rumour: *Shóhrut-luggna*; to be rumoured or reported: *Shóhrut-kurna*; to divulge, publifh, report.

شهریار (*shúhryár*) A prince, a king; literally, friend of the city.

شهوت (*shúhwut*) Luft, fenfuality, lafcivioufnefs.

شهید (*shúheed*) A martyr: *Shúheed-kurna*; to martyr: *Shúheed-hona*; to be martyr'd.

شیب (*shaib*) A defcent, declivity; under, below.

شیت (*shiut*) Will, defire.

شیخ (*shaikh*) A venerable old man; a man of authority; a chief; one of the Mahommedan fects.

شیر (*sheer*) A lion, a tyger.

شیرازه (*shirázeh*) The ftitched work on the back of a book.

شیره (*sheereh*) Juice of fruit, new wine, muft.

شیرین

شيرين (_Shireen_) Sweet, pleasant, delicate, gentle: _Shireeni_; sweetness; sweetmeats.

شيشه (_sheesheb_) A glass, a bottle, flask, phial: In Hindvi, lead.

شيطان (_shytán_) Satan, the devil: _Shytáni_; diabolical.

شيعي (_sheea_) A follower of the sect of Ali.

شيفته (_shuifteh_) Mad, enamoured.

شيوه (_shaiwúh_) Habit, custom, manner of acting; amorous looks, blandishments.

ص

صابون (_sáboon_) Soap.

صاحب (_sáhub_ or _sáheb_) Lord, master, Sir. — Used in composition, it denotes possession; as, _Siheb é Jumál_; beautiful: _Saheb é Dowlut_; possessed of wealth, opulent, a rich or powerful man, &c.

صادر (_sádir_) Produced, derived, happened, arrived, descended.

صادق (_sádik_) True, just, sincere, ingenuous.

صاف (_sáf_) Pure, clear; sincere: _Sáfi_; pureness, cleanness: _Sáf-kurna_; to clean, cleanse, purify.

صالح (_sáleh_) Good, proper, just, fit, adviseable; a man of virtue or probity.

صبا (_sábá_) The zephyr, a gentle breeze.

صبح or صباح (_subéh_ or _subéh_) The morning, the dawn: _Subéh-sádik_; the break of day (or true dawn) in opposition to _Subéh-kázib_, the twilight (or false dawn).

صبر (_subr_) Patience: _Subr-rukhna_ or _kurna_; to have patience, to suffer, to bear with: _Bé-subr_; without patience, impatient.

صبي (_súbi_) A youth: _Súbyut_; a girl or damsel.

صحاب

صحاب (*sĭhāb*) Companions, plural of *Sáhub* or *Sáheb*.

صحابت (*sŭhábut*)
صحبت (*sohbut*) } Society, companionship, friendship.

صحرا (*sŭbrá*) A desert, a plain.

صحن (*subn*) A court, court-yard, area.

صحیح (*sŭheeh*) Right, exact, true, just, certain, authentic, perfect: *Sáheeh-kurna*; to correct; to authenticate; to sign.

صحیف (*sŭleefeh*) A page, leaf, book, letter.

صدا (*sŭdá*) Sound, voice, noise, echo.

صداقت (*sŭd kut*) Sincere friendship, truth, sincerity, fidelity.

صدر (*sŭdr*) Chief, supreme.

صدف (*sŭdf*) A shell, a shell-fish, a pearl, mother of pearl.

صدق (*sĭdk*) Truth, veracity, sincerity.

صدمہ (*sŭdmeh*) A blow, collision: *Sudmeh-lugna*; to strike against.

صراف (*surráf*) A banker, a money-changer.

صرف (*surf*) Expence, disbursement; grammar: *Sirf*; pure, unmixed; purely, merely, only: *Surf-kurna*; to expend, exhaust; waste.

صرف (*surfeh*) Surplus, redundancy, addition.

صعب (*săab*) Hard, difficult, arduous: *Súsubut*; difficulty, trouble.

صغیر (*sŭgheer*) Small, slender; junior, inferior.

صف (*suff*) A series, order, rank, row, file (of soldiers, &c.): *Suff é Jung*; order or line of battle: *Suff-suff*; rank and file.

صفا (*sŭfá*) Purity, clearness, polish.

صفت (*sĭfut*) Quality, attribute, property; description; an adjective: *Sifut-kurna*; to describe, to ascribe good qualities to; figuratively, to praise.

صفحہ (*sŭfheh*) A side or page.

صفر (*sŭfur*) The second month of the Mahommedan year.

صفی (*sŭfi*) Pure, clear, bright, just, sincere.

صیقل or صقل (*sukl or sykul*) Polishing, furbishing (a sword, &c.): *Sykul-gur* or *Syklee-gur*; a furbisher (of swords, &c.); an armourer: *Sykul-kurna*; to furbish, polish.

صلابت

صلابت (*sulábut*) Firmnefs, hardnefs; majefty, dignity; formidable, ftrong.

صلات (*sulát*) Prayer, benediction; the firft chapter of the Koran.

صلاح (*suláh*) Rectitude, probity, that which is proper to be done, good advice: *Suláh-déna*; to give good advice, direct, guide, inftruct, counfel.

صلح (*sulah*) Peace, pacification; compact, treaty; concord, reconciliation: *Sulah-kurna*; to make peace.

صلوت (*suloot*) Prayer, benediction; compaffion.

صلہ (*silléh*) Conjunction; gift, prefent; reward, premium.

صلیب (*suleeb*) A crofs or crucifix.

صمت or صمات (*sumut* or *sumát*) Silence; filent: *Súmoot*; filent.

صمیم (*sumeem*) Pure, unmixed, fincere.

صناعت (*finaat*) Art; profeffion, trade.

صندل (*sundul*) The fandal wood.

صندوق (*sundook*) A cheft, a cafket, a coffer; a coffin: *Sundookchéh*; a fmall cheft.

صنعت (*sunat*) Art; profeffion, trade.

صنم (*sunum*) An image, an idol; figuratively, a miftrefs or lover.

صنوبر (*sunubur*) Fir, cyprefs.

صواب (*suwáib*) Rectitude, juftnefs of acting or thinking.

صوب (*soub*) Side, track, way.

صوت (*soat*) Sound, voice, clamour, noife.

صورت (*scorut*) Vifage, countenance; image, form, figure; face, picture, portrait; ftate, cafe; a fpectre or ghoft.

صوفی (*sofi*) Wife, intelligent, pious, devout: Ufed alfo ironically, to fignify a perfon who affects purity of manners.

صوم (*soam*) A faft: *Syam*; fafting.

صیاد (*syád*) A fowler, a hunter.

صیان (*syán*) Keeping: *Syánut*; defence, guarding, keeping, preferving: *Syánut-kurna*; to defend, fupport, guard, &c.

صید (*syed*) The chace, hunting; prey, game.

ض

ض

ضابط *(zábit)* A poſſeſſor, holder, maſter.

ضابطہ *(zúbtéb)* Rule, cuſtom, manner, regulation.

ضامن *(zámin)* A ſurety, a ſecurity: *Zámin-bóna*; to be bail or ſurety for a perſon: *Zámini*; bail, ſurety: *Zámini-déna*; to anſwer for a perſon: *Zámini* is of two kinds; viz. *Mál-zámini*, which is a pecuniary ſurety or engagement, and *Házir-zámini*, which is an engagement for the appearance of a perſon.

ضایع *(záyé or záya)* Periſhed, loſt, deſtroyed, ruined: *Záya-kurna*; to ſpoil, ruin, deſpoil: *Záya-bóna*; to periſh, decay, be ſpoiled, ruined or loſt.

ضبط *(zubt)* Check, controul, keeping in ſubjection, poſſeſſion, ſway, government: *Zubt-kurna*; to take poſſeſſion of, to confiſcate, to forfeit: *Zubti*; confiſcation, forfeiture.

ضحا *(zóha)* Breakfaſt-time; that part of the day which is about half way between ſun-riſe and noon.

ضر *(zidd)* Contrary, oppoſite; contention, oppoſition: *Zydd-kurna*; to contend, oppoſe, contradict, reſiſt, quarrel.

ضرب *(zurb)* A blow, ſtroke; force, violence, beating; ſtruck, coined (money): *Dárúl-zurb*; the mint.

ضرر *(zúrur)* Loſs, damage, injury, detriment, ruin: *Zúrur-luggna*; to ſuffer a loſs, injury, &c.: *Zúrur-poanchhána*; to injure, hurt, damage.

ضرور *(zúroor)* Neceſſary, expedient, neceſſity: *Zúroor-bóna*; to be neceſſary, expedient, requiſite: *Zúroorut or Zúroori*; neceſſity, want, indigence: *Bizzúroor*; of neceſſity, by compulſion, neceſſarily, unavoidably: *Já or Jáe-zúroor*; a privy: *Zúrooriát*; neceſſaries.

ضعیف

ضعیف (*zueef* or *zdif*) Weak, infirm, impotent, feeble, wretched: *Zueefut*; weaknefs, feeblenefs, wretchedness.

ضلال (*zuldl* and *zalálut*) Error; deviating from, or lofing, the right way; ruin, perdition.

ضلع (*zillia* or *zila*) Side, part, quarter, region, diftrict.

ضلل (*zúlul*) An error.

ضمن (*zimn*) The middle or interior part; an interval; moment, conjuncture, period.

ضمیر (*zúmeer*) The mind, heart, thought.

ضوابط (*zúrwábit*) Plural of *Zábteb*; cuftoms, regulations, &c.

ضیا (*zid*) Light, fplendour, brilliancy.

ضیافت (*ziáfut*) A feaft, an entertainment, a banquet: *Ziáfut-kurna*; to make or give an entertainment: *Bábut e ziúfut*; fometimes, inftead of making an entertainment in honour of a perfon, an inferior fends to his fuperior a fum of money *Bábut e Ziáfut*, or, by way of entertainment.

ضیق (*zeek* or *zyek*) Anguish: *Zeek* or *Zeekúlnufs*; the afthma.

ط

طاس (*tás*) A cup or goblet.

طاعت (*táut*) Obedience, fubmiffion.

طاق (*tdk*) A nich; an arched ftructure, a cupola; unique, odd: *Tdk o jooft* or *Tdk ki jooft*; the fame as *odd or even*.

طاقت (*tákut*) Power, force, ftrength; patience.

طالب (*tálib*) Afking, demanding; one who demands or requires: *Talib-ilm*; a ftudent.

N

طالع

طالع *(tála)* Fortune, fate, deftiny.

طامع *(táma)* An ambitious or covetous perfon.

طاهر *(tábir)* Pure, holy, chafte, clear, unfullied: *Táhirut* or *Túbáiut*; purity, purification, &c.

طاير *(táir)* Flying; a bird.

طايفه *(táiféh)* A troop, band, company; a people, tribe, nation; a fet of dancers; a dancing girl; plural *Túwáif.*

طب *(tibb)* Medicine: *Ilm e Tibb*; the medical art: *Túbeeb*; a phyfician, a doctor.

طبع *(túba)* Nature, genius, quality, temperament, difpofition, humour: *Khoofh-túba*; good-natured, fweet-tempered.

طبق *(túbuk)* Condition, ftate; confecutive, one thing following another: *Tibk*; way, mode, ufage.

طبقه *(tubkéh)* A tribe, a clafs or order of men.

طبل *(tubl)* A drum: *Tubluk*; a little drum.

طبيب *(túbeeb)* A phyfician.

طبيخ *(túbeekh)* Cooked, dreffed.

طبيعت *(túbiut)* Nature, conftitution, humour, difpofition; temperament or ftate of the body.

طراز *(tiráz)* An ornament or decoration, as fringe, lace, &c.; any painted ornament.

طراوت *(túráwut)* Frefhnefs, verdure; frefh.

طرب *(túrib)* Chearfulnefs, mirth, gladnefs, joy.

طرح *(túréh)* Pofition, difpofition, manner, arrangement, form; kind, fort.

طرز *(turz)* Form, manner, habit.

طرف *(túruf)* Side, quarter, part, corner; region, place; towards: *Hur-túruf* or *Cháro-túraf*; on all fides, every way: *Bur-túraf*; difmiffed, turned afide or turned off: *Bur-túruf-kurna*; to difcharge, difmifs, turn away.

طرفه *(toorféh)* Any thing new or rare and agreeable; wonderful, furprifing.

طرفرار

طرفدرار (*túruf-dár*) A partizan, a follower: *Túruf-dári*; fiding with, adhering to, efpoufing a party: *Túruf-dari-kurna*; to fide with, to affift, to be partial to.

طرہ (*toorréh* or *túrré*) A waving ringlet, a tuft of hair.

طریق (*túreek*) A way, road, path; manner, mode, cuftom, fafhion, inftitution, rite: *Túreekut*; mode of action, plan of conduct, &c.

طعام (*túám* or *taam*) Victuals, food, meat, viands, refrefhment.

طعن (*taan* or *tánéh*) Accufation, reproach, afperfion, reviling: *Túán*; a flanderer, afperfer: *Tánéh-kurna*; to revile, charge, accufe, reproach, upbraid, flander.

طفل (*tifl*) An infant, a child, a little boy: *Tiflius* and *Tifligi*; child-hood, infancy; alfo *Túfoolut* and *Túfooliut*.

طلا (*tilá*) Gold.

طلاق (*túlák*) A divorce, repudiation.

طلاوت (*túlárwut* or *túláwéh*) Beauty, grace, elegance.

طلایہ (*túláiyéh*) The picquets of an army; reconnoitring parties.

طلب (*túlub*) Demand, requeft, application, petition; calling or fending for, or requiring one's prefence; wag.s, what is due to one, what a perfon has a right to demand: *Túlub-kurna*; to require, demand; fend for, fummon: *Túlub-tukfeem-kurna*; to diftribute pay or wages: *Túlub-powna*; to receive one's wages: *Túlub-monggna*; to demand one's pay: *Túlub-déna*; to pay off, to difcharge the wages due to a fervant.

طلم (*túlúb* or *túllut*) Pleafant, agreeable, favoury.

طلسم (*tilfim*) A Talifman.

طلق (*tulk*) Repudiated: *Tulk-kurna*; to divorce.

طلف (*túluf*) A gift: *Túluf* or *túlúfa*; gratis.

طلوع (*túloo* or *túlooa*) The rifing (of the Sun): *Túloo-hona*; to rife, to be rifen.

طمانیت (*túmániut*) Reft, repofe, tranquillity.

طمع (*tíma*) Avarice, avidity, covetoufnefs; ambition, wifh: *Túma-kurna*; to wifh for, covet, defire.

طمن

طمن *(tumn)* Quiet, quiefcent.

طناب *(túnáb)* A tent-rope.

طنبور *(tumboor)* A mufical inftrument; a drum; (a tent): *Tumboor-wála*; a drummer.

طنز *(tunz)* Mirth, joking, pleafantry; ridiculing, laughing at: *Tun-náz*; jocofe, playful, facetious; giving one's felf airs in walking, or the like.

طور *(toor or towr)* Mode, manner, fashion.

طوطی *(túti)* A parrot, a paroquet.

طوفان *(túfán)* A deluge; a ftorm; the univerfal deluge; figuratively, a difturbance, a tumult; alfo, a calumny; as, *Túfán-ootta-owna*; to raife a difturbance, to fet people by the ears; to calumniate.

طوق *(towk)* Power; a chain or collar.

طول *(túl or tool)* Length; latitude; long, prolix: *Tool-kurna*; to lengthen, to fpin out, to delay.

طومار *(túmár)* A roll, a volume, a bundle of papers.

طویل *(túweel)* Long, tall.

طویلة *(túwailéh)* A ftable, a ftall.

طهارت *(tubárut)* Purity, cleannefs, fanctity.

طی *(ty)* Rolling or folding up: *Ty-kurna*; to fold, to twift, roll up; to travel.

طیب *(ty-yib)* Odour, perfume; agreeable, fweet-fcented, delightful: *Ty-yibát*; good or pious works; delights.

طیر *(tyre)* Flying, a bird.

طینت *(teenut)* Nature, conftitution, complexion, temperament, difpofition.

ظ

ظالم (*zálim*) A tyrant, oppressor; unjust, tyrannical, barbarous, oppressive.

ظاهر (*zábir*) The exterior, the outward or external part; apparent, manifest, clear, evident: *Zábira*; seemingly, apparently, outwardly: *Zábir-kurna*; to disclose, reveal, open, manifest, shew: *Zábir-bona*; to be clear, evident, manifest; revealed, disclosed.

ظرافت (*zúráfut*) Ingenuity, genius, address, wit; elegance, gracefulness, sweetness, politeness; also *Zúrifut*: — *Zúreef*; ingenious, witty, &c.

ظروف (*zúroof*) Properly plural of *Zurf*, a plate, a dish, a vessel; vessels, dishes, pots, &c.

ظفر (*zúfur*) Victory, conquest, triumph.

ظل (*zill*) A shadow, a shade; protection, guard: *Zilúllah*; the shadow of God (a title).

ظلم (*zúlm* or *zoolm*) Tyranny, oppression, injustice, cruelty, outrage, barbarity: *Zúlm-kurna*; to oppress, injure, tyrannize, wrong.

ظلمت (*zúlmut*) Darkness, obscurity.

ظن (*zunn*) Opinion, thought, judgment; suspicion, jealousy: *Zunn-rukbna*; to suspect, be jealous of: *Zunn-déna*; to give one's opinion; plural, *zúnoon*.

ظهر (*zóhr* or *zóhrut*) Mid-day.

ظهور (*zúhoor*) Appearing; appearance, manifestation: *Zúhoor-hóna*; to appear, to come forth, to be evident, to happen, to spring up.

ظهير (*zúheer*) An assistant, supporter.

ع

ع

عابِر (*ábid*) An adorer, or fervant of God.

عابِر (*ábir*) Paſſing ; a paſſenger.

عاجِز (*ájiz*) Weak, impotent, diſtreſſed, powerleſs, dejected : *Ajizi* ; weakneſs, diſtreſs, perplexity : *Ajiz-kurna* ; to diſtreſs, perplex, puzzle, humble.

عاجِل (*ájil*) Haſtening, fleeting, tranſitory.

عارت (*ádut*) Cuſtom, mode, uſage, habit, practice.

عادِل (*ádil*) Juſt, equitable ; a juſt perſon.

عار (*ár*) Reproach, diſgrace, infamy, ignominy, diſhonour : *Ar-luggna* ; to be diſgraceful or diſhonourable : *Ar-kurna* ; to diſgrace, render infamous, &c. : *Ar-rukhna* ; to regard as infamous, to be aſhamed of.

عارض (*áriz*, or *árizut*, or *árizéh*) An accident, event ; a misfortune or evil : *Ariz* ; the cheek : *Arizun* ; accidentally.

عارِف (*árif*) Knowing, intelligent, wiſe.

عاريت (*áriut*) Any thing borrowed or lent : *Ariut-déna* ; to lend ; *Ariut-léna* ; to borrow.

عازِم (*ázim*) Deſigning, intending, undertaking, determining.

عاشِق (*áſhik*) A lover, an enamorato : *Aſhik-hona* ; to be in love : *Aſhiki* ; love.

عاشورا (*áſhoora* or *áſhooréh*) The firſt ten days of the month of Mohurrum, during which the Mahommedans obſerve a ſolemn mourning in commemoration of the patriarchs or Imams *Húſun* and *Hooſain*, ſons of Ali.——This period is alſo called *Dúba*, which, as well as *Aſhoora*, ſignifies Ten.

عاصي (*áſi*) A ſinner, an offender ; ſinning, offending.

عاطِر (*átir*) Odoriferous ; benevolent, generous, noble : *Khátir-átir* ; of a generous or noble mind.

عافيت

عافيت (*áfiut*) Health; safety; also *Khyre-áfiut* or *Khyre o áfiut*: *Khyre-áfiut poochna*; to afk after one's health: *Khyre-áfiut?* Are you well?—Alfo, the anfwer,—Very well.

عاقبت (*ákibut*) The end, conclufion; confequence, iffue, fuccefs, accomplifhment; *Akibut-undaifh*; prudent, provident, looking to futurity.

عاقل (*ákil*) Wife, fagacious, fenfible; a wife or fenfible perfon.

عالم (*alum*) The world, univerfe; a great number of people: *Alim*; learned, wife; a learned perfon (from *Ilm*, knowledge, fcience): *Alum-idn*; mortals, the inhabitants of the earth.

عالي (*áli*) High, fublime, eminent, grand; prefixed or added to many words, it forms titles of dignity, refpect, &c. denoting fuperiority and eminence; as, *Ali-jáh*, *Ali-fhán*, *Ali-kudr*, *Ali-mik-dár*, *Ali-mukdn*, *Jináb-ali*, &c.

عام (*ámm*) Common, public, univerfal, popular, vulgar; the multitude, the common people.

علمره (*ámiréh*) Royal, imperial; abundant, rich, inhabited.

عامل (*ámil*) A collector of the revenues; making, performing.

عاير (*áid*) Incurring; turning towards, returning, happening; connected, related: *Aid-bona*; to incur; to have a reference to, to be connected with, to happen.

عبارت (*ibádut*) Divine worfhip, adoration: *Ibádut-kurna*; to worfhip, adore: *Ibádut-gáh*; a place of worfhip: *Ibád*; worfhippers: *Ibádillah*; fervants of God.

عبارت (*ibárut*) Speech, a word; dialect, idiom; phrafe: a trope or figure; plural, *Ibárát* or (Hind.) *Ibárut-ón*.

عبث (*úbus*) Vain, idle, foolifh.

عبد (*ubd*) A fervant (of God).

عبرت (*ibrut*) An example, that which inftructs, particularly what deters: *Ibrut-léna*; to take example, to be deterred by: *Ibrut-bona* or *lugna*; to be an example, to be the means of deterring or difluading.

عبودت

عبووت (*úboodut* or *úboodiut*) Servitude, fubmiffion, devotion, fubjection, profound reverence.

عبور (*úboor* or *úboor*) Paffing, croffing (a river); a ford or pafs:
Uboor-kurna; to crofs or pafs (a river).

عتاب (*itáb*) Generally pronounced (though improperly) *útáb*; re-
prehenfion, reproach; difpleafure, anger: *Utáb-kurna*; to fpeak
fharply to, to reprehend feverely, to be angry with, to rail,
to ftorm, to fume.

عجیب (*újeeb*) ⎞ Wonderful, furprifing, aftonifhing; any thing rare,
عجب (*ujub*) ⎠ new, or furprifing; plural, *Ujáib*: — *Ujub-ádmi*;
a ftrange, fingular fort of man: *Ujub-lugna*; to
feel ftrangely; to appear furprifing.

عجز (*ijuz*, properly *újuz*) Weak, impotent, humble, fubmiffive; weaknefs, humblenefs, wretchednefs: *Ijuz* or *Ijúzi-kurna*; to humble one's felf, to be very fubmiffive, to folicit with humility
or meannefs.

عجل (*újul*) Hafte, fpeed; alfo *Ujálut*: — *Ujool*; making hafte,
fpeedy.

عجم (*újum*) Perfia: *Ujum* or *Ujúmi*; Perfian.

عرالت (*údulut*) Juftice, equity, law; juft, right, equitable; a court
of juftice: *Událut-kurna*; to adminifter juftice, to try by law.

عراوت (*udáwut*) Enmity, hatred, animofity, rancour, oppofition:
Udáwut-rukhna; to hate, to be at enmity with: *Udáwut-lugna*
or *purbhna*; to fall out, to quarrel, to proceed to hoftilities,
to conceive a hatred.

عزر (*údud*) Number: *Udud-kurna*; to number, reckon.

عدل (*údul*) Juftice, equity, rectitude, probity.

عدم (*údum*) Privation, inexiftence, nothing; without: *Udum-kurna*;
to annihilate.

عدن (*údun*) The garden of Eden, Paradife.

عدو (*údoo*) An enemy.

عدول

عدول (*údool*) Returning, deviating; turning, receding: *Udool-e-boo-kum*; disobedience of orders; deviating from commands or instructions.

عديل (*údeel*) Alike, equal (in weight, &c.); a distributer of justice; just, a just person.

عديم (*údeem*) Destitute, deprived; not to be found.

عزاب (*úzzib*) Pain, torment, torture; punishment.

عزر (*úzr* or *oozr*) An excuse, apology, pretext: *Oozr-kurna*; to make an excuse, to apologize for, to beg pardon; to pretend.

عرابه (*uráibéh*) A wheeled carriage (of a gun, &c.).

عراق (*Irák*) Parthia: *Iráki*; a breed of horses.

عرب (*Urub*) An Arabian: *Urúbi* or *Urbi*; Arabic, especially the Arabic language.

عربده (*urbúdéh*) A conflict, dispute, battle; antipathy.

عرش (*urfb*) A throne; the roof of a house; the ninth heaven.

عرصه (*urféh*) Interval, period of time; a plain; a court or area.

عرض (*úruz*) An accident; any thing that befals a person; disease, sickness: *Urz*; breadth, amplitude, width; a proposition, a representation, a memorial, a petition, a request: *Urz-kurna*; to state, represent, exhibit, explain, address, bespeak, petition: *Urz-dáfbt* and *Urzi*; a petition, an humble memorial; also, a letter from an inferior to a superior.

عرف (*úrf* or *oorf*) Known; the name by which a person or thing is commonly known.

عرق (*úruk*) Sweat, perspiration.

عروج (*úrooj*) Ascent, rising; reaching the summit.

عروس (*úroos*) A bride; nuptials: *Uroofi*; nuptial, a marriage feast.

عروض (*úrooz*) Prosody.

عز (*uzz*) Glory, dignity, grandeur.

عزت (*izzut*) Honour, esteem, respect, reverence, glory, grandeur.

عزل (*uzl*) Removal (from office).

O

عزم

عزم (*úzim*) Defign, intention, purpofe, refolution, undertaking: *Uzum-kurna*; to defign, refolve on, undertake.

عزيز (*úzeez*) Precious, dear, valuable, beloved; venerable, refpeftable; a friend, a beloved or refpected perfon.

عزيمت (*úzeemut*) Refolution, determination, undertaking.

عساكر (*úfákir*) Armies, troops; plural of *Uſkur*.

عسرت (*úfrut* or *oofrut*) A ftate of hardfhip, indigence or difficulty; difficulty: *Uſeer*; difficult.

عسل (*úful*) Honey.

عشرت (*ifhrut*) Pleafure, delight, enjoyment of life.

عشق (*ifhk*) Love, tender paffion or affection: *Ifhk-rukhna*; to be in love, to love: *Ifhk-lugna* or *purrbna*; to fall in love.

عشوه (*ifhwih*) Blandifhment, ogling, coquetting, amorous playfulnefs.

عصر (*ufr*) Time, an age.

عصمت (*ifmut*) Chaftity, continence; defence, protection.

عصي (*úfi* and *úfián*) Sinful, offending, rebelling; fin, rebellion.

عصيب (*úfeeb*) Strong, vehement, intenfe, hard, difficult.

عضو (*úzoo* or *oozoo*) A member, a joint.

عطا (*útá*) A prefent, gift, donation, favour: *Utá-kurna*; to give, confer a benefit, favour, &c.; to make a prefent, to beftow one's bounty: *Utá-bukhſh*; liberal, bountiful, beftowing prefents; plural, *Utáyá*.

عطار (*uttár*) A druggift, a perfumer.

عطر (*útur*) Odour, perfume, fragrance; ottar of rofes.

عطسه (*utféh*) Sneezing.

عطف (*utf*) Favour, affection, kindnefs; a copulative conjunction; as *Wá-utf*; the copulative *and*.

عظم (*uzm*) Greatnefs.

عظما (*oozúmá*) The great, the grandees.

عظمت (*úzámut*) Greatnefs, grandeur, magnitude, magnificence.

عظيم (*úzeem*) Great, grand, high in dignity and power.

عنو

عفو (*úfoo*) Pardon, abfolution, forgivenefs: *Ufoo-kurna*; to pardon, forgive, abfolve, excufe, fpare.

عقب (*úkub*) The rear; behind, after: *Ukub-jdna*; to follow, go after: *Ookb* or *Ookúb*; the end or iffue of any thing: *Ukib*; offspring, children.

عقر or عقدر (*ukd* or *oakdéb*) A knot, a chain, a connection, a compact, league, alliance: *Ukd e nikáb*; a marriage-contract.

عقل (*ukl*) Intellect, knowledge, judgment, fenfe, underftanding, wifdom, genius; opinion, guefs, conjecture: *Ukli*; judicious, fenfible, wife· *Ukl-kurna*; to guefs, judge, conjecture, imagine.

عقوبت (*úkoobut*) Punifhment, chaftifement, torment, torture.

عقیدت (*úkeedut*) Faith, belief, taken into the heart.

عقین (*úkeek*) A red gem, a cornelian.

عقیم (*úkeem*) Having no children, barren.

عکس (*uks*) Reflection, refraction; the contrary, oppofite: *Bur-uks*; on the contrary, in oppofition to.

علا (*úlá*) Glory, fublimity, exaltation, eminence; fuperior, above.

علاج (*iláj*) A medicine, a remedy: *Bé-iláj*; incurable, without remedy: *Iláj-kurna*; to cure: *Iláj-déna*; to apply a remedy.

علاقت (*ildkut*, or *ilákéb*, or *úlákéb*) Relation, connection, attachment, intereft, communication, correfpondence; appertaining, belonging, relating to; ftation, office, bufinefs, engagement.

علامت (*úlámut*) A fign, mark, fymptom.

علت (*illut*) Pretence, caufe, reafon.

علف (*úluf*) Grafs, forage, hay.

علق (*úluk*) Hanging, depending, fufpended; adhering.

علم (*ilm*) Knowledge, fcience, art, learning; *Ilmi*; fcientific: *Ulum*; a ftandard, enfign, flag, banner.

علیا (*úlúmá* or *oolúmá*) The wife, the learned; doctors, fages.

علوفه (*úlooféb*) The fubfiftence of an army, ftipend, falary.

علی (*áli*) High, eminent; the proper name of a man; the fourth caliph, and fon-in-law of Mahommed: *Ulá*; in, from, by, according to, above, upon, &c.; an Arabic particle, used in forming a variety of adverbs.

عليل (*uleel*) Weak, sick, indisposed.

عم (*umm*) An uncle, a father's brother: *Umm-zádéb*; a cousin-german, a paternal uncle's son.

عماد (*imád*) Lofty columns or pillars; figuratively, confidence, reliance, trust, support.

عبارت (*imárut*) An edifice, an inhabited place, a habitation.

عباري (*úmdri*) The canopy of the litter or seat fixed on an elephant or camel; a litter, with a canopy annexed; the litter, without the canopy, being called, in the Hindvi, *Howdah*, or *Howduj*.

عمده or عمدت (*oamdut* or *oamdéh*) Confidence, reliance, trust; a prop, pillar, or support; a minister of state: *Oamdéh*; great, powerful, in high trust or office.

عمر (*omur, úmur,* or *oomur*) Life, age, time: *Omur-dúrás*; (a prayer) May your life be long! *Omur* or *Omar*; the second caliph or successor of Mahommed.

عمق (*oomúk*) Depth, profundity; a deep, abyss, gulph.

عمل (*úmul*) An action, operation, work, deed; possession: *Umul-kurna*; to take possession: *Umul-déna*; to put in possession: *Umul-dúr*; a receiver or tax-gatherer: *Umúli*; practical, artificial (in opposition to theoretical).

عموم (*úmoom*) Common, general, universal; also, *Umeem*.

عميق (*úmeek*) Deep, profound.

عناصر (*únáfir*) Plural of *Oonsúr*; elements: *Urbai-Unáfir*; the four elements.

عنان (*inán*) The reins, a bridle.

عنايت (*inaut* or *ináyut*) Favour, kindness; a gift or present: *Inaut-kurna*; to confer a favour, to give, grant, bestow; plural, *Ináyát*.

عنبر (*umbur*) Ambergris.

عندليب (*undúlaib*) A nightingale.

عنفوان

عنفوان *(oonfúwán)* The flower of youth, the beginning (of any thing).

عنقا *(unka)* A fabulous bird.

عنقریب *(unkúreeb)* Soon, shortly, nearly.

عنكبوت *(unkúboot)* A spider.

عنوان *(únwán)* Kinds, sorts, variety.

عوام *(úwám)* The vulgar, the populace, the common people, opposed to *Khúwás*, the nobles, the gentry, or the superior order of people : *Uwámúnás* ; the vulgar or populace.

عود *(ood)* The wood of aloes.

عورت *(owrut)* A woman, a wife.

عوض *(iwuz)* Exchange, compensation, recompence, return ; retribution, reward (bad or good) : *Iwúzi* ; exchanging, the thing given, or taken, or offered in exchange : *Iwúzi-léna* ; to take satisfaction or revenge.

عون *(own)* Aid, assistance ; a defender, an aider.

عهد *(ubd)* Compact, contract, obligation, treaty, promise ; time, season, period, conjuncture : *Ubd o pymán* ; a treaty : *Ubd o pymán-kurna* ; to conclude a treaty.

عهده *(obdéb)* Place, situation, condition, rank ; a post, station, office ; commonly, but erroneously, pronounced *Hoodab* : *Obdéb-dár* ; filling or holding a station, place, or office ; an officer : *Obdéb-búrái* : being equal to any particular situation, capability of performing an action or surmounting a difficulty, executing a business, or filling an arduous situation successfully.

عیار *(úyár)* A mark, proof, test, standard : *Iyár* ; a cheat, impostor : *Iyári* ; imposture.

عیال *(iyál)* Family, children, domestics.

عیان *(iyán)* Clear, manifest, public, conspicuous : *Iyánun* ; visibly, manifestly, clearly.

عیب *(ibe or iyb)* Vice, fault, defect : *Ibe-joo* ; malevolent, malignant : *Ibe-geer* ; a satirist, a slanderer, a critic : *Ibe-koajbna* ; to seek for faults.

عیر

عِيْر *(eed)* A feſtival, ſolemnity, holiday (in general); alſo, a particular feſtival ſo called.

عِيْسي *(eeſd* or *Huxrut Eeſd)* Jeſus Chriſt: *Eeſirwi*; a Chriſtian or follower of Jeſus.

عِيْش *(iſhe* or *iyiſh)* Pleaſure, delight: *Iſhe o iſhrut*; the pleaſures or luxuries of life, living joyouſly: *Iſhe-kurna*; to take one's pleaſure, to delight one's ſelf, to live luxuriouſly, to purſue pleaſure.

عِيْن *(ine)* The eye; a fountain; the extreme point or extremity (of any thing); original, genuine, eſſential.

غ

غار *(ghár)* A cavern, a den, a hole, a pit.

غارت *(ghárut)* Rapine, plunder, booty: *Ghárut-kurna*; to plunder, deſpoil, lay waſte: *Ghárut-gur*; a plunderer, a marrauder, a robber: *Ghárut-gúri*; plundering.

غازي *(gházi)* A conqueror, a victor, a hero, a champion.

غافل *(gháfil)* Inattentive, negligent, incautious, inconſiderate, careleſs; a negligent perſon; ſee *Ghuflut:* — *Gháfil-bona*; to be inattentive, careleſs, negligent.

غالب *(ghálib)* A conqueror; overcoming, overpowering, excelling, victorious: *Ghálib-bona*; to overcome, conquer, excel: *Gháliba* or *Ghálibun*; chiefly, principally, apparently, probably, more than likely.

غايب *(ghàib)* Abſent, inviſible, latent, concealed, vaniſhed: *Ghàib-bona*; to diſappear, to vaniſh, to be inviſible: *Ghaiibúnéb*; inviſibly, concealedly, ſecretly.

غايت *(gháyut)* The end, extremity, termination; extremely, exceedingly.

غبار

غبار (*ghúbár*) Duſt; foulneſs, impurity, (water, &c.); figuratively, vexation, affliction.

غدر (*ghudr*) Perfidy, treachery, infidelity, ingratitude.

غزا (*ghizá* or *ghizzá*) Aliment, meat or drink.

غرب (*gharb*) The ſetting of the ſun.

غربا (*ghúrúbá*) Poor people, the poor; plural of *Ghúreeb*.

غربال (*ghirbál*) A large ſieve.

غرض (*ghúraz*) Inclination, wiſh, deſire; deſign, view, intention, end, machination; intereſtedneſs, felfiſhneſs; hatred, ill-will, ſpite: *Bé-ghúraz*; without any ſelfiſh view, diſintereſtedly: *Ghúraz* or *Ghúraz-yéb*; upon the whole, to ſum up all, the fact is this: *Ghúraz-rakhna*; to have an intereſted view, to covet or aim at.

غرق (*ghúruk*) Drowned, immerſed: *Ghúruk-kurna*; to drown, immerſe, ſubmerge: *Ghúruk-bona*; to be drowned, to ſink, &c.

غروب (*ghúroob*) Setting (the ſun); the Weſt.

غرور (*ghúroor* or *ghúroori*) Pride, haughtineſs, preſumption, arrogance, vain-glory, vanity: *Ghúroor-lugna* or *bona*; to be proud, arrogant, vain, haughty: *Ghúroor-ſé*; haughtily, arrogantly, proudly, vainly.

غرّه (*ghúrréh*) The beginning or firſt day of a month.

غريب (*ghúreeb*) A poor or indigent perſon; poor, indigent; rare, curious, ſtrange, uncommon, extraordinary: *Ghúreeb-niwáz*; kind or bountiful to the poor, courteous to ſtrangers, hoſpitable.

غريو (*ghúrio*) A guggling noiſe in the throat, and the like; crying, growling; clamour, exclamation.

غزال (*ghizál*) A young deer juſt begun to walk; the ſun; a delicate young man.

غزل (*ghizul*) An ode; the Hindvi ode is called *Raikhtéh* (a Perſian participle ſignifying *poured, ſcattered, diffuſed, ſhed*).

غسل

غسل (*ghúsil*) Washing, bathing, (the body): *Ghúsil-kurna*; to wash, to bathe (the body): *Ghúsil-khánéb*; a bath, a bagnio: *Ghussál*; one whose business it is to wash the bodies of the dead.

غصر (*ghússéb* or *ghossab*) Anger, rage, wrath: *Ghússab-lugna*; to fall into a passion: *Ghússab-hona*; to be angry, enraged, or in a passion: *Ghússab-kurna*; to enrage; to fly out against a person: *Ghússab-wur* or *Ghússáwur*; a passionate or angry man.

غضب (*ghúzub*) Anger, rage, passion, wrath.

غفران (*ghúfrán*) Pardon, remission (of sins); also, *Ghifrut*, *Ghúfoor*; merciful, clement, forgiving (God).

غفلت or غفل (*ghúfl* or *ghúflut*) Carelessness, negligence, inattention, inadvertency, imprudence: *Ghúflut-kurna*; to neglect, to act carelessly or inattentively.

غلاف (*ghiláf*) A pillow-case; (a scabbard, a knife-case).

غلام (*ghúlám*) A slave, a servant, a boy: *Ghúlámi*; servitude, slavery.

غلبه (*ghúlúbéb* or *ghulbéb*) Victory, conquest, predominance, superiority; a crowd, a multitude: *Ghulbéb-kurna*; to over-power, to over-run, to subdue, to predominate.

غلط (*ghúlut*) An error, mistake, blunder, solecism: *Ghúlut-kurna*; to make a mistake, to blunder.

غلطان (*ghultán*) Rolling, wallowing.

غلغل (*ghúlghúl*) A tumult, confusion, vociferation, clamour, noise, uproar.

غله (*ghulléb* or *ghullah*) Grain (in general).

غليظ (*ghúleez*) Filth, dirt; vile, nasty, filthy: *Ghúleez-hona*; to be covered with filth: *Ghúleez-kurna*; to dirty, make nasty, &c.

غم (*ghumm*) Grief, sorrow, sadness, anguish, affliction, mourning (for a deceased person): *Ghumm-kurna*; to grieve, lament, bemoan: *Ghumm-lugna*; to be plunged in grief, &c.: *Ghumkeen*; sorrowful, sad: *Ghumm* or *Ghimm* (hence, probably, the Hindvi *Gám* or *Ghám*); intense heat.

غنا

غنا (*ghiná*) A fong; from hence, perhaps, the Hindvi *Ghána* or *Gána*: — *Ghúnna*; content: *Mútúghunni*; contented, a contented man.

غنايم (*ghúnáim*) Spoils, prey; enemies.

غنچه (*ghúnchéh*) A rofe-bud.

غني (*ghúni*) Rich, opulent; a rich man.

غنيمت (*ghúneemut*) Affluence, plenty, wealth; a bleffing, a fortunate or propitious circumftance; booty, fpoil, plunder.

غور (*ghowr*) Deep, profound thinking; confideration, deliberation; attending to, taking care of, providing for: *Ghowr-purdákht*; taking an intereft in a perfon's fuccefs; patronizing, befriending: *Ghowr-kurna*; to weigh, confider, reflect (deeply); to take care of a perfon's interefts: *Ghowr-fé*; with deep attention or confideration: *Bé-ghowr*; haftily, without confideration.

غوط (*ghotéh*) Plunging, diving, fubmerging; a plunge, &c. (in the water).

غوغا (*ghowghá*) A noife, cry, clamour, uproar.

غول (*ghool* or *ghoal*) A column or divifion of an army; an imaginary demon that haunts woods and deferts, and leads travellers out of their way.

غياث (*ghyás*) Affiftance, redrefs.

غيب (*ghibe*) Invifible, abfent: *Alum é ghibe*; the other world: *Ghybut*; abfence, invifibility: *Ghybi*; invifible, concealed; divine.

غير (*ghyre*)' Another, different; an alien, a ftranger; without, except: *Bú-ghyre* (in Hindvi, corruptedly, *Biggur*); without; otherwife: — *Ghyre* is ufed in forming a variety of compounds; as, *Ghyre-wájibi*; without reafon or juftice, injuftice: *Ghyretaamul*; without hefitation or delay, &c.

غيره (*ghyréh*) Other, others, divers: *O-ghyréh* or *We-ghyréh*; et cetera.

غيرت (*ghyrut*) Emulation, fhame, a nice fenfe of honour or fhame; jealoufy, fhame: *Ghyrut-lugna*; to be afhamed of, to blufh, or be moved with an honeft fhame.

ف

ناتحہ (*fátibéb*) The first chapter of the Koran; a prayer: *Fátibeb-*
purrbna; to say or read prayers (especially from the first chapter of the Koran); the prayers read or repeated over the dead
are called *Fátibéb*.

فاجر (*fájir*) Sinful.

فاحش (*fábish* or *fábisbéb*) Shameful, wicked, obscene, enormous,
vile; an adultress, a whore: *Kar e fábisbéb*; whoredom, adultery.

ناختہ (*fákhtéb*) A ring-dove.

فاخر (*fákbir*) Precious, valuable, honourable, distinguished; *Fákhiréb*;
honourable: *Kbilaat-fákhireb*; a rich dress given to a person
by way of honouring him.

فارسی (*fárfi*) Persian, Persick, especially the Persian tongue; written
and pronounced, also, *Párfi*.

فارغ (*fárigh*) Free, disengaged, at leisure; having no connections to
embarrass one: *Fárigh-bál*; content, happiness; contented,
at ease.

فاسد (*fáfid*) Corrupted, depraved, bad, vile, vicious.

فاسق (*fáfik*) A worthless fellow, a scoundrel, a liar; a prevaricator,
a refractory, disobedient person.

فاش (*fáfh*) Manifest, public, clear, evident, known: *Fáfh-kurna*;
to reveal, divulge, &c.

فاصلہ (*fáfiléb*) Distance (between two places).

فاضل (*fázil*) Excellent, virtuous, learned; a sage.

فاعل (*fáil*) An agent; making, that which acts: *Fúili*; efficient,
effective, active.

فال (*fál*) An omen, presage, augury.

فام

فام (*fám*) Joined to nouns of colour implies a tendency to such colours, and seems equivalent to the English termination *ish*; as
Seeah-fám, blackish, &c.

فاما (*fúummá* or *fúammá*) But, yet, &c.; see اما *Ummá*.

فانوس (*fánoos*) A sort of glass candle-shade used in India; a lantern.

فاني (*fáni*) Frail, transitory, inconstant: *Jéhán-fáni*; this transitory
world.

فايده (*fáidéh*) Profit, gain, advantage, utility, emolument: *Fáidéh-
mund* or *Múfeed*; advantageous, profitable, useful: *Fáidéh-
milna* or *powna*; to profit, to benefit, to gain: *Fáidéh-purrhna*;
to be of advantage, to reap advantage, to turn out emolumentary or beneficial.

فايض (*fáiz*) Abundant, exuberant, excellent.

فتح (*fútéh* or *fútah*) Victory, conquest: *Fútah-kurna*; to conquer:
Fútah-powna; to obtain a victory.

فترت (*futrut*) Languor, debility, relaxation, intermission.

فتنه (*fitnéh*) Sedition, mutiny, insurrection, tumult; discord, disturbance, misunderstanding, variance: *Fitnéh-oottaouna*; to ex-
cite a mutiny, &c., to create discord, raise a disturbance, &c.

فتوي or فتوا (*futwá*) A judicial or religious decree: *Futwá-déna*;
to pronounce a decree or judgment, according to the law of
the Koran.

فتوت (*fútoowut*) Liberality, generosity.

فتور (*fútoor*) Weakness, languor, infirmity (especially after any exertion).

فتيله (*fúteeléh*) Properly, a match; a sort of candle.

فجر (*fújir*) The dawn or crepuscule.

فجور (*fújoor*) Very wicked, adulterous.

فحش (*fuhsh*) Obscenity, shameful discourse or action.

فخر (*fúkhur*) Glory, honour; pride, vanity, ostentation, boasting:
Fúkhur-kurna; to boast, to glory in.

فداي or فدا (*fidá* or *fidáii*) Sacrifice, consecration, devoting: re-
demption, ransom: *Fidá-kurna*; to sacrifice, devote.

فر. (*fur*) Splendour, glory, luftre, power, dignity, grace, beauty.

فراخ (*furàkh*) Large, broad, wide, extensive, plentiful : *Furàkhi* ; amplitude, largeness, abundance, plenty.

فرار (*firàr*) Flight ; also, *Firàri*.

فراز (*furàz*) For *ufràz*, exalting, elevating ; as *Sur-furàzi* for *Sur-ufràzi* ; ennobling, honouring, promoting, raifing ; also, above, upon, the top or fummit, height.

فراست (*firàfut*) Sagacity, penetration, judgment, ingenuity, underftanding.

فراش (*furràfh*) One whofe employment is to fpread carpets, pitch tents, and the like.

فراغت or فراغ (*furàgh* or *furàghut*) Ceffation from labour or bufinefs, reft, repofe, leifure ; eafe, happinefs : *Furàghut-léna* ; to take repofe, to relax, to ceafe from labour, &c.

فراق (*firak*) Separation, abfence.

فراموش (*furàmoafh* or *furàmoafbi*) Forgetfulnefs : *Furàmoafh-kurna* ; to forget.

فراوان (*firàwàn*) Much, abundant, copious : *Firàwàni* ; abundance.

فراهم (*furàhum*) Collected, gathered together : *Furàhum-kurna* ; to collect, affemble, &c.

فربه (*furbéh*) Fat.

فرجام (*furjàm*) The end, conclufion, iffue ; advantage, happinefs.

فرح (*furùh*) Gladnefs, chearfulnefs, happinefs, joy, delight.

فرخ (*furrùkh*) Happy, fortunate : *Furkhúndéh* ; happy, profperous.

فرد (*furd*) A fheet or roll of paper containing an account, or the like ; a fingle thing.

فردا (*furda*) To-morrow ; figuratively, the laft day.

فردوس (*firdoas* or *firdows*) Paradife, a garden.

فرز (*furz*) Separating, diftinguifhing.

فرزام (*furzàm*) Worthy, fuiting, befitting.

فرزانه (*furzànéh*) Wife, learned, of a firm mind, perfevering.

فرزند (*furzund*) A fon, a daughter, a child.

فرسخ

فرسح (furjukh or furfung) A parafang, a league.

فرش (furfh) A cufhion, mat, carpet, or any fimilar houfehold furniture.

فرشته (furifhteh) An angel.

فرصت (furfut) Occafion, opportunity, conveniency, reft, repofe, leifure : Furfut-powna ; to find an opportunity or occafion.

فرض (furz) A duty, · divine command, religious precept (the obfervation of which is indifpenfable).

فرق (furuk) Difperfion : Furuk-kurna; to difperfe : Furk ; feparation,
diftinction, divifion, diftance, difference, difcrimination ; the
top of any thing : Furk-kurna; to feparate, divide, diftinguifh,
&c.: Furk-jana ; to go or ftep afide, to remove to fome diftance : Furk-rubna ; to abfent one's felf, to ftay away, to ftay
at a diftance.

فرقه (firkeh) A body, a fect, a tribe, a band, a troop.

فرمان (furman) A mandate, command, order ; patent, commiffion,
royal letter : Furman-burdar ; obedient, a fubject : Furman-
burdari ; obedience, fubjection.

فرمایش (furmaifh) An order, commiffion ; any thing ordered or
commiffioned ; pleafure, will, commands.

فرنگستان (Frungiftan) Europe ; the country of the Franks : Frungi
or Fringi ; an European.

فرود (furoad) Defcending, alighting, ftopping, putting up : Furoad-
ana; to defcend, alight, ftop: Furoad; the place where a
perfon ftays or fojourns.

فروز (furoaze) Kindling, inflaming, &c. : Ufed in forming a variety
of compounds.

فروش (furoafh) A feller, felling : Khoad-furoafh ; a boafter.

فروغ (furoagh) Splendour, light, brightnefs.

فرومانده (furomandeh) Weak, fatigued, oppreffed, helplefs.

فرومایه (furomaieh) Mean, ignoble, fordid, worthlefs, low.

فرنك

فرهنگ (*furhungg*) Wisdom, science, manners, politeness; a dictionary (especially a Persian one).

فریاد (*furyád*) An exclamation, cry for help, clamour, lamentation, complaint: *Furyád-kurna*; to complain, to exhibit a complaint, to cry out for justice: *Furyádi*; a complainant, a plaintiff.

فریب (*fúraib*) Fraud, deceit, deception, treachery, imposture: *Fúráibi*; a cheat, an impostor, a deceiver: *Fúraib-kurna*; to deceive, impose on: *Fúraib-khána*; to be deceived, to allow one's self to be imposed on.

فساد (*fúsád*) War, horror, disturbance, villany, wickedness, corruption, depravity, malignity; sedition, mutiny.

فسق (*fisk* and *fúsook*) Iniquity, sin, falsehood.

فسیح (*fúseeh*) Ample, large, capacious.

فشان (*fishán*) Scattering, strowing, shedding; a Persian participle used in forming compound epithets.

فصاحت (*fúsáhut*) Eloquence, elegance, whether in speaking or writing.

فصد (*fusd*) Bleeding, opening a vein: *Fusd-kurna*; to bleed, let blood.

فصل (*fusl*) A section, article, chapter, or other division of a book; a season of the year; one of the seasons or periods appointed for the collection or settlement of the revenues.

فصیح (*fúseeh*) Eloquent, rhetorical, elegant.

فضاحت (*fúzáhut* or *fúzeehut*) Disgrace, ignominy, infamy, dishonour.

فضال (*fúzáléh*) Remainder; remains; also, *Fuzléh*.

فضایل (*fúzáil*) Virtues, excellencies; learning.

فضل (*fuzl*) Excellence, virtue, wisdom, learning, &c.; increase; a gift, favour, benefit.

فضول (*fúzool*) Exuberant, excessive.

فضیح (*fúzeeh*) Ignominious, infamous, disgraceful.

فضیلت (*fúzeelut*) Excellence, virtue, perfection, wisdom.

فطر

نطر (*futr* or *fitr*) Breaking (a fast) : *Eedúl-fitr* ; the festival of breaking the fast of Rumzân : *Fitréh* ; creation, nature ; alms given on the *Eedúl-fitr*.

نعال (*fuál*) An action : *Fiál* ; actions, deeds, works : *Fiil e naik* ; good actions : *Fiál e bud* or *Bud-fiál* ; bad deeds.

نعل (*fál*) Acting : *Fiul* ; an action, work.

نغان (*fighán*) Complaint, lamentation.

نغفور (*fughfoor*) The general name of the Chinese emperors.

نقط or نقر (*fukud* or *fúkut*) Only, solely, singly, no more, simply.

نقر (*fúkir* or *fukr*) Poverty, indigence.

نقرا (*fúkúrá*) The poor, the indigent, the lower people ; plural of *Fúkeer*.

نقره (*fikréh*) A sentence, or member of a sentence.

نقه (*fikéh*) Knowledge of religion and law, divinity, theology.

نقير (*fúkeer*) Generally written *Faquir* ; a poor man, a beggar ; a religious order of mendicants : *Fúkeeri* ; poverty, beggary : *Fúkeer-kurna* ; to beggar, impoverish.

نقيه (*fúkeeh*) A Mahommedan lawyer, or theologian.

نقر (*fikr*) Thought, reflection, consideration, opinion, deliberation, counsel ; care, solicitude : *Fikr-kurna* ; to consider, reflect, think ; devise, contrive, conceive ; to attend to, take care of, be solicitous or anxious about, to provide for : *Fikr-mund* ; thoughtful, serious, anxious : *Bé-fikr* ; inconsiderate, unthinking ; unconcerned.

نلان (*fúlan* or *fúlán·* or *fuláni*) A term equivalent to the English *such-a-one* : the name of any unknown or undefined person.

نلك (*fúluk*) The sky, the firmament, the heavens.

نلوس (*fúloos*) Small coins ; a pice, or small copper coin, of which fifty generally make a rupee.

نن (*funn*) Science, learning, knowledge, art.

ننا (*fúnii*) Mortality, frailty, corruption : *Dárúl-fúna* ; this frail house, the world.

فنوس

فانوس (fánoos) See فانوس.

فنون (fúnoon) Sciences; plural of *Funn*.

فوت (fowt) Death : *Fowt-kurna* ; to die.

فوج (fowj) An army, a body of men.

فوجدار (fowj-dár) A kind of high sheriff, or chief magistrate of a county, province, or district, and often the collector of the revenues : *Fowjdári* ; the office of a *Fowjdar* ; the court in which he presides, the jurisdiction of a *Fowjdar*.

فور (fowr) Celerity, haste : *Fil-fowr* and *Fowrun* ; instantly, immediately, quickly.

فوق (fowk) Superiority, excellence.

فهرست (fúhrist) A table of contents, an index, a catalogue, a list.

فهم (fuhm) Understanding, intellect, comprehension : *Taiz-fuhm* ; of a quick understanding.

في (fi or fee) An Arabic particle, prefixed to a great variety of words, and signifying *in, into, among, of, to, with, for, by,* &c. ; also equivalent to *each*, as in *Chár roopeh fi mun*, i. e. four rupees each maund.

فياض (fyáz) Liberal, generous, bountiful ; copious, plentiful, profuse.

فيروز (feeroze) Victorious, triumphant ; also *Feerozi* : — *Feeroze-mund* ; a conqueror ; victorious.

فيصل (fyful) Decision, decree, determination ; also *Fyfúleh* :—*Fyful* or *Fyfúleh-kurna* ; to settle, determine, decide.

فيض (fyze) Favour, bounty, grace ; plenty, abundance.

فيل (feel) An elephant : *Feel-bán* ; an elephant-keeper.

فيلسوف (filefoof) A philosopher : *Filefoofi* ; philosophy ; art, cunning.

ق

ت

قابض *(kábiz)* Taking, seizing; an aftringent.

قابل *(kábil)* Capable, able, qualified, fkilful; an able, fkilful, or clever perfon: *Kábiliut*; fkill, capacity, ability.

قاتل *(kátil)* A murderer; killing, mortal, deadly: *Zúhur-kátil*; a deadly or mortal poifon.

قادر *(kádir)* Potent, powerful, capable, able; one of the attributes of the deity.

قاصد *(kásid)* A courier, a meffenger.

قاصر *(kásir)* Defective, infufficient, failing.

قاضي *(kázi)* A cazi or cadi, a mayor or judge.

قاطع *(kátai)* Cutting, refcinding; definitive, decifive, categorical, peremptory: *Kátai últúreek*; a cut-purfe, a highwayman, an affaffin.

قاعده *(káideh)* A rule, cuftom, practice, ufage, mode, manner; ftile, method, order: *Bé-káideh*; without method, form, or order; irregular, informal: *Káideh-purrhna*; to become a cuftom.

قاف *(kaf)* A fabulous mountain mentioned by poets.

قافله *(káfiléh)* A caravan, a body of travellers.

قافيه *(káfiéh)* Rhime, metre.

قال *(kál)* A word, a faying: *Keel o kál*; much converfation.

قالب *(kálib)* A model, mould, form; the body.

قالي *(káli)* A large carpet; *Káleechéh*; a fmall carpet; corruptedly, *Gúleechéh*.

قامت *(kámut)* The ftature, fhape, form, figure, body.

قانت *(kánit)* Obedient to God, devout; filence.

قانع *(kánai)* Contented, fatisfied.

ﺭ

قانون

قانون *(kánoon)* A canon, rule, regulation, law, ſtatute, ordinance, conſtitution : *Kánoon-go*; a revenue officer whoſe duty it is to ſee that juſtice is done to the huſbandmen and farmers, according to the conſtitutions of the empire ; literally, a pronouncer of the law.

قاهر *(kábir)* Subduing, triumphing ; violent, forcible ; alſo *Kábireh.*

قايل *(káil)* Conſenting, agreeing, acquieſcing ; convinced, confuted : *Káil-kurna* ; to convince, confute, ſilence, make agree or acquieſce : *Káil-hona*; to be convinced, to agree, concur, acquieſce.

قايم *(káim)* Standing, firm, fixed, durable, conſtant : *Káim-mukám* ; a regent, a vicegerent, a lieutenant : *Káim-hona* ; to be firm, fixed, eſtabliſhed.

قبا *(kubd)* A veſt quilted with cotton.

قباحت *(kubábut)* Vileneſs, deformity, badneſs, baſeneſs ; ſpoiling, ruining.

قبالہ *(kubáleh)* Any contract, eſpecially of bargain and ſale.

قبر *(kubr)* A ſepulchre, tomb, monument.

قبض *(kubz)* Taking, ſeizing ; poſſeſſion ; conſtipation ; ſtoppage, coſtiveneſs (of the bowels).

قبضہ *(kubzeh)* The hilt of a ſword, a handle ; poſſeſſion, power ; a receipt.

قبل *(kubl)* Before, anterior, prior.

قبلہ *(Kibleh)* Mecca ; *Kibleb* or *Kibléh-gáh* ; figuratively, a patron, protector, a perſon to whom one looks for ſupport, a father : *Kibléh-núma* ; a compaſs.

قبول *(kubool)* Conſenting, granting, approbation, conceſſion, receiving favourably, accepting : *Kúbool-kurna* ; to agree, conſent, allow, admit, accept, receive : *Kúbooliut* ; a receipt, acceptation.

قبیح *(kúbeeh)* Vile, deteſtable, deformed, bad, ugly, ſhameful, baſe.

قبیلہ *(kúbeeleh)* A wife ; kindred ; plural, *Kúbáil* ; wives or family, including wives, children, &c.

قتل

قتل (kutl) Slaughter, murder, death: *Kutl-kurna*; to murder, flay, kill, flaughter.

قحط (kuht) Scarcity, want, famine.

قد (kudd) Stature; the body.

قدح (kúdéh) A cup, a bowl, a glafs, any drinking veffel.

قدر ((kúdur) Fate, deftiny, providence: *Kudr*; quantity, meafure; dignity, rank, ftation; worth, value: *Kudr-dán*; one acquainted with the true worth or character of a perfon; hence, figuratively, a patron.

قدرت (kúdrut) Power, potency, force, ability, authority.

قدس (kúdús) Holy, pure; fanctity, holinefs.

قدم (kúdum) A foot, a ftep, a footftep: *Kúdim*; prior, preceding, antecedent: *Kúdum-kurna*; to ftep, to move, to march: *Kúdum-oottaouna* (in military exercife) to raife the foot well: *Kúdum-léna*; to take, or fall into, the ftep.

قدوه (kidóh, or kidoob, or kidwéh) A pattern or model, an example, a leader (in good qualities).

قدورت (kúdoorut) Ability, power.

قدوس (kúddoos) Pure, holy, bleffed (one of the names of God).

قدوم (kúdoom) Traces, marks, effects.

قديم (kúdeem) Ancient, old, former.

قرابت (kúrábut) Relationfhip, confanguinity, kindred, affinity, propinquity.

قرابه (kúrrábéh) A large flaggon or veffel for holding wine.

قرار (kúrár) Agreement, promife; conftancy, firmnefs; fixing one's abode, reft, quiet: *Kúrár-kurna* or *déna*; to promife, pledge one's felf: *Bur-kúrár*; confirmed, firm, re-eftablifhed: *Kúrári*; conftancy, firmnefs: *Bé-kúrári*; inconftancy, ficklenefs.

قران (korán) The koran; reading: *Kirán*; conjunction of the planets.

قراول (kúráwul) Pickets, out-guards or centinels, reconnoitring parties: *Kúráwúli*; reconnoitring, fkirmifhing.

قرب (koorb) Vicinity; propinquity, kindred: *Koorúbd*; relations, kindred.

Q 2

قربان

قربان (*koorbán*) A sacrifice, victim, oblation: *Koorbán-kurna*; to sacrifice, offer up, devote.

قرص (*koors*) The sun or moon's orb.

قرض (*kurz*) Debt, money borrowed or lent; a loan: *Kurz-léna*; to borrow money: *Kurz-monggna*; to ask the loan of money: *Kurz-dár*; a debtor; in debt.

قرطاس (*kurtás*) Paper (especially coarse, thick paper).

قريب (*kúreeb*) Near, nearly, almost, about; at hand.

قرين (*kúreen*) Connected, joined, next, contiguous; a friend, companion.

قريه (*kúriyéh*) A village, a town.

قرمساق (*kúrumsák*) A pimp.

قساوت (*kúsáwut*) Hardness of heart.

قسر (*kusr*) Violence, compulsion (retaliation, vengeance, see قصر).

قست (*kist*) Share, portion; division; such a part of the revenue as is payable at a stated period, according to a previous agreement: *Kist-bundi*; the settlement or payment of the revenues by instalments.

قسم (*kism*) Kind, sort, species: *Kúsum*; an oath: *Kúsum-khána* or *léna*; to swear, to take an oath.

قسمت (*kismut*) Fate, fortune, destiny, luck; portion, lot.

قصاب (*kussáb*) A butcher.

قصاص (*kisás*) Retaliation, revenge.

قصبه (*kusbéh* or *kúsúbéh*) A town (the middle of a city). Whether the word *Kusbi* (a courtezan or woman of the town) be derived from *Kusbéh*, or from کسب *kusb* (gaining a livelihood by business or labour, or by following a trade) I confess myself unable to determine.

قصه (*kisséh*) A tale, fable, apologue, story, history; a thing, affair, business, &c.; *Kisséh-khán* or *Kisséh-khwán*; a story-teller (a sort of employment in India).

قصد (*kusd*) Intention, design, scope, view, profit, attempt, endeavour, resolution, determination: *Kusd-kurna*; to form a design, to attempt,

attempt, &c.: *Kufd-rukhna*; to intend, to have in view: *Kufd-fé*; intentionally, on purpofe.

قصر (*kufr*) Deficiency, fhortnefs; failing; a palace (retaliation, vengeance: *Kufr-léna*; to revenge, retaliate, take fatisfaction.— I am not quite clear whether this Hindvi expreffion be derived from the Arabic قصو or قسر; but if from either, it moft probably is borrowed from the latter).

قصف (*kúfuf* and *kúfeef*) Weaknefs, languor; broken, fplit.

قصور (*kúfoor*) Failure, deficiency, defect, omiffion, neglect; fault, offence, fin: *Kúfoor-lugna*; to be deficient, neglectful: *Kúfoor-kurna*; to fail, omit, neglect; to commit a fault, to offend.

قصيده (*kúfeedéh*) A fpecies of poetical compofition:—It differs from the *Gbúzul* or ode in three particulars; it is longer, it admits of rather a greater variety of fubject, and its meafure is, for the moft part, more full and folemn.—The *Kúfeedéh*, as well as every other fort of rhythmical compofition in ufe among the Perfians, is imitated by the Hindvi poets.

قضا (*kúzá*) Fate, deftiny, fatality, decree; death.

قضيه (*kúziyéh*) A difturbance; an affair, bufinefs, matter, fact (in a bad fenfe).

قطار (*kitár*) A ftring of camels.

قطب (*kootub*) The polar ftar, the north pole.

قطره (*kutréh*) A drop; plural *Kutrát*:— *Kutréh-kutréh*; drop by drop.

قطع (*kúta*) Cutting; Hindvi, *kátta* and *káttna*:— *Kúta-kurna*; to cut, to cut off; to terminate, ftop fhort, break off; to finifh, perform (a journey): *Kúta-nízur*; turning away the eyes, abandoning a perfon.

قطعه (*kitah*) A fegment, fection, part, divifion, fragment;—a fhort piece of poetry, an unfinifhed or imperfect *Gbúzul* or *Kúfeedéh*, for the moft part of a ferious caft.

قعب (*káb*) A cavern, a pit, a furrow.

قعر (*kár*) A gulph, an abyfs; the bottom (of a well, &c.).

قنا

تغا (*kifá*) The nape of the neck, the back of the head; also *Kúfún*.

تغتان (*kuftán*) A robe of honour.

تغس (*kúfus*) A cage, a lattice, a net-work.

تغل (*kúfl* or *koofl*) A lock; a bolt.

قلب (*kulb*) The heart, mind, soul; the kernel, marrow; plural, *Kuloob*:—*Kulb* or *Kulb-gáh*; the middle, center (of an army): bad money; false, counterfeit: *Kulbi*; cordial, hearty.

قلبر (*kulbéh*) A plough: *Kulbéh-ráni*; ploughing.

قلت (*killut*) Penury, scarcity, want, indigence.

قلعر (*kúlah*) Generally written *Killa* or *Killah* by Europeans; a fort, a fortress, a castle; plural, *Kúlaját*:—*Kúlah-dár*; the governor or commander of a fortress: *Kúlah-dári*; the government or command of a fortress.

قلعی (*kúly*) Tin: *Kúlygur*; a tin-man: *Kúly-kurna*; to tin, to line a pot, kettle, &c. with tin.

قلم (*kúlum*) A pen (whether quill or reed): *Kúlum-túráfh*; a pen-knife; also, figuratively, the stubble that remains after cutting down the grain: *Kúlum-dán*; a pen-case, an ink-stand; *Seeah-kúlum* or *Seeih-kúlum*; pen and ink; called, also, *Kúlum-duwdt* or *Dawát-kúlum*.

قلمرو (*kúlum-ro*) Empire, dominion, jurisdiction.

قلمون (*kúlamoon, bo-kúlamoon*, or *abú-kúlamoon*) The camelion.

قلندر (*kúlundur*) A religious order among the Mahommedans.

قلی (*kúli*) A kind of soap-ashes: *Kooli*; a slave, a labourer, a porter, a cooley.

قلیل (*kúleel*) Little, small, moderate, few.

قمار (*kimár*) Dice, or any game of hazard: *Kimár-báz*; a gambler; *Kimár-bázi*; gaming, gambling.

قمر (*kúmur*) The moon: *Kúmúri*; lunar: *Kúmri* or *Koomri*; a female turtle-dove.

قمیص (*kúmees*) Erroneously called *Kameej*; a shirt, or any kind of inner garment of linen.

قناعت (*kúnaat*) Content, happiness, moderation, continence.

قنر

قند *(kund)* Sugar, fugar-candy, loaf-fugar.

قنديل *(kundeel)* A candle, lamp, chandelier.

قنوط *(kánoot)* Defpair.

قواعد *(kuwáid)* Plural of *Káidéb*; rules, cuftoms, habits, &c.; the manual exercife: *Kúwáid-kurna*; to exercife, to perform, or go through the manual and evolutions: *Kúwáid-ka-din*; a field-day.

قوال *(kúwál)* Loquacious; eloquent; a finger.

قوام *(kúwám)* Juftice, equity.

توت *(koot)* Subfiftence, nourifhment, fufficient to live on: *Kúwut* or *Koowut*; power, force, ftrength, vigour; faculty, virtue: *Ná-kúwut*; weak, feeble; weaknefs, debility.

توس *(kows)* A bow; Sagittarius: *Koos*; a hermit's cell.

قول *(kowl)* An agreement, compact, contract; a word, a faying: *Kowl-náméb*; a treaty, the writing or inftrument given or exchanged by contracting parties.

قوم *(koam* or *kome)* A tribe, nation, people.

قوي *(kúwi)* Strong, powerful, robuft, vigorous, firm.

قهر *(kubr)* Violence, feverity, fubjection; rage, indignation; punifhment, chaftifement.

قهوة *(kúhwéb)* Coffee.

قي *(ky)* Vomiting: *Ky-kurna*; to vomit.

قياس *(kyás)* Judgment, conjecture, guefs, opinion: *Kyás-kurna*: to guefs, conjecture, fancy, judge, fuppofe, imagine.

قيام *(kyám)* Refidence, fettlement, fixture.

قيامت *(kyámut* or *kiámut)* The refurrection, the laft day.

قير *(kyd* or *kyde)* Imprifonment, reftraint, reftriction: *Kyde-mé*; imprifoned,—in prifon, in arreft: *Kyde-kurna*; to imprifon, to reftrain the perfon: *Kydi*; a prifoner.

قيصر *(kyfur)* The general name of the Greek or Turkifh fovereigns; Cefar.

قيل

قیل (*keel*) A word, fpeech, or faying: *Kál o keel* or *Keel o kál*; converfation, dialogue, difpute, controverfy.

قیمت (*keemut*) Price, value, worth: *Keemúti*; valuable, precious, dear: *Keemut-lúgáowna*; to fix a price upon a thing: *Keemut-boalna*; to tell or declare the price of a thing.

ک

کبیر (*kábir*) Great, grand, illuftrious; a great man.

کابین (*kábeen*) A marriage portion or fettlement.

کاتب (*kátib*) A fcribe, a writer.

کاخ (*kákh*) A palace.

کاذب (*kázib*) A liar; falfe.

کار (*kár*) A work, aćtion, deed; thing, affair, bufinefs; occupation, employ, profeffion, art, labour: *Kár* and *Gár* joined to abftract nouns and the participles of verbs, form a great variety of perfonal nouns: *Kár o bár*; occupation, employment, bufinefs: *Dur-kár*; neceffary, requifite, wanted: *Surkár* or *Sircar* (as commonly written) placed at the head of affairs; or, the fource or head of bufinefs: See سرکار.

کارخانه (*kár-khánéh*) A work-fhop, a work-houfe.

کارد (*kárid*) A knife, a dagger.

کارزار (*kárzár*) A battle, combat, confliċt.

کارگر (*kárgur* or *kári-gur*) A workman, a labourer, an artificer, an artift.

کاروان (*kárwán*) A caravan: *Kárwán-fúrái*; a caravanfera or public building for the reception of caravans.

کاست (*káft*) Diminutiou; lofs, damage.

کاس س

كاس or كاسه (*kás* or *káséb*) A cup; a goblet; a plate, a saucer.

كاغذ (*kághiz*) Paper; a bundle of papers, or a single paper.

كافر (*káfir*) An infidel, an unbeliever: *Káfir* or *Káfiri*; a Caffre.

كافور (*káfoor*) Camphire.

كافي (*káfi*) Sufficient, enough.

كاكل (*kákúl*) A lock of curling hair, a ringlet.

كالبد (*kálbud*) The human body, a figure, form.

كام (*kám*) Desire, wish; the palate: *Kám-ráni*; happiness, felicity, attainment of one's wishes.

كامل (*kámil*) Perfect, compleat; finished entirely, compleatly versed in science, perfectly good or virtuous.

كامياب (*kámyáb*) Happy, successful, fortunate.

كان (*kán*) A mine: *Káni*; mineral; in Hindvi *Kbán*.

كانا (*kána*) Foolish, stupid; a stupid fellow; in Hindvi, deaf, and thence, figuratively, a dull person, or one of dull apprehension.

كاه (*káh*) Grass, hay: *Kah-gil* or *Kbúgil*; straw mixed with clay for plastering walls, &c.

كباب (*kúbáb*) Roasted (meat): *Kúbáb-kurna*; to toast: *Kúbábi*; an Indian dish, so called.

كبر (*kibr*) Greatness, illustriousness, nobility; great: *Kúbúra*; the great, great or illustrious men, grandees, nobles.

كبك (*kubk* or *kubk-dúri*) A kind of partridge.

كبوتر (*kúbootur*) A pigeon.

كبود (*kúbood*) Azure, blue.

كبير (*kúbeer*) Large, great, immense; full grown.

كبيسه (*kúbeeséb*) Intercalary: *Sál-kúbeeséb*; leap-year.

كتاب (*kitáb*) A book; a letter or epistle: *Kitáb-kbánéb*; a library: *Kitábus*; writing; an inscription, motto, or the like, worked in a vest, handkerchief, &c. or painted upon the walls or ceiling of a room.

كتاره (*kútáréb*) A sort of weapon; this is properly Hindvi.

R

كتب

كتب (*kútúb* or *kitb*) Books, writings: *Kútúb-khánéh*; a library or book-cafe.

كتخدا (*kut-khóda* or *kud-khódd*) The master of a family: *Kud-khóda* or *kud-khódái*; marriage, matrimony.

كتف (*kútif* or *kitf*) The shoulders, the shoulder-blades.

كتوال or كوتوال (*kutwál* or *koatwál*) A sort of superintendant of the police: *Koatwáli*; the office of *Kutwál*: — *Kutwáli-chú-bootréh*; the hall or court of the *Kutwál*; generally, an open edifice in the center of the market-place.

كثافت (*kúsáfut*) Density, thickness, fulness, repletion: *Kúseef*; thick, dense.

كثرت (*kusrut*) Multitude, plenty, abundance, excess; a great number or great deal, a throng or crowd (of people); an overflowing, superfluity.

كثير (*kúseer*) Many, much, copious, abundant, numerous, excessive, superfluous.

كج (*kuj*) Crooked, bent, curved, distorted: *Kúji*; crookedness.

كحل (*kuhl*) Black-eyed, of the colour of antimony; a barren or scarce year; a collyrium.

كد (*kudd*) Trouble, labour, diligence, endeavour.

كدبانو (*kudbánoo*) A noble lady, a mistress of a family.

كدو (*kúdoo*) A gourd, a pompion.

كدورت (*kúdoorut*) Foulness, impureness (water, or the like); figuratively, perturbation, oppression of spirits, affliction, anguish.

كده (*kúdéh*) A house; in composition, a noun of place; as *My-kúdéh*; a tavern or place where wine is kept or sold.

كذب (*kúzib*) Lying: *Kuzzáb*; a liar: *Kizb*; a lie.

كرامت (*kúrámut*) Generosity, munificence, nobleness, excellence: a miracle: *Kúrámát*; miracles.

كرانه or كران (*kúrán* or *kúránéh*) A shore, &c.; See كنارة *kúnáréh*.

كراهت (*kúráhut*) Dislike, disgust, aversion: *Kúráhut-lugna* or *rukhna*; to dislike, detest, abhor, loathe.

كرايه

كرايه (kiráyeb) Hire, the price paid for labour, the rent of a house, &c.: Kiráyeb-kurna or déna; to hire, to rent, to let: Kiráyeb-léna; to hire, to take (a house, &c.).

كردار (kirdár) Action, deed (good or bad); manner, conduct.

كردكار (kirdgár) God, the omnipotent.

كرسف (kirsúf or kirsúf) Cotton, or the like, put into an ink-holder.

كرسي (kúrsí) A chair, a throne.

كرشمه (kúrushmeb) Amorous gesture or look, blandishment; a wink, a glance.

كركره (kurkúreb) Laughing immoderately.

كرم (kúrum) Generosity, liberality, beneficence, grace, favour, courtesy, kindness, benignity: Kirm; a worm: Kirmuk; a small worm.

كرور (kúroar) A hundred thousand.

كروه (kúrêb or korôb) A cofs, a measure equal to from three to four thousand Guz, or from one and a half to two miles.

كريم (kúreem) Generous, liberal, benign, benevolent, courteous, gracious, kind.

كريه (kúreeb) Detestable, odious, abominable, disgusting.

كز (kuz) Contraction of كزاز, from, by, &c.

كزج (kuzj) Crooked, distorted: See كج.

كس (kus) A man, a person, one: Kús or Koos; pudenda.

كساحت (kúsáhut) Lameness in the hands or feet; sweepings; removing dust, &c. from a house or street.

كساد (kúsád) Not being in demand, use, or currency; badness of markets, and the like.

كسب (kusb) Trade, business, occupation; gain, acquisition (by labour).

كسل (kúsul) Laxness, relaxation, sickness: Kúsul-mizáj; sick, ill; bad health, illness.

كسوف (kúsoof) An eclipse of the sun; an eclipse of the moon being called خسوف khusoof.

كش

كش (*kush*) The Persian participle *drawing, pulling, carrying, bearing,* &c. from which a great variety of compounds is formed; as *Dil-kush,* drawing or attracting the heart (i. e. engaging): *Sur-kush*; drawing in the head, or rearing, extending, or tossing the head (i. e. refractory, stubborn, rebellious), &c.

كشا (*kúshá*) The Persian participle *opening, displaying,* &c. used in composition; as *Dil-kúshá,* opening (i. e. exhilerating) the heart: *Kishwur-kúshá*; opening (i. e. conquering) countries.

كشاو (*kúshád* or *kúshádéh*) Open, uncovered, expanded; wide, ample, extensive; displayed, revealed: *Kúshádigi*; openness, amplitude, expansion.

كشاف (*kushsháf*) A discoverer, a solver, an explainer.

كشان (*kúshán*) See كش *kush.*

كشاكش (*kúshákush* or *kúshákúshi*) Attraction, allurement.

كشت (*kisht*) A sown field.

كشتي (*kishti*) A boat: *Kúshti*; wrestling: *Kúshti* or *kooshti-kurna*; to wrestle.

كشش (*kúshish*) Attraction, allurement.

كشف (*kushf*) Opening, revealing, manifesting, showing, explaining.

كشمش (*kishmish*) Dried grapes, raisins.

كشور (*kishwur*) A climate, a country.

كعب (*kábéh*) The square temple at Mecca.

كف (*kuf*) The hand, the palm; froth, foam.

كفا (*kúfá*) Adversity, vexation; affliction, disease.

كفاره (*kúfáréh*) Atonement, expiation (for a sin).

كفاف (*kúfáf*) A bare competency, just enough to support one.

كفالت (*kúfálut*) Security, pledge, pawn.

كفايت (*kifáit*) Sufficiency, enough; sufficient: *Kifáit-bona* or *lugna*; to be sufficient, to suffice.

كفر (*kúfr*) Ingratitude, unthankfulness, incredulity.

كفش (*kúfsh*) A slipper, a shoe, a sandal.

كفن (*kúfun*) A winding-sheet, the clothes of a corpse.

كفگير

کفیل (*kúfeel*) A fecurity, furety, hoftage.

کل (*kúll*) The whole, all, univerfal: *Kúlli*; univerfality, the whole, or total: *Kúlliát*; the entire works of an author.

کلابه (*kúlábeh*) A clew, a hank, a fkein of thread; a reel, a wheel for winding thread; alfo *Kúláweb*.

کلام (*kúlám*) A word, a fpeech: *Kúlám-kurna*; to fpeak, relate, ftate: *Háfil-kúlám*; in a word, to fum up all.

کلان (*kúlán*) Great, large, big.

کلاه (*kúláh*) A cap, a cowl, a night-cap; in general, any head-drefs.

کلک (*kilk*) A pen (properly the reed of which the pen is made).

کلمه (*kúliméh* or *kulméh*) A word, faying, vocable; plural *Kulmát*.

کلید (*kileed*) A key.

کم (*kum*) Lefs, deficient, defective, wanting: *Kúmi*; fmallnefs, deficiency: *Kum-kurna*; to leffen, diminifh, reduce, curtail, fhorten, abridge: *Kumtur*; mean, low.

کمال (*kúmál*) Perfection, excellence; plural, *Kúmálát*: — *Kúmáliut*; perfection, excellence.

کمان (*kúmán*) A bow: *Kúmán-gur*; a bow-maker.

کمخاب (*kumkháb*) A fort of gold or filver flowered filk, corruptedly called *Kinkob* or *Kingkob*.

کمر (*kúmur*) The loins, the waift, the middle: *Kúmur-bufteh*; ready, prepared (for any bufinefs or enterprize): *Kúmur-bund*; a girdle, zone, belt.

کمند (*kúmund*) A toil, a noofe.

کمیاب (*kumyáb*) Rare, difficult to be found or procured: *Kumyábi*; rarity, fcarcity.

کمیت (*kúmait*) A bay horfe.

کمینگاه (*kúmeengáh*) An ambufh, a lurking-place.

کمینه (*kúmeenah*) Low, mean, bafe, abject: *Kúmeenah-loag*;·the plebeians, the vulgar: *Kúmeenah-ádmi*; a low perfon, a dirty fellow.

کنار

کناره or کنار (*kúnár* or *kúnáréh*) A brink, shore, margin, edge, coast; side, part: *Kúnáréh-jána*; to go ashore, or to make for the shore, to land; also, to go or step aside: *Kúnári* or *Kindri*; a sort of broad border or edging, made of gold or silver thread, and used by women.

کنایت (*kináyet*) An allusion, metaphor, rhetorical figure.

کنز (*kunz*) Treasure.

کنون (*kúnoon*) Contraction of اکنون *uknoon*; now, presently.

کنیز (*kúneez* or *kúneezuk*) A female slave, a maid servant.

کوتاه (*kotáh*) Short, contracted; *Kotáhi*; shortness, contraction: *Kótáh-núzur*; short-sighted, undiscerning.

کوتوال (*koatwál*) See کتوال *Kutwál*.

کوش (*kows*) A shoe, especially that kind the heels of which are shod with iron.

کوثر (*kowsur*) A nectar-flowing river in Paradise.

کوچ (*kooch*) Marching, decamping: *Kooch-kurna*; to march, to move to another place: *Kooch o múkám*; marching and halting: *Colh kooch ki múkám*; does (the army) march or halt to-morrow?

کوچک (*kóchuk*) Little, small.

کوچه (*koochéh*) A lane, a street (the diminutive of *Kooe*).

کودک (*kóduk*) A boy, a youth.

کور (*koar*) Blind: *Koari*; blindness.

کوز (*kooz* or *koozah*) A flaggon, jug, cup: a hunch-back.

کوس (*koos*) A large brass drum.

کوشش (*kúshish*) Endeavour, labour, study, effort, application: *Kó-shish-kurna*; to labour, attempt, endeavour, try.

کوکب (*kowkub*) A star, a constellation; plural, *Kúwákib*.

کوکنار (*koaknár*) Poppy.

کوکو (*kúkoo*) A ring-dove or wood-pigeon.

کوه (*koh*) A hill: *Kóhistán*; a hilly country.

کوی (*koo* or *kooe*) A street.

کهتر

كهتر (*kaihter*) Lefs, very fmall, junior; mean, low: *Kaihtúri*; lownefs, littlenefs; minority.

كهربا (*kúhrúbá*) Amber (attracting ftraws).

كهكشان (*kúhkúfhán*) The galaxy, or milky way.

كهنه (*kóhnéh*) Old, ancient.

كي (*ky*) A great king, but efpecially the Perfian kings of the fecond
or Kyanian dynafty, called *Kyáns*.

كياست (*kiáfut*) Ingenuity, quicknefs of parts.

كيد (*kide*) Deceit, fraud, treachery.

كيسه (*keefah*) A purfe.

كيسو (*keefoo*) A ringlet, a lock.

كيفيت (*kyfiyut*) Account, relation, ftate of a cafe or fact; condition,
ftate, circumftances; quality, mode.

كيميا (*keemiya*) Chymiftry, alchymy; the philofopher's ftone.

كين (*keen* and *keenah*) Hatred, enmity, rancour, malice, revenge;
ufed in compofition, it forms a clafs of adjectives; as *Ghumkeen*, forrowful, &c.

گ

كازر (*gázir*) A wafherman or wafherwoman.

گاو (*gáo*) A cow: *Nur-gáo*; a bull or bullock: *Gáo-maifh*; a buffalo.

گواره (*gáwáréh* or *gábwúréh*, or *ghúwáréh*) A cradle.

گاه (*gáh*) Time, place; ufed much in compofition: *Gábi* or *gáb-gáh*;
fometimes, now and then.

گبر (*gubr*) A guebre, an idolater, a worfhipper of fire, a pagan, an
infidel.

كرا

كرا‍ (*gúdii*) Poor, indigent, begging ; a beggar, a poor man : *Gúdii* ; poverty, indigence, the condition of begging : *Gúdii-kurna* ; to beg : *Gúdii-kurna* ; to impoverish, reduce to beggary, ruin.

كداز (*gúdáz*) Melting, diſſolving, uſed ſometimes in compoſition ; as *Dil-gúdáz* ; melting the heart.

كذار (*gúzár*) Paſſing, performing, executing, paying ; uſed much in compoſition : *Gúzir* ; a paſſage ; *Gúzur* or *Gúzur-gáh* ; a ford, a ferry, a paſs or paſſage : *Gúzur-bán* ; a perſon having charge of a place where a toll is collected, a keeper of the roads : *Gúzur-júna* ; to paſs, paſs by ; to elapſe : — From hence, alſo, the Hindvi verb *Gúzurna.*

كذارش (*gúzárish*) Repreſentation, addreſs, ſtatement of one's caſe : *Gúzárish-kurna* ; to repreſent, relate, ſtate.

كذاف (*gúzáf*) Vain, idle, impertinent, or ſilly diſcourſe.

كر (*gur*) Contraction of اكر *úgur* ; if ; alſo a particle much uſed in forming perſonal nouns, and ſignifying a performer, maker, workman, or the like ; as *Sikli-gur* ; (a furbiſher) : *Kúmán-gur* ; a bow-maker, &c. — From theſe perſonal nouns are likewiſe formed a claſs of abſtract nouns, by the uſual addition of ى or *i* ; as *Sikligúri* (the buſineſs of a poliſher) ; *Sipáh-gúri* (the military profeſſion), &c.

كرامي (*girámi* or *gúrámi*) Dear, precious, excellent, honoured, re- vered : *Girámi-kudr* ; a perſon of dear eſtimation, honoured rank, &c.

كران (*girán*) Dear, of high price, heavy : *Giráni* ; dearneſs, ſcarcity, a famine : *Girán-máéb* ; precious, valuable, of great worth, a moſt valuable perſon, a man of a noble nature.

كرچه (*gurchéh*) Contraction of اكرچه *althougb.*

كرد (*gurd*) Duſt : *Gird* ; round, circular ; around, about ; a circuit, circle ; circumference.

كرداب (*girdáb*) A whirlpool.

كردان ((*gurdán*) Turning, revolving, winding.

كردباد

کرد باد (*gird-bad*) A whirlwind.

کردش (*gurdish*) Turning round, reversion, revolution, motion (particularly circular).

کردن (*gurdun*) The neck, the throat.

کردون (*gurdoon*) The firmament, the heavens : fortune, chance ; a chariot.

کرده (*gúrdeh*) The kidnies ; figuratively, an appellation of fondness, and equivalent to " My soul !"

کرز (*gúrz*) A mace, a battle-axe.

کرسنگی (*gúrsinúgi*) Hunger: *Gúrsineh* ; hungry, starved.

کرفتار (*giriftár*) Involved (in trouble); a captive, prisoner : *Giriftári* ; captivity ; embarrassment, being involved in difficulties or trouble.

کرم (*gurm*) Warm, hot ; choleric, passionate : *Gurm-mizáj* ; of a warm or choleric temper : *Gurmá* or *Gurmi* ; heat, warmth ; summer, sultriness.

کرو (*giró*) A pledge, a pawn, security : *Giró-déna* or *rukhna* ; to pawn, to pledge : *Giró-léna* ; to take in pawn ; *Giró-mé* ; pawned, in pawn.

کروه (*giróh* or *goróh*) A company, band, tribe, troop, body.

کرویده (*girweedéh*) Attached to, following, admiring, attracted, captivated.

کره (*girih* or *giréh*) A knot, a joint ; a button ; a division of a *Guz* or yard.

کریا (*giria* or *girya*) Crying, weeping : *Giria-kurna* ; to cry, weep : *Girián* ; shedding tears, crying.

کریبان (*guraibán*) The collar of a garment, &c.; figuratively, the neck.

کریز (*gúraiz*) Flight.

کریه (*giriyéh*) A plaint, lamentation, cry.

کز (*guz*) A measure something under a yard.

کزند (*gúzund* or *gúzund*) Misfortune, calamity, loss, injury.

کزین (*gúzeen*) Choosing, preferring, electing : *Gúzeen* and *Gúzidéh* ; chosen, selected, &c.; used in composition, as *Khilwut-gúzeen* ; solitary, fond of retirement.

S

کنسار

كسار (*gúsár*) Removing, carrying away; as *Ghum-gúsár*; removing grief, i. e. a friend, or friendly.

كستاخ (*gustákh*) Presumptuous, bold, arrogant, assuming, impudent, disrespectful, impolite, rude: *Gustakhi*; presumption, insolence, boldness, &c.: *Gustukbi-kurnu*; to act or behave presumptuously, &c.

كستر (*gústur*) Spreading, strewing, scattering, diffusing; used in composition; as *Kurum-gústar*; spreading generosity, a liberal or bountiful person.

كشت (*gusht*) Walking, perambulation, wandering: *Gusbt-kurna*; to walk about, to stroll, &c.

كفتوكو (*goaft o goo*) Talk, discourse, conversation: *Goaftúr*; speech, manner of talking.

كل (*gúl*) A rose, a flower (in general): *Gúl-áb*; rose-water; also, the rose itself: *Gulábi*; belonging to a rose or to rose-water; of a rose-colour: *Gil*; clay, earth, mould, mud.

كلبن (*gúlbún*) A rose-bush, a stalk, a shoot.

كلدستہ (*gúldustah*) A handful of flowers or roses, a nosegay, a bouquet. There are several other compounds formed from *Gúl*; as *Gúl-zár*; a flower-bed: *Gúlrúkh*; rosy-cheeked, &c.

كلستان (*gúlistán*) A rose-garden; a celebrated Persian book, by Shaikh Sadi.

كلشكر (*gúlshukur*) Conserve of roses.

كلشن (*gúlshun*) A garden, a delightful place.

كلقند (*gúlkund*) Candied conserve of roses.

كلو (*gúloo*) The gullet, throat, windpipe: *Gúloo-bund* or *Gúla-band*; a neck-cloth, a stock: — This word is generally, though improperly, pronounced *Gúla*.

كلہ (*gilắh*) A complaint, lamentation, accusation: *Giléh-kurna*; to complain, find fault, accuse, upbraid, reproach, backbite.

كم (*gúm* or *goom*) Lost, wanting, missing; strayed, absent, wandering: *Gúm-kurna*; to lose, to miss: *Gúm-júna*; to lose one's way, to be lost.

كماشتہ

کماشته (gúmáſhtéh) An agent, a factor.

گمان (gúmán) Doubt, ſuſpicion; opinion: Bud-gúmán; ſuſpicious, jealous, malignant: Gúmán-kurna; to ſuſpect, doubt, fancy, ſuppoſe, imagine: Gúmán-léjána; to ſuſpect, diſtruſt, to be jealous of: Gúmáni; ſuſpicious, diſtruſtful; fancied, imagined.

گمراه (gúm-ráh) Loſing the way, wandering, deviating: Gúm-ráhi; deviation, error, ſeduction.

گناه (gúnáh) A crime, ſin, offence: Gúnáh-gár; an offender, criminal, ſinner: Gúnáh-gári; guilt, ſinfulneſs: Gúnáh-kurna or Gúnáh-gári-kurna; to ſin, commit a crime or fault.

گنبد (gúmbud or gúmbuz) An arch, cupola, dome, tower.

گنج (gunj) A market-town, particularly a place where grain is ſold. —The names of many villages in India are terminated by this word, which properly ſignifies a treaſure or place where treaſure is depoſited; alſo, a caſe for holding any thing, but eſpecially a knife-caſe.

گنجایش (gúnjáiſh) Capable of containing or holding; room.

گنده (gundah) Fetid, ſtinking.

گندم (gundúm) Wheat.

گنگ (Gung) The river Ganges: Goong; dumb; hence, probably, the Hindvi Goanga; dumb, or a dumb perſon.

گو (goo) A ball; any thing globular: Go; a ſpeaker; uſed in compoſition; as Dúroagh-go; a liar, or ſpeaker of lies.

گوار (gúwár and gúwára) Digeſting, digeſtion, digeſtable; figuratively, agreeable, pleaſant.

گواه (guwáh) An evidence, witneſs: Guwábi; evidence, teſtimony: Guwábi-déna; to give evidence, to bear witneſs, to atteſt or confirm.

گور (goar) A ſepulchre, a monument: Goriſtán; a burying-place.

گوز (gowz or gooz) A walnut.

گوش (goaſh) The ear: Goaſh-máli; (rubbing the ears) reproof, chaſtiſement: Goaſh-máli-kurna; to reprove, chaſtiſe.

کوشت (*goasht*) Flesh, meat.

کوشواره (*goashwáréh*) An ornament belonging to a turban.

کوش (*góshéh*) A corner, an angle; a retired spot: *Góshéh-nushéen*; a recluse, a hermit.

کول (*góléh*) A cannon ball: *Góli*; a musquet ball.

کون (*goon*) Added to nouns, implies a similitude of colour; as *Laléh-goon*; of the colour of a tulip, &c.: *Goondgoon*; of various kinds or colours.

کونه (*goonéh*) Colour, form, species, figure, mode, manner, kind.

کوهر (*góhur*) A gem, a jewel, a precious stone; essence, substance, nature.

کویا (*góyá*) A particle of similitude; thus, in this manner, as you would say, or, as one might say.

کبهر (*gobr*) See کوهر.

کیاه (*geeáh*) Green herbage, grass.

کیتی (*gaiti*) The world, the universe.

کیر (*geer*) Taking, seizing, holding; used in composition, as *Alam-geer*, subduing the world, &c.

کیهان (*gyhán*) The world.

ل

لا (*lá*) A particle prefixed to Arabic substantives, denoting privation.

لابت (*lábut*) A place abounding in black stones; figuratively, an idol.

لابد (*lábud*) Necessarily, infallibly, unavoidably.

لاجرم (*lájúrum*) Of necessity, compelled, compulsively.

لازم (*lázum*) Necessary, proper, fit, indispensable; inseparable: *Lázum-bona*; to be necessary, requisite, fit, proper, indispensable: *Lá-zimut*; expediency, necessity, fitness.

لاس

لاش (*láſh*) A dead body, a corpſe.

لغبر (*lághbur*) Lean, meager, thin.

لاف (*láf*) Boaſting, vanity, vain-glory.

لاک (*lák*) Lack or lac, a tincture ſo called.

لاکلام (*lá-kúlám*) Without diſpute or altercation ; there is no more to be ſaid.

لاکن (*likin*) But, &c. : See لیکن *leikin*.

لالہ (*láléb*) A tulip.

لامسہ (*lámiſéb*) Feeling, touching.

لمع (*lámai*) Splendid, ſhining, bright.

لیق (*láik*) Worthy, deſerving, meriting, ſuitable, fit for, able, qualified.

لب (*lub*) The lip : *Lúb.ilub* ; full to the lip, running over.

لبادہ (*lubádéb*) Properly a woollen coat ; a gown, wrapper, or great coat.

لباس (*libás*) A garment, veſt, &c. ; a dreſs.

لحاظ (*libáz*) Obſerving or regarding attentively (eſpecially with the corner of the eye) ; watching, looking after.

لحاف (*libáf* or *libáféb*) A blanket, a coverlet.

لحظ (*lubzéb*) Properly, a look or glance ; figuratively, a moment, or, in the twinkling of an eye.

لحم (*lubm*) Fleſh, meat : *Lúbeem* ; fleſhy, a fat man.

لحن (*lúbn*) Melody, a ſound, a tone ; plural, *Lúbán*.

لخت (*lukbt*) A piece, part, portion ; ſome, ſomewhat.

لزت (*luzzut* or *luzzab*) Taſte, flavour, favour ; pleaſure, delight, ſweetneſs ; plural, *Luzzát*.

لزیز (*lúzeez*) Pleaſant, delightful, ſweet, agreeable to the palate.

لرزہ (*lurzéb*) Tremor : *Tup-lurzéb* ; an ague, a cold fit : *Lurzán* ; tremulous, trembling.

لزوم (*lúzoom*) Neceſſity ; expediency, behoving.

لس (*luſs*) Licking : *Luſs-léna* ; to lick.

لسان (*liſán*) The tongue ; language, idiom, dialect.

لشکر

لشكر (*luſhkur*) An army; a laſcar or native artill·ry-man: *Luſhkúri*; belonging to an army.

لطافت (*lútáfut*) Grace, elegance, beauty (eſpecially of the delicate or minute kind).

لطف (*lootf*) Gentleneſs, graciouſneſs, goodneſs, courteſy, favour, kindneſs, benignity, bounty, generoſity: *Lootf-kurna*; to favour, &c.

لطيف (*lúteef*) Soft, gentle, lovely, benign, affable, kind, &c.: *Lúteeſab*; a pleaſantry, joke, a witty or facetious thing; plural, *Lutáif*.

لعاب (*láub* or *looáb*) Spittle, ſaliva.

لعب (*láb*) Playing; a play or game; alſo *Lábut* or *Lábéh*.

لعل (*lál*) A ruby.

لعنت (*lánut*) An imprecation, curſe, anathema: *Lánútálláh*; the curſe of God: *Lánut-kurna*; to curſe, to execrate.

لغام (*lúghám* or *lúgúm*) Reins, a bridle.

لغت (*lóghut*) A word, phraſe, idiom; a dictionary or lexicon, eſpecially an Arabic one; a tongue or language; plural, *Lóghát*.

لغز (*lúghuz*) Any ambiguous or obſcure expreſſion or phraſe; an enigma, a riddle.

لغافر (*lif·féh*) The cover of a letter.

لغظ (*lufz*) A word, a vocable.

لقا (*liká* or *lúká*) The face, form, viſage, appearance.

لقب (*lúkub*) A nickname, a ſurname, an addition; plural, *L7káb*, titles or appellations of honour; but commonly uſed for the ſingular, like many other Arabic plurals.

لقمان (*lókmán*) A famous Eaſtern fabuliſt (ſuppoſed by ſome to be Æſop).

لك (*luk*) A hundred thouſand, a lack.

لكام (*lúgám*) A bridle.

لكد (*lúkud*) A kick.

لكنت (*lúknut* or *lúknéh*) A heſitancy in ſpeech, ſtammering.

لحم

لمحه *(lumbéh)* A moment, an inftant ; properly, a glance with the eye, or a wink.

لمس *(lúmis)* The touch, feeling, handling.

لمع *(lúma)* Splendour, brilliancy ; fhining, glaring.

لند *(lund)* Membrum virile.

لنک *(lung)* Lame :—Hence the Hindvi *Lungra* :—*Loang* or *Loong* ; a fort of girdle wrapped round the waift and between the thighs, inftead of drawers ; in Hindvi *Lungoat*, petticoats, being called *Lunga*.

لنکر *(lungur)* An anchor : *Lungur-dálna* ; to anchor, to caft anchor : *Lungur-oottíowna* ; to weigh anchor.

لوا *(láwá)* A ftandard or banner.

لواحق *(líwáshik)* Domeftics, followers, family, dependents.

لوازم *(líwázim* or *líwázimát)* Neceffary things, requifites.

لوح *(lób)* A table, plank, board, efpecially on which any thing is infcribed.

لولي *(loóli)* A finging girl or boy ; handfome, delicate ; plural, *Looliún*.

لهب *(lúbub)* Flame ; flying or afcending (duft) : *Lóbáb* ; blazing, flaming.

لهذا *(lúbázá)* Therefore, confequently.

لياقت *(liákut)* Dignity, worth, merit, excellence, fitnefs, fuitablenefs.

لیک *(leik* or *leiken)* But.

لیل *(lile)* The night : *Lile o nihár* ; night and day.

لیلي *(Lieli)* A lady celebrated by the poets as the miftrefs of Mujnoon.

لیمون *(leemoon)* A lime or lemon.

لیم *(leem)* Concord, peace.

م

ما *(má)* The perſonal pronoun plural *we*, uſed for the moſt part, in
the Hindvi, with the ſubſtantive مردم *murdum* (man or men);
as *má-murdum*, we men or people; ſpoken generally or inde-
finitely.

ماب *(madb* or *múáb)* A receptacle, a repoſitory, a center or point to
which any thing returns, or a place in which it is contained.
—This is a noun of place, of which there are great numbers
in Arabick, as well as of nouns of time and of inſtrument,
which begin with this letter (م). Such words are chiefly uſed
in compoſition; as *Izzut-múáb*; the ſeat of magnificence, the
reſidence of glory (or reverence); alſo, ſimply, magnificent,
illuſtrious (honoured or revered).—*Richardſon's Dictionary.*

ماباقي *(má-báki* or *mábúki)* The reſt, the remainder.

مات *(mát)* Aſtoniſhed, confounded, reduced to the laſt extremity:
Shah-mát; (at cheſs) checkmate.

ماتم *(mátum)* Mourning: *Mátum-poorſi;* condoling with a perſon on
the death of a friend or relation, compliments of condolance:
Mátum-kurna; to mourn: *Mátum-poorſi-kurna;* to condole
with a perſon on the death of a relation or friend.

مائر *(múáſur)* Signs, marks, memorials; worthy actions.

ماجرا *(májúrá)* An event, incident, occurrence, affair, accident, tranſ-
action, any thing paſt.

ماچين *(Máicheen)* The empire of China.

مادّه *(máddéh)* A matter, point, ſubject, article, affair: *Mádéh;* a female: *Nur ki mádéh;* Is it a male or female?

مادح *(mádih)* Praiſing, an encomiaſt.

مادر *(mádur)* A mother: *Mádúri;* maternal.

مارب

مارب (*muárub*) Wants, necessities.

ماش (*mísh*) Pease, pulse.

ماضي (*mázi*) The past.

مآل (*muál*) End, termination, issue; tendency: *Khyre-muál*; of a happy issue or tendency.

مال (*mál*) Wealth, possessions, effects, property: *Máldár*; wealthy, rich, opulent: *Máldári*; opulence.

مالش (*málish*) Rubbing, wiping: *Málish-kurna*; to rub, to wipe.

مالک (*málik*) An owner, master, possessor, proprietor, lord; an independent person, a free agent: *Málik-bona*; to possess, to govern, to be independent, to be at liberty to act according to one's pleasure.

مالوف (*muáloof*) Familiar, having contracted a close acquaintance, living in habits of friendship.

مامور (*muámoor* or *mámoor*) Ordered, commanded, fixed, determined, defined; usage, established custom.

مامون (*mámoon*) Rendered secure, safety: *Mámun*; a place of safety.

ماندہ (*mándéh*) Fatigued, tired, harrassed, low-spirited: *Mándéh-bona*; to be fatigued, tired, &c.: *Mándúgi*; fatigue, lassitude, indisposition, low spirits.

مانع (*mánai*) Prohibition, interdiction, opposition, hindrance, obstacle, impediment: *Mánai-kurna*; to prohibit, oppose, refuse, &c.

مانند (*mánund*) Like, resembling; resemblance, similitude: *Mánund-purrhna, lugna,* or *bona*; to resemble.

مانوس (*mánoos*) A companion, associate, friend; familiar, intimate.

ماوا (*máwá*) A mansion, habitation.

ماہ (*máh*) The moon, a month: *Máh-táb*; moonlight, the moon: *Máh-tábi*; a blue light.

ماہر (*máhir*) Skilful, ingenious, sagacious; a master of any art.

ماہواره (*máhwáréh* or *máhgánéh*) Monthly, monthly wages or pay; also *Dur-máh* or *Dur-máhéh*.

T

ماي

ماهي (*mahi*) A fish: *Mahi-muratib*; a dignity or honorary order conferred by the Emperor of Hindostan.

ماهیت (*mahiyut*) Quality, value, essence, the true worth or virtue of a thing or person.

مایل (*mail*) Inclined towards, taking delight in, affectionate, having a partiality for, inclination, propensity: *Mail-lugna*; to have an affection for, to be inclined or disposed towards, to conceive a liking or attachment.

مایوس (*mayoos*) Desperate, hopeless.

مایه (*mayeh*) Wealth, stock, money; measure, quantity, origin, principle, essence; ferment, leaven.

مباوا or مباد (*mubad* or *mubadi*) Let it not be! God forbid! Left.

مبارز (*mubariz*) A warrior, a combatant, a hero: *Mubaruzut*; war, battle.

مبارک (*mubaruk*) Happy, fortunate, blessed, sacred: *Mubaruk-bad*; congratulating, felicitating, wishing all happiness: *Mubaruk-badi*; congratulation, felicitation, commemoration of any joyful event: *Mubaruk-badi-kurna*; to congratulate, felicitate, make rejoicings: *Mubaruk* or *Mubaruk-bad*; joy be to you!

مبالغه (*mubalugheh*) Dwelling, insisting, or speaking largely on a subject, exaggeration; endeavour, diligence, unwearied application.

مبتدا (*mubtuda*) The beginning, a thing begun: *Mubtudi*; beginning; a beginner, a learner.

مبتلا (*mubtula*) Afflicted, unfortunate; misfortune, distress, ruin.

مبدا (*mubda*) The beginning, origin, principle, source (of any thing).

مبدل (*mubuddul*) Changed, altered; exchanged.

مبذول (*mubzool*) Expended, bestowed.

مبرهن (*muburhun*) Demonstrative; evident, manifest.

مبلغ (*mublugh* or *moblugh*) Money; a sum.

مبین (*mubeen*) Manifest, clear: *Mubiyun*; explained, illustrated, an illustrator.

متابع

متابع (*mútábai*) A follower, imitator; obedient: *Mútábiut*; obedience, submiffion, conformity: *Mútábiut-kurna*; to obey, follow, conform one's felf to.

متاخر (*mútúakhir*) The laft, the lateft; behind; modern.

متادى (*mútúaidi* or *mútáidi*) Prepared, ready; performing.

متاع (*mútá*) Goods, valuables, wealth; profit, gain, advantage.

متامل (*mútúamil*) Confidering, weighing deliberately.

متحرک (*mútúhurrik*) Moved, moveable: *Ghyre mútúhurrik*; immoveable.

متحرم (*mútúhurrim*) Revered, refpected; prohibited, unlawful.

متحمل (*mútúhummil*) Bearing (a burden), fupporting, enduring, fuffering patiently.

متحیر (*mútúbiyur*) Aftonifhed, wondering, confounded.

مترحم (*mútúrubbim*) Compaffionate, merciful, tender, affectionate.

متردد (*mútúruddid*) Repulfed, rejected; oppofed, refifted.

مترصد (*mútúruffid*) Watching, expecting.

مترضی (*mútúruzzi*) Contenting, fatisfying.

مترقب (*mútúrukkib*) Expecting, watching, obferving, defiring.

متزاید (*mútúzáid*) Increafing, multiplying; increafed.

متساوى (*mútúfáwi*) Equal, parallel; right, ftraight.

متسلم (*mútúfullim*) Delivered, configned.

متسلى (*mútúfulli*) Confoled, fatisfied, comforted.

متصدع (*mútúfudda* or *mútúfudhiah*) Importuning, troubling, plaguing.

متصدى (*mútúfuddi*) A clerk, a writer.

متصرف (*mútúfurrif*) Poffeffing, occupying; a poffeffor, mafter.

متصل (*mútttúfil*) Near, contiguous, adjoining.

متصور (*mútúfúwur*) Imagining, conceiving; imagined; imaginable, poffible.

متضرب (*mútúzurrib*) Agitated, difturbed, uneafy.

متضلم (*mútúzullim*) Darkened, obfcure; oppreffed, injured.

متعاقب (*mútúaikib*) Succeffive, following, purfuing.

متعال (*mútúál*) High, fublime: *Khóda-mútúil*; the moft high God.

متعبر

متعبد (mútúabbid) Devout, religious.

متعجب (mútúajjib) Admiring, wondering.

متعدر (mútúaddid) Many, various, a great number.

متعدي (mútúadi) An active, transitive, or causal verb.

متعلق (mútúallik) Belonging to, depending upon, touching, concer-
ning; a kinsman, a member of a family; plural, *Mútúallikán*,
domestics, women, children.

متعين (mútúyin) Constituted, appointed, determined, fixed, deputed:
Mútúyinéb; a command, station, post.

متغير (mútúghiyir) Disturbed, stupified.

متفرق (mútúfurrik) Separate, divided, distinct, different, dispersed,
scattered, dissipated.

متفق (múttúfik) United, agreed, consenting, corresponding, concur-
ring: *Múttúfik-bona*; to be united, to be of one mind, to
agree, to conspire, &c.

متفكر (mútúfukkir) Contemplative, considering; serious, thoughtful,
pensive, grave.

متقدم (mútúkuddim) Ancient, anteriour, antique, preceding; a chief,
president, governor: *Mútúkuddimeen*; the ancients.

متقرب (mútúkurrib) Approaching or fearing (God); having access to
a king, a royal favourite.

متكبر (mútúkubbir) Proud, haughty, arrogant, lofty, insolent, over-
bearing.

متكلم (mútúkullim) Speaking; a speaker, orator, declaimer.

متلف (mútlif) Consuming, ruining; a consumer, a prodigal.

متمادي (mútúmádi) Persevering, continuing, prolonging.

متمرد (mútúmurrid) Stubborn, disobedient, refractory.

متمكن (mútúmukkin) Powerful, having great authority; placed, established, residing.

متمني (mútúnmumi) Wishing, desiring, hoping.

متناهي (mútúnáhi) Finished, terminated, arrived at the utmost extreme.

متواتر

متواتر (*mútúwátir*) Successively, one after another; also, *Mútúwárid* and *Mútúwáli*.

متوصل (*mútúwuſſil*) Connected, related, joined to, depending on; a connection, dependant; plural, *Mútúwuſſílán*, dependants, domestics, family.

متوطن (*mútúwuttin*) Inhabiting, residing; an inhabitant.

متوفر (*mútúwuffir*) Many, numerous, plentiful, copious.

متوفي (*mútúwuffi*) Dead, defunct.

متوقع (*mútúwukkai*) Expected, expecting.

متوقف (*mútúwukkif*) Slow, tardy, delaying, lingering, expecting, waiting for.

متوكل (*mútúwukkil*) Trusting in God, placing confidence in another, resigned to one's fate.

متولد (*mútúwullid*) Born, generated.

متهور (*mútúbawir*) Violent, furious, rash.

متين (*mútern*) Strong, firm, solid.

مثال (*miſál*) Similitude; like, resembling: *Bé-miſál*; Incomparable, without parallel.

مثقال (*miſkál*) A dram and a half weight.

مثل (*múſul*) An example, comparison, simile; adage, proverb, apologue: *Múſul* or *Múſulun*; for example, as for instance: *Miſl*; similitude; like, resembling: *Muſlut*; an example, an instance.

مثلث (*múſullis*) Triangular, triple.

مثمر (*múſmir*) Fruitful, bearing plenty of fruit: *Múſummur*; fruit ripe for gathering.

مثنوي (*múſniwi*) That sort of poetical composition in which the couplets rhime regularly, as in English heroic verse. Neither the Persian ode nor elegy is ever of this species:—The subject of the *Muſnawi* is, properly, moral; for although Firdoſi's celebrated poem is in this regular kind of versification, yet the term *Muſniwi* is not correctly applicable to it.

مجادل (*mújádil*) Contention, dispute; a conflict.

مجاز

مجاز (*mújáz* or *mújázi*) Feigned, not true, hyperbolical, metaphoric.

مجال (*mújál*) Power, ability, strength: *Ká* or *Kia Mújál*; It is out of your power (literally, what power ?).

مجامعت (*mújámúat*) Copulation.

مجاوز (*mújáwiz* or *mújáwizat*) Passing, transgressing, exceeding bounds, &c.

مجتبی (*mújtubi*) Elected, chosen.

مجترم (*mújturim*) Guilty, acknowledging a crime.

مجبر (*mujbur*) An asylum, shelter, place of concealment.

مجد (*mujd*) Glory, grandeur, greatness.

مجدد (*mújuddid*) Renewing, making afresh.

مجزوب (*mujzoob*) Drawn, attracted; defective.

مجرا (*mújra*) Allowance, premium, deduction: *Mújra-déna*; to give or allow part out of a whole (sum): *Mújra* or *Mújrái*; paying one's respects or obeisance to a superiour: *Mújra-kurna*; to pay one's respects or obeisance, to wait on or visit (a superiour).

مجرب (*mújurrib*) Trying, proving; expert, skilled, experienced.

مجرد (*mújurrid* or *mújurrud*) Solitary, alone, unmarried; only, solely; bare, naked: *Bú-mújurrid* or *Bú-mújrid*; immediately upon; instantly, in the same moment.

مجرم (*mújrim*) A criminal, sinner, malefactor: *Mújurrum*; mulcting, fining.

مجروح (*mujrooh*) Wounded.

مجسم (*mújussum*) Incorporated, embodied, incarnate; grown large, corpulent, massy.

مجلا (*mújullá*) Polished, furbished; illustrated, manifested.

مجلد (*mújullid*) A book-binder: *Mújullud*; a volume or book (bound).

مجلس (*mujlis*) An assembly, convivial meeting, a company; a congregation, convention.

مجمد (*mújummud*) Congealed.

مجمل (*mújmil*) A summary, compendium, abstract; collected into a small compass, brought into one point of view.

مجموع

مجموع (*mujmúa*) A collection, magazine, compendium; collected, affembled, convened, contained; all, the whole.

مجنون (*mujnoon*) Infane, mad; in love; the name of a celebrated Eaftern lover.

مجنس (*mujunnis*) A horfe of a mixed breed, between a *Tazi* and a *Túrki*: Ranged in claffes or fpecies; compofed of different kinds.

مچنک (*muchung*) A jew's harp.

مجهود (*mujhood*) Care, trouble, diligence: *Mújhid*; vexing, difturbing.

مجهول (*mujhool*) Unknown; ignorant, ignorance.

مجید (*mújeed*) Glorious, honourable, noble.

محابا (*múhába*) Refpect, regard: *Bé-múhába*; without refpect (of perfons or circumftances); friendfhip, affection.

محاربت (*múhárubut* or *múhárubéh*) War, battle, combat: *Múhárib*; a warriour, a combatant.

محاسبت (*múhásubut*) Computation, calculation.

محاش (*múháfh*) Goods, effects, furniture.

محاصره (*múháfúréh*) A fiege, blockade, circumvallation: *Múháfúréh-kurna*; to befiege.

محاضره (*múházúréh*) Arraigning, or pleading againft, one; citing (before a judge).

محافظت (*múháfúzut*) Care, prefervation, fafety, cuftody, guardianfhip.

محال (*múhál* or *móbál*) Impoffible; a place, a diftrict: *Mobálát*; places, diftricts; impoffibilities.

محاوره (*múháwúréh*) Dialogue, converfation; phrafeology.

محب (*móhib* or *muhib*) A lover, a friend: *Mohibánéh*; friendly, affectionate.

محبت (*móhubbut*) Love, affection, friendfhip.

محبوب (*múhboob*) Beloved; a fweetheart, miftrefs, or object of one's affections.

محبوس (*múbboos*) Imprifoned, confined, arrefted.

محتاج (*múhtáj*) Neceffitous, indigent, in want of; an indigent perfon.

محترم

محترم (m'btúrim) Honoured, revered, venerable, sacred.

محتسب (móhtúsib) A public officer whose duty it is to watch and correct the conduct and manners of the people; literally, an accountant or reckoner.

محتشم (móbtúsbim) Powerful, great, having many followers.

محتمل (móbtúmil) Probable, possible; conjectured; suffering patiently.

محجوب (múhjoob) Veiled, covered; modest, bashful.

محجور (múhjoor) Forbidden, prohibited.

محدود (múhdood) Limited, bounded.

محراب (méhráb) A kind of altar in the Mahommedan mosques, where the priest prays with his face turned towards Mecca.

محرر (múburrur) Written, inscribed.

محرک (múburrik) A mover, persuader, exciter, promoter.

محرم (múburrum) The first month of the Mahommedan year; forbid, interdicted; venerable, dignified: *Múhrum*; a confidant, an intimate friend; one permitted to enter the Haram; that part of the female dress which braces and conceals the breasts.

محروس (múhroos) Guarded, preserved: *Múhroosuh*; a garrisoned or fortified city.

محروم (múhroom) Debarred, excluded; prohibited, forbidden; unfortunate, deprived or destitute of the means of supporting life.

محزون (múhzoon) Grieved, afflicted, vexed.

محشر (múhshur) The last judgment, a place of assembly.

محصل (móhussil) Collecting, gathering, acquiring; a collector (of revenue): *Móhussul*; collected.

محصن (mohsun) Chaste, continent.

محصور (múhsoor) Besieged, surrounded; detained, restrained.

محصول (múhsool) Customs, duties, postage of letters; the produce of any thing.

محض (múhz) Pure, unmixed; merely, purely, solely; sincere.

محضر (múhzur) Presence, appearance (before a judge or prince); the record of a court of judicature, or the decree of a *Cazi* or judge.

محضور

محظور (*mŭhzoor*) Forbidden, unlawful; plural, *Múhzoorát*; illicit things.

محظوظ (*múhzooz*) Glad, chearful, delighted, contented, pleafed.

محفّ (*mihŭffab* or *móbaffab*) A litter for women.

محفل (*múhfil*) A place of meeting, an aſſembly, congreſs, &c.

محفوظ (*múhfooz*) Guarded, preſerved, kept ſafe.

محقّق (*móbukkŭk*) Confirmed, certified, verified.

محكم (*móbkum*) Strengthened, firm, fortified, ſtrong; firmly, ſtre-
nuouſly, ſtrongly.

محكوم (*múhkoom*) Inveſted with ſupreme power; alſo, condemned,
ſentenced; commanded, ordered: *Múbkŭmab*; a tribunal or
court of juſtice.

محلّ (*múhull*) A place, ſtation; diſtrict, quarter; an abode: *Múhul-
lab*; a quarter of a town, a pariſh.

محمّد (*Móbummud*) Praiſed; Mahommed, the Arabian prophet.

محمل (*múhmil*) A camel litter or camel ſaddle: *Móbummil*; bearing,
a carrier: *Múbmool*; loaded, charged.

محنت (*maihnut* or *méhnut*) Labour, toil, trouble, hardſhip, difficulty, care, misfortune, miſery: *Méhnut-kurna*; to labour,
to toil: *Méhnut-khynchna*; to endure hardſhips, to ſuffer great
diſtreſs, to undergo great difficulties.

محو (*múbo* or *múhv*) Erazing, cancelling, defacing: *Múho-kurna*;
to eraze, cancel, rub out.

محيط (*mobeet*) Containing, ſurrounding; comprehending, knowing:
Búbr-mobeet; the ocean.

مخادم (*múkhadim*) Servants, domeſtics, miniſters.

مخارج (*múkhárij*) Expences, diſburſements.

مخاطب (*mókhátib*) A ſpeaker: *Mókhátub*; a perſon addreſſed or
ſpoken to: *Mokhátúbit*; ſpeech, diſcourſe, ſpeaking.

مخاطره (*múkhátúrb*) Danger, peril, hazard.

مخالف (*mókhálif*) Adverſe, oppoſing, diſſentient, contrary; an ad-
verſary, an enemy: *Búd e mokbálif*; a contrary or foul wind:
Múkbálifut; oppoſition, contrariety, repugnance; variance, enmity.

U

مخبر

مخبر (*mukhbir*) Announcing, fignifying, certifying, telling news.

مختار (*moakhtár*) At liberty to chufe; chofen, felected; a free agent; independent, powerful; a minifter, a manager or chief director: *Moakhtár-kurna*; to invest with power or authority: *Moakhtári* or *Moakhtiári*; free-agency, or free-will, independence, power, authority, having the chief or fole direction of affairs.

مخترع (*moakhtúra*) An inventor, an author.

مختصر (*moakhtúsur*) Abbreviated, abridged, contracted; an epitome, a compendium, an abstract, a digeft.

مختلف (*moakhtúlif*) Diverfe, difcordant, different, various, clafhing, jarring.

مختوم (*mukhtoom*) Sealed, figned.

مخدوم (*mukhdoom*) A lord, a mafter.

مخزن (*mukhzun*) A ftorehoufe, magazine, cellar, repofitory.

مخسور (*mukhfoor*) Injured, damaged.

مخصوص (*mukhfoos*) Peculiar, particular, proper, efpecial, intimate : *Mukhfoofiyut*; property, peculiarity.

مخضر (*mókhuzzur*) Verdant.

مخطوب (*mukhtoob*) Affianced, betrothed, promifed.

مخطور (*mukhtoor*) Thought, imagined, conceived, fuppofed.

مخفف (*mókhuffuf*) Alleviating, making light : *Mukhfoof*; alleviated, a confonant having a fhort for a long vowel.

مخفى (*mukhfi*) Hid, concealed, covered, occult, private, clandeftine; fecretly.

مخل (*mókhill*) Difturbing, fpoiling, ruining; a difturber.

مخلد (*múkhullud*) Eternal, durable, permanent.

مخلص (*moukhlis*) Sincere, pure, candid, real, loyal, unfeigned; a friend.

مخلوط (*mukhloot*) Mixed, blended; confufed.

مخلوق (*mukhlook*) Created, formed, produced : *Mukhlookát*; creatures, created beings.

مخبر

مخمر (moakhmir or múkhmir) Leavening: Mókhummir; fermenting, leavening: fermented; intoxicated: Mukhmoor; drunk, crop-fick.

مخمس (múkhummus) Pentangular.

مخمل (mikhmul, pronounced generally Mukhmul) Velvet (fatin).

مخنث (múkhunnis) An hermaphrodite.

مخيل (mókhy-yil) Imagining, fancying, conceiving.

مخيم (mókheem) Pitching a tent.

مد (mudd) Extenfion, production, lengthening.

مداخل (múdákhil or múdákhilut) Entering into, engaging or taking part in, intermeddling.

مدار (múdár) A center, a place of turning or returning: Múdárúl-mohám; the center of affairs; i. e. a minifter.

مدارا (múdárá or múdárát) Affability, courtefy, civility, humility (with a bad view); deceit, diffimulation.

مدارج (múdárij) Steps, degrees.

مدام (múdám) Always, perpetual, continual, lafting.

مداوره (múdáwúréh) Going about, furrounding, compaffing, adjufting (a bufinefs).

مدايح (múdáyéh) Laudable actions.

مدبر (múdubbir) A counfellor, director, administrator, minifter; dif-pofing in order, regulating; plural, Múdubbirán.

مدت (múddut) A space of time; a long time.

مدح (múdah) Praife, eulogium, commendation.

مدخل (múddúkhil) Entering, entered: Mudkhool; entered, put in, inferted.

مدد (múdud) Affiftance, help, aid, fuccours: Múdud-gár; an affiftant: Múdud-déna or kurna; to aid, affift, help, fuccour.

مدرسه (múdrúfah) An academy, college, public fchool.

مدرک (múdrik) Comprehending, comprehenfive: Múdruk or Mudrook; comprehended, underftood.

مدعات (múdát) An invitation, invocation, calling.

مرعي

مدعى (*múdduy* or *múddye*) An adversary, an enemy: *Múddúi* or *Múddú*; an intention, defign, purpofe, meaning; view, object; fcope.

مدرفع (*múduffa*) Repulfed: *Múduffai*; repelling.

مدفون (*mudfoon*) Buried, interred, concealed.

مدور (*múdowwir* or *múdúwir*) Round, circular.

مدروش (*mudboafh*) Aftonifhed, confounded: *Mudbófhi*; aftonifhment.

مديد (*múdeed*) Long, extenfive.

مدينه (*Múdinah*) A city, but efpecially Medina in Arabia.

مذاب (*múzáb*) Liquid, melted: *Lál-múzáb*; a liquid ruby; i.e. red wine.

مذاق (*múzák*) Tafting, tafte; the palate; alfo *Múzákéh* or *Múzákut*.

مذبوح (*muzboob*) Slaughtered, facrificed.

مذكر (*múzukkur*) Of the mafculine gender: *Múzkir*; mentioning, praifing.

مذكره (*muzkúrah*) Mentioning, relating: *Muzkoor*; before mentioned: *Muzkoordt*; difcourfes, relations, matters mentioned.

مذلت (*múzullut*) Bafenefs, contempt.

مذمت (*múzummut*) Scorn, contempt, blame, reproach: *Muzmoom*; fcorned, defpifed: contemptible, blameable.

مذهب (*muzhub*) A religious order or inftitution, a fect; religion.

مرات (*mirát*) A looking-glafs or mirror: *Murrát*; times, turns.

مراتب (*murátib*) Times; alfo ranks, degrees, &c.; plural of *Murtúbah*.

مراجعت (*murójúat*) Return: *Murójúat-kurna*; to return, to come or go back.

مراحل (*murahil*) Journies, day's journies, travelling ftages.

مراحم (*murábim*) Favours, kindnefles, gifts.

مراد (*murád*) Defire, inclination, will, wifh, defign, meaning.

مراسم (*murásim*) Laws, ufages, cuftoms.

مراعات (*murá-át*) Taking care of, attending to, liftening; favours.

مراقبت (*murákubut*) Watching, obferving, attending to.

مربه (*murubbah*) A preferve, a confection.

مربع

مربع (*múrubba*) Square, quadrangular.

مربي (*múrubbi*) A patron, guardian, protector.

مرتب (*múruttib*) Ordering, regulating; a director or regulator; *Múruttub*; put in order, regulated.

مرتبه (*murtúbah*) Rank, degree, dignity, office; a step, a time or turn.

مرتضي (*múrtúzá*) Chosen, approved; the title of Ali, the son-in-law of Mahommed, who is called *Múrtúzáli*.

مرتفع (*múrtúfa*) Elevated, exalted, high, sublime, aggrandized.

مرتكب (*múrtúkib*) Engaging in, commencing; committing a crime.

مرثيه (*murfiah*) A monody, an elegy, a dirge.

مرجان (*murjín*) Coral.

مرحب (*murhub*) Large, spacious, wide; amplitude, extent, largeness.

مرحل (*murhul*) A day's journey: *Murhúlah*; a day's journey, an inn or halting-place for travellers.

مرحمت (*murhúmut*) Pity, compassion, mercy, clemency, favour: *Bé-murhúmut*; unmerciful, inhuman: *Murhúmut-kurna*; to give, bestow; to have compassion.

مرحوم (*murhoom*) A deceased person, the deceased; literally, one whom God has taken to his mercy.

مرخص (*múrukhkhis*) Permitted, allowed (to depart); you have leave to go.

مرد (*murd*) A man: *Murdáneh*; manly, masculine, bold, brave: *Murdánugi*; courage, manliness.

مردار (*múrdár*) Carrion; impure, foul.

مردك (*murduk*) A little man, a contemptible fellow.

مردم (*murdum*) A man; men, people: *Murdum* or *Murdum e chushm*; the pupil of the eye: *Murdúmi*; manliness, humanity, courtesy: *Murdah-ádmi*; a man of honour, a genteel man.

مردود (*murdood*) Repulsed, confuted, rejected.

مرده (*múrdéh*) Dead, defunct; a dead person or body, a corpse.

مرز (*murz*) A region, district; also *Murzúboom*.

مرزبه

مرزبه (*murzúbéh*) A way, mode; regimen, government.

مرسل (*múrſul*) An ambaſſador, prophet; *Múrſúlah*; an epiſtle, a letter;
　a necklace.

مرسوم (*murſoom*) Accuſtomed, preſcribed.

مرشد (*mûrſhid*) A guide to the right way, i. e. to ſalvation.

مرصع (*mûruſſa*) Covered with gold, ſet with jewels.

مرض (*múrun*) Diſeaſe, indiſpoſition, malady, diſtemper.

مرضي (*murzi*) Pleaſure, will, ſatisfaction, concurrence; agreeable,
　acceptable.

مرطوب (*murtoob*) Moiſt, full of humours.

مرغ (*moorgh* or *múrgh*) A bird; a cock: *Múrghi*; a hen.

مرغوب (*murghoob*) Deſireable, eſtimable, amiable.

مرفوع (*murfooa*) Exalted, raiſed high, honoured.

مرفه (*mûruſſah*) Quiet, tranquil, contented.

مرقب (*murkub*) A place of obſervation.

مرقد (*murkud*) A ſepulchre, a tomb, a monument.

مرقوم (*murkoom*) Written, deſcribed, inſcribed; above-mentioned.

مرگ (*murg*) Death.

مركب (*múrukkib*) Compounded, compoſed, a mixture: *Murkib*;
　riding, mounted on.

مركز (*murkuz*) A center: *Murkooz*; concentered: *Murkooz e khátir*;
　the object or deſire of the mind.

مرمت (*múrummit*) Reparation, mending: *Múrummit-kurna*; to re-
　pair, to mend, to put in order.

مرمر (*murmur* or *ſung-murmur*) Marble.

مرواريد (*murwáreed*) Pearls.

مروت (*múrúwut*) Humanity, generoſity, manhood, manlineſs: *Bé-
　múrúwut*; inhuman, barbarous, cruel, uncivil, rude; gene-
　rally pronounced *Múrúwut*.

مرور (*múroor*) Paſſing, elapſing; a paſſage, paſs, tranſition.

مرهم (*murhum*) A plaſter, any dreſſing for wounds.

مرهوب (*murhoob*) Terrible, dreadful.

مرهون (*murhoon*) Pledged, pawned.

مربه

مرید (múreed) A difciple, a follower; defirous, willing.

مریض (múreez) Sick, infirm.

مریم (Múrium) Mary: *Bibi Múrium*; the Virgin Mary.

مزاج (mizáj) Temper, difpofition; the temperament, conftitution, habit of body, the ftate of one's health: *Mizáj kyfa?* How are you?

مزاحم (múzáhim) Inconvenient, hindering, molefting, troubling: *Múzáhim-kurna*; to moleft, hinder, to be troublefome: *Múzáhúnut*; annoyance, impediment, obftacle, difturbance, hindrance.

مزار (múzár) A place of vifitation or pilgrimage; hence, a fepulchre, a tomb.

مزبور (múzboor) Written, above-mentioned, before-mentioned: *Múzbur*; a pen.

مزد or مزج (múzd or múzjd) A reward, premium, falary, wages: *Múzjd* or *Múzjdah*; joyful tidings.

مزدور (múzdoor) A hired labourer, corruptedly pronounced *Mújoor*.

مزرع (múzra) A field fown, or ready prepared for it.

مزور (múzúwur) A lie, a falfehood; falfified, falfe.

مزه (múzah) Tafte, flavour, relifh: *Bé-múzah*; infipid, taftelefs, without flavour: *Múzúgi*; fweetnefs, flavour.

مزه (mizjéh or mizjgan) The eye-lafhes.

مزید (múzeed) Increafe, augmentation.

مزبر (múzeer) Intrepid, bold, ftout-hearted.

مزین (múzíyun) Adorned.

مس (mis) Brafs: *Míjí*; brazen.

مساس (múfás) A foundation.

مسافت (múfáfut or múfáfah) Diftance, part of a road or journey.

مسافر (múfáfir) A traveller: *Múfáfirut*; travelling.

مساکت (múfákut) Avarice, ftinginefs.

مساکن (múfakin) Habitations, manfions.

مسالک (múfálik) Ways, paths.

مساوات (múfáwát) Equation, equality, evennefs: *Múfáwi*; equal, parallel; neutral.

مساورت

مساورت (*músŏwúdit*) Contending for superiority or dominion.

مسايل (*músáil*) Questions, demands, propositions.

مست (*mŭst*) Drunk, intoxicated; hot, libidinous: *Mŭsti*; intoxication, drunkenness; lust, carnal desire: *Mŭstánéh*; intoxicated, lewd; a drunkard, a lewd person.

مستاجر (*mústájir* or *mústuájir*) A tenant, a farmer of land.

مستجاب (*mústujáb*) Acceptable, agreeable, approved.

مستحسن (*mústuhsun*) Approved, laudable, beautiful.

مستحكم (*mústuhkim*) Firm, established, strong.

مستزاد (*mústuzúd*) Increased; a species of poetical composition in which a half verse is added sometimes to every hemistich, but most commonly to every distich of the *Ghúzul* or ode.

مستطاب (*mústutáb*) Good, agreeable, pure, excellent.

مستعار (*mústuár*) Borrowed.

مستعد (*mústuúde*) Prepared, ready, arranged.

مستعصي (*mústŭsy*) Rebellious, stubborn, sinful.

مستعمل (*mústŭmil*) Using, practising: *Mústámul*; practised, used.

مستغفر (*mústughfir*) Penitent.

مستغني (*mústughni*) Content, satisfied; rich.

مستفاد (*mústŭfúd*) Received, acquired, benefited: *Mústúfeed*; acquiring, gaining, profiting.

مستقبل (*mústukbil*) Future, the future tense of a verb.

مستقر (*mústŭkirr*) Remaining firm, constant, stable, confirming.

مستقيم (*mústŭkeem*) Right, straight, standing erect, faithful, loyal.

مستمد (*mústŭmidd*) Asking assistance or aid.

مستمر (*mústúmirr*) Firm, constant, durable.

مستوجب (*mústowjib*) Deserving, meriting, proper, worthy of, fitting; an author, cause, motive.

مستور (*mŭstoor*) Covered, concealed, veiled: *Mŭstoorát*; women (especially of the Haram).

مستولي (*mŭstooli* or *mŭstowli*) Overcoming, subduing, taking possession of, surmounting.

مستوي

مستوي (*mústúwi*) Equal, ſtraight, direct.

مسجد (*musjid*) A moſque, temple, or place of worſhip: *Musjid e jámai*; the great moſque where prayers are ſaid every Friday.

مسجع (*músujjúa* or *músujja*) Rhythmical, periods ſimilar in rhyme and cadence.

مسجل (*miſsujjul*) Proved, authenticated by a judge.

مسخرب (*muſkhúrab*) A droll, a wag, a facetious perſon; a pleaſantry: *Muſkhúrab-kurna*; to play the droll, to be facetious, to joke.

مسدود (*muſdood*) Shut, obſtructed, cloſed.

مسرت (*múſurrut*) Chearfulneſs, gladneſs, joy.

مسرف (*múſrif*) Prodigal, extravagant.

مسرور (*muſroor*) Glad, chearful, exulting, gay, delighted, pleaſed.

مسطر (*muſtur*) A rule with which they draw lines; ſtraight and pa-rallel threads fixed or ſewed on ſtrong paper are generally uſed for this purpoſe.—The word is commonly pronounced *Miſtur*.

مسطور (*muſtoor*) Written, delineated, ſpecified, expreſſed, before-mentioned.

مسعود or مسعد (*múſúd* or *múſaood*) Happy, fortunate, propitious, auguſt.

مسكن (*muſkin*) A dwelling, a habitation.

مسكنت (*muſkúnut*) Humility; poverty, miſery.

مسكين (*muſkeen* or *miſkeen*) Poor, humble, ſuppliant; a poor man, a beggar, a miſerable wretch.

مسلب (*múſúléb*) A queſtion, propoſition, thing.

مسلح (*múſullab*) Armed for war: *Múſúlib*; (warlike) ſtores, arms, preparations.

مسلسل (*múſulſil*) Enchained, linked, ſucceſſive, conſecutive.

مسلط (*múſullut*) A governor, ruler; ſuperiour, ruling over.

مسلك (*muſluk*) A way, path, track; an inſtitution, regulation, rule of conduct.

مسلم (*muſlim*) A Muſulman: *Múſullim*; keeping ſafe, preſerving: *Múſullum*; ſecure, ſafe.

X

مسلمان

مسلمان (*músúlmán*) A Mufulman, a true believer: *Músalmáni*; belonging to the true faith; the true or Mahommedan faith.

مسلوب (*myfloob*) Provided, furnifhed; arranged, fettled (bufinefs).

مسمي or مسي (*músummus*) Named, called, denominated: *Músummit*; names, denominations.

مسمار (*mifmár*) A nail, peg, pin, ftake: *Mifmár-kurna*; to deftroy, level, raze (walls, or a building).

مسموع (*mufmooa*) Heard, audible.

مسند (*mufnud*) A throne, a cufhion on which they fit or recline: *Mufnud-núfbeen*; fitting on the throne, i. e. a reigning prince.

مسواك (*mifwák*) A brufh with which they rub the teeth: *Mifwák-kurna*; to rub or clean the teeth with the particular kind of brufh called *Mifwak*, which is made of a certain fort of tree.

مسودہ (*músúwúdah*) A fketch or rough draught of a letter, or the like: *Músúwúdub-kurna*; to prepare the draft of a letter, &c.

مسهل (*múf-hil*) Laxative, loofe, fluxed.

مسیحا or مسیح (*Múfeeh* or *Múfeeha*). The Meffiah, Jefus Chrift.

مشابہ (*múfbábih*) Like, refembling: *Múfbábúhut*; fimilitude, refemblance, comparifon: *Múfbábúhut-kurna*; to compare to, to make a fimile: *Múfbábúhut-purrhna*; to refemble: *Múfbubbah*; compared, made to refemble, imitated, counterfeited.

مشانمت (*múfbátúmut*) Reproaching, abufing, reviling.

مشار (*múfbar*) Signified, indicated: *Múfbárúmiléh*; aforefaid, abovementioned, the perfon beforementioned.

مشاركت (*múfbárúkut*) Community, fociety, affociation.

مشام (*múfbám*) The fmell.

مشاہدہ (*múfbáhúdéh*) Sight, vifion; ocular demonftration: *Múfbáhúdeh-kurna*; to contemplate, view, look at.

مشاہرہ (*múfbáhúreh*) Monthly allowance or wages.

مشت (*moofbt*) The hand, the fift: *Múfbt* or *Múfbta*; a handful.

مشتاق (*múfbták*) Defirous, wifhing, longing.

مشترک (*múfbtúrik*) A partner, an affociate, an accomplice.

مشتری

مشتری (*múshturi*) A buyer; the planet Jupiter.

مشتمل (*múshtumil*) Comprehending, containing, comprizing.

مشتهي (*múshtúbi*) Loving, defiring, wifhing.

مشجر (*múshujjir*) Abounding in trees: *Mushjur*; a grove.

مشرب (*mushrib*) Drinking, imbibing; nature, temper, humour.

مشرف (*múshrif*) An infpector, examiner, obferver: *Múshurruf*; ennobled, honoured, exalted.

مشرق (*mushrik*) The Eaft: *Mushriki*; oriental, eaftern.

مشروح (*mushrooh*) Explained, illuftrated.

مشعر (*múshir*) Signifying, denoting, indicating, bearing the marks of.

مشعل (*múshál*) A torch, a flambeau, a link: *Múshál-chi* or *Múshálji*; a link-boy or torch-bearer.

مشغول (*mushghool*) Bufied, employed, diligent, engaged.

مشفق (*múshfik*) A friend, my friend! properly, pitying, compaffionate, fhowing favour, kind, courteous.

مشق (*mushk*) A copy to write after.

مشقت (*múshukkut*) Affliction, adverfity, diftrefs, difficulty, inconvenience, trouble.

مشک (*mushk*) Pronounced commonly *Múshuk* or *Músuk*; a leather bag for carrying water: *Múshk*; mufk: *Múshkeen*; mufky.

مشکل (*múshkil*) Difficult, intricate, hard; arduous; a difficulty: plural, *Múshkilát*; difficulties, troubles, &c.

مشموم (*mushmoom*) Odoriferous.

مشورت (*mushwúrut*) Counfel, confultation: *Mushwúrut-kurna*; to confult, deliberate.

مشوش (*múshúwush*) Difturbed, confufed, uneafy; uneafinefs, perplexity, confufion.

مشهود (*mush-hood*) Attefted, proved, evinced; clear, manifeft.

مشهور (*mush-hoor*) Celebrated, illuftrious, famous; known, confpicuous, publifhed, divulged: *Mush-hoor-kurna*; to publifh, to make known, to celebrate.

مشیت (*múshiut*) Will, pleafure, defire, wifh.

مشیر

مشير (musheer) A counsellor.

مصاحب (musáhib) A companion, a friend, a favourite; living in the family of a person on terms of intimacy: Músáhubut; companionship, society, fellowship.

مصاف (musáff) A field of battle; the ranks of an army drawn up for engagement: Musáfft; confronting in battle.

مصالحت (músálúhut or músalúbah) Reconciliation, pacification, accomodation.

مصحف (mus-buf) A book, a page: Ul-musbuf; the Koran.

مصحوب (mus-hoob) Accompanied, accompanying; by, or by the hands of (a letter or the like dispatched).

مصدر (musdur) An origin, source, spring; the infinitive of a verb.

مصدق (músuddik) Verifying: Musdook; verified, true.

مصر (Misr) Egypt: Musr; a large city.

مصراع (misrai) A hemistich, a verse or line.

مصرف (musruf) Expence, disbursement, cost, charge: Musroof; expended, disbursed, employed, directed.

مصطفي (múslúfá) Chosen, selected; one of the names of Mahommed.

مصلحت (muslúhut) Counsel, consultation; measures proper to be pursued: Muslúhut-kurna; to consult, deliberate.

مصنع (músunnaa) Factitious, artificial: Musnaoa; formed, made, created.

مصنف (músunnif) An author.

مصور (músow-wur) Figured, formed, painted; imagined.

مصيبت (múseebut) A misfortune, disaster, calamity, trouble, affliction, adversity.

مضاربه (múzáribeb) A battle, conflict, combat.

مضاعف (múzáuf) Doubled, increased, multiplied.

مضاف (múzuf) Annexed, added, related.

مضايقه (múzáikah) Consequence, significance, importance: Ka or Kia múzáikah; What does it signify? Koochh múzáikb nhy; it
does

does not fignify; it is of no confequence : *Múzáikab* ; oppreffion, penury, want, neceffity.

مضبوط (*muzboot*) Strong, firm, ftout, robuft.

مضطرب (*múztúrib*) Agitated, difturbed, afflicted, chagrined.

مضمر (*múzmur*) Concealed, conceived (in mind).

مضمون (*muzmoon*) Senfe, fignification, contents (of a letter).

مطا (*mútá*) Favour, protection.

مطابق (*mútábik*) According or agreeable to, conformable, fuitable,
anfwering to or agreeing with : *Mútábikut* ; conformity.

مطاع (*mútá*) Obedience ; obeyed.

مطالب (*mútálib*) Demands, requifitions ; plural of *Mutlub.:—Mútá-
lúbit* or *Mútálúbeh* ; afking, requiring.

مطالع (*mútáliah*) Confideration, contemplation ; reading, perufing,
ftudying : *Mútáliah-kurna* ; to read, perufe, examine, to ftudy.

مطايبت (*mútáyúbit*) Jefting, joking, pleafantry.

مطبخ (*mútbukh*) A kitchen.

مطرب (*mutrib*) A mufician, a finger.

مطلب (*mutlub*) Defire, wifh, demand, propofition, queftion ; meaning, intention.

مطلع (*mutla*) Arifing (the fun, &c.) ; the opening or beginning of a
poem ; informed.

مطلق (*mútluk*) Not in the leaft, never ; abfolute, univerfal, free,
unreftrained ; entirely, altogether, abfolutely.

مطلوب (*mutloob*) Demanded, required, wanted, neceffary.

مطمين (*mútmiyin*) Quiet, fecure, enjoying repofe and eafe.

مطیع (*mútia*) Obedient, fubmiffive, obfequious.

مظفر (*múzuffur*) A conqueror ; victorious.

مظلل (*múzullul*) Shaded.

مظلم (*múzlim* or *muzlim*) Dark : *Muzlúmut* ; oppreffion, tyranny,
injuftice.

مظلوم (*múzloom*) Injured, oppreffed.

مغ

مظهر (muzbur) The place where any object or thing appears; figuratively, an object.

معابد (muábid) Servants (of God); sacred places.

معارض (muáriz) An adversary, competitor, opponent: Muáruzut; opposition, contradiction.

معاش (muásh) Life, living; means of living.

معاصر (muásir) Cotemporary.

معاف (muáf) Absolved, spared, dispensed with, exempted from; pardoned: Muáf-kurna; to absolve, pardon, forgive; exempt, excuse, dispense with: Muáfi; exemption, immunity; pardon, forgiveness.

معالجه (muálujéb) Cured; a cure, remedy.

معاملت (mudmúlut or mádmúleb) Business, affair, transaction; negociation: Mudmúlut-kurna; to do or settle business, to transact an affair, to accommodate matters, to negociate, to treat.

معاودت (muáwúdit) Returning, coming or going back.

معاوضت (mudwúzit) Retaliating, returning like for like.

معاونت (muáwúmut) Aid, succour, help, favour, grace: Muáwin; assisting, an assistant.

معاین (mudyun) Seen: Muáyúneb; beholding.

معبد (mábid) A temple, church, place of worship.

معبر (mábur) A pass, a ferry, a ford.

معتاد (mútád) Custom, habit, use.

معتبر (mótúbir or muotúbir) Respectable, worthy of consideration, creditable, deserving belief, reputable.

معتدل (mótúdil) Temperate, mild, equal, moderate.

معترض (mctúriz) Opposing, hindering; interposing.

معتقد (mútúkid) A believer, a faithful friend, or servant.

معتمد (mótúmid) One in whom confidence is placed; a trust-worthy man.

معده (mádéb) The stomach.

معدلت

معدالت (*mádulut*) Juſtice, equity, rectitude: *Mú-uddul*; juſt, equitable.

معدن (*mádin*) A mine, a quarry.

معذور (*mázoor*) Excuſed, excuſable: *Mázoor-kurna*; to excuſe.

معرفت (*múrifut*) Knowledge, acquaintance (eſpecially in a religious ſenſe); virtue, piety; by means of, through, through the channel or medium of, by.

معروض (*márooz*) A repreſentation, ſtatement, relation, petition.

معروف (*mároof*) Known, well known; any thing (eſpecially a name) commonly known.

معزز (*mú-uzzuz*) Honoured, revered, glorious, venerable, magnificent.

معزول (*mázool*) Diſplaced, removed, diſmiſſed, turned out: *Mázool-kurna*; to remove from an office or poſt: *Múzooli*; removal, diſmiſſion (from office).

معسور (*máfoor*) Difficult: *Múfurut*; difficulty.

معشر (*máfhur*) A company, troop, ſociety, body of men.

معشوق (*máfhook*) A lover, a miſtreſs, a beloved object.

معطر (*múattur*) Perfumed, fragrant.

معطل (*múattul*) Abandoned, deſerted, neglected; obſolete, fallen into diſuſe.

معظم (*mózum*) The ſuperiour, the greater: *Múazzum*; honoured, great, reſpectable.

معقول (*mákool*) Reaſonable, juſt, fit, pertinent, conſiſtent with reaſon: *Mákool-kurna*; to bring to reaſon, to make one think or act reaſonably.

معلم (*mú-ullim*) A preceptor, tutor, ſchool-maſter, profeſſor: *Mú-ullum*; taught, inſtructed; a ſcholar.

معلول (*málool*) Indiſpoſed, diſeaſed, diſtempered.

معلوم (*máloom*) Known, notorious, clear, evident, obvious, apparent, conſpicuous; knowledge, acquaintance: *Máloom-kurna*; to know, to recognize, to underſtand, comprehend; to imagine, ſuppoſe, believe, think.

معلى

معلي (múalla) Elevated, exalted, high, eminent, sublime.

معما (mú-umma) An enigma.

معمار (miümár or memár) An architect.

معمور (mámoor) Cultivated, inhabited, peopled; delightful.

معنوي (mánuwi) Essential, intrinsic, real; significant.

معني (máni) Sense, meaning, signification: Bé-máni; without meaning, vain, foolish, idle, useless: Mániyut; sense, reality.

معود (mú-owwud) Exercised, trained.

معون (máoon) Aid, assistance, favour.

معهود (máhood) Agreed, established, fixed, appointed, determined,
promised.

مع or معر (myh or my) With, together with, along with.

معيشت (mú-eeshut) Living, the means of living.

معين (mú-ïyun) Fixed, determined, destined, assigned, allotted, stated:
Múïyuneh; that which is allotted, fixed, stated, or assigned:
Múïyun or Múïyuneh-kurna; to fix, determine, assign, state, &c.

مغ (mugh) A tavern-keeper; one of the Magi; Mugh-búchah; the
son of a tavern-keeper; figuratively, a frequenter of taverns.

مغاک (múghák) A ditch, a furrow, a pit.

مغرب (mughrub) The West: Mughrúbi; Western.

مغرور (mughroor) Proud, arrogant, haughty, presumptuous: Mugh-
roori; pride, arrogance, &c.

مغز (mughz) The brain; marrow, kernel, pith.

مغزب (mughzub and mughzoob) Irritated, angry, enraged.

مغفر (mighfur) A helmet.

مغفرت (mughfirut or mughfirah) Pardoning, remitting of sins:
Mughfoor; pardoned; figuratively, deceased, the deceased or
dead.

مغل (Moghul) A Mogul or Tartar: Moghuláneh; Tartarian, belonging to, or in the manner of, the Moguls or Tartars: Moghu-
búcheh; of Mogul descent, a Mogul youth, a Mogul.

مغلوب (mughloob) Conquered, overcome, subjected.

مغناطيس

مغناطیس (*mughnátees*) The magnet or loadstone.

مغنی (*múghunni*) A singer, a musician.

مغیب (*múghy-yib*) Hidden, concealed : *Múghy-yibat*; secrets, mysteries, concealed things.

مغیر (*múghy-yir*) Changed, altered.

مفاجات (*múfájat*) Sudden death.

مفاخره (*múfakhúrut* or *múfakhúrah*) Glorying, boasting ; aspiring to an equality, emulating : *Múfákhir*; glorious, honourable, dignifying : *Mufukhkbur*; glorified, exalted, dignified, honoured.

مغارقت (*múfúrúkut*) Separation, alienation, distance, absence.

مفاصل (*múfúfuleb*) Distance (between two places).

مفاضل (*múfúzúleh* or *múfúzúlet*) Contending for excellence.

مغاوضت (*múfáwúzut*) Explaining, consulting on business, retribution.

مفایش (*múfáisheb* or *múfáishit*) Boasting, vaunting, contending for superiority.

مفت (*múft* or *mooft*) Gratuitously, without payment, for nothing.

مفتوح (*mufteob*) Taken, subdued (as a town).

مفتی (*múfti*) Giving a decree according to law ; a Mufti.

مفرد (*múfrud*) Singular, alone, solitary, unique.

مفرق (*mufrik*) The crown of the head; plural, *Múfúrik*.

مفروح (*mufrooh*) Glad, rejoicing.

مغروض (*mufrooz*) Necessary to be observed, as being ordained by God; required by duty : *Mufroozát*; the divine commands.

مغروق (*mufrook*) Separated, divided.

مفسد (*múffid*) A seditious person, a corrupter, an author of evil.

مفصل (*múfufful*) Distinct; diffusive, fully, distinctly, at large ; particularly, or dwelling upon particulars; the districts whence the land revenue arises.

مفلس (*múflis*) Poor, indigent.

مفوض (*múfuwuz*) Committed or resigned to the care of, delivered or made over.

مفهوم (*mufhoom*) Understood, comprehended.

مغیر

مفید (*múfeed*) Useful, profitable, salutary.

مقابل (*múkábil*) Opposite, over-against, confronting, collating or comparing: *Múkábúlah*; comparison, opposition, collation, facing or confronting (as in battle): *Múkábúlah-kurna*; to compare, collate; to confront, to meet, to face (as in battle).

مقاتلت (*múkátúlut*) Slaughter, carnage; a battle, conflict.

مقارنت (*múkárúnut*) Conjunction, connexion, contiguity.

مقاصد (*múkásid*) Designs, enterprizes, attempts, undertakings.

مقاعد (*múkáid*) A guardian, keeper, preserver.

مقال (*múkál* or *múkáleh*) Speech, discourse, saying, sentence, a word; plural, *Múkálát*.

مقام (*múkám*) A place of residence, a dwelling, habitation, mansion, abode; a halt or halting-place: *Múkám-kurna*; to halt; a musical mode or tone: *Káim-múkám*; a vicegerent, a successor, a substitute: *Múkámát*; halting-places, halts; musical modes, of which there are twelve.

مقاول (*múkáwúleh*) An agreement, a compact.

مقاومت (*múkáwúmit*) Opposition, resistance.

مقبره (*mukbúrah*) A sepulchre, tomb, burying-ground.

مقبول (*mukbool*) Agreeable, acceptable, pleasing.

مقتدا (*múktúdá*) Followed, imitated, imitable: *Múktúdi*; an imitator, a follower.

مقتصر (*múktúsur*) A compendium, a summary.

مقتضا (*múktúzá*) Exacted, required; exigence, necessity, expediency; agreeable or according to, necessarily or in consequence of.

مقدار (*mikdár*) Quantity, measure, space, number.

مقدس (*múkuddus*) Sanctified, holy, consecrated: *Bytúl-múkuddus*; Jerusalem: *Mukdis*; a holy place.

مقدم (*mukdim*) Coming, arriving (off a journey), arrival: *Múkuddum*; antecedent, prior, preceding; a revenue officer.

مقدمه (*múkuddúmah*) An affair, matter, business; plural, *Múkuddúmát*.

مغرور

مقدور (*mukdoor*) Power, ability, capacity, poſſibility : *Bé-mukdoor* ; powerleſs, unable, helpleſs, without authority.

مقر (*múkurr*) A reſidence, ſtation, place of reſt.

مقراض (*mikráz*) Sciſſars, ſhears.

مقرب (*múkrub*) Approached, approximated ; eſteemed, honoured.

مقرر (*múkurrur*) Eſtabliſhed, confirmed, fixed, certain, infallible, certainly : *Múkurrur-kurna* ; to fix, ſettle, eſtabliſh, appoint, to ratify, confirm : *Múkurrúri* ; certainty ; confirmation, eſtabliſhment.

مقرون (*mukroon*) Near, conjoined, connected, related.

مقسوم (*mukſoom*) Diſtribution, diviſion : *Mukſoom-kurna* ; to diſtribute, divide.

مقصد (*mukſud*) An intention, deſign, meaning, purpoſe ; alſo *Mukſood*.

مقطر (*múkuttir*) Diſtilling, dropping.

مقطع (*mukta*) The laſt verſe in an ode.

مقهور (*mukhoor*) Conquered, ſubdued ; diſtreſſed, oppreſſed, vexed ; figuratively, an enemy ; plural, *Mukhoorán* (the enemy).

مقيت (*múkeet*) Powerful ; a guardian, keeper.

مقيد (*múky-yud*) Diligent, fixed, attentive, bound; dedicated to ; noted, ſigned, regiſtered ; diligence, cloſe attention, care.

مكاتبت (*múkátúbit*) Correſponding by letter.

مكار (*múkkár*) A cheat, an impoſtor, a deceiver, a pretender.

مكافات (*múkáfát*) A recompence, retribution, reward.

مكان (*múkán*) A place, ſtation, ſpot, dwelling.

مكه (*Mukkéb*) The city of Mecca.

مكتب (*muktub* or *muktub-kbánéb*) A writing-ſchool : *Muktib* ; a writing-maſter : *Muktoob* ; written, a letter.

مكتفي (*múktúfi*) Content, having enough.

مكدر (*múkuddur*) Diſturbed, vexed, afflicted.

مكر (*mukr*) Fraud, impoſture, deceit, pretence : *Mukr-kurna* ; to pretend ; to deceive, impoſe on, &c.: *Múgur* ; except, unleſs, only ; yet, notwithſtanding, however.

Υ 2

مكرد

مكرر (*múkurrur*) Repetition, repeated, dwelt on; repeate.lly, again and again.

مكرم (*múkurrum*) Noble, illustrious, venerable, revered, respected, honoured: *Mukrúmut*; honour, glory, &c.

مكروه (*mukrooh*) Odious, hated, detestable, abominable, ugly, vile.

مكس (*múgus*) A fly.

مكشوف (*mukshoof*) Revealed, disclosed, open.

مكيدت (*múkeedut*) Deceiving, defrauding, ensnaring.

مكين (*múkeen*) Inhabiting; fixed, established.

ملاح (*mullah*) A seaman, sailor, mariner.

ملاحت (*múlábut*) Beauty, elegance, goodness.

ملاحظ (*múl.ibúzah*) Contemplation, observation, consideration: *Múlábúzah-kurna*; to regard or observe attentively, to peruse, to read.

ملاذ (*múláz*) An asylum, refuge, protection; a protector.

ملازم (*múldzim*) A servant, an attendant; plural, *Múlázimán: Múlázúmut*; service, attendance; assiduity, diligence: *Múlázúmut-kurna*; to wait upon, to pay one's respects (to a superior).

ملاطفت (*múlátúfut*) Courtesy, graciousness, favour, benignity.

ملاقات (*múlikát*) A meeting, interview: *Múlikát-kurna*; to meet, to have an interview, to encounter, to visit: *Múláki*; meeting, encountering with.

ملال (*múlál*) Sadness, affliction, anguish, languor; also *Múlilut*.

ملام (*múlim* or *múlámet*) Reproach, reprehension, blame, accusation: *Múlimet-kurna*; to blame, reproach, revile, censure.

ملائك (*múláik*) Angels; plural of ملك *Múluk*.

ملايم (*múláim*) Mild, gentle, soft, easy, affable; tender, delicate: *Múlúmit*; gentleness, softness, tenderness, mildness, &c.

ملت (*millut*) Religion, faith; a nation, people.

ملتزم (*múltúzim*) Constrained, compelled; necessarily, following; convicted.

ملتمس (*múltúmis*) Begging, praying, supplicating.

ملتوي .

ملتوی (*múltúwi*) Delaying, spinning out.

ملجا (*muljá*) An asylum, a place of refuge, a retreat.

ملحق (*múlhuk*) Joined, added, annexed, adhering.

ملخ (*múlukh*) A locuft.

ملزوم (*mulzoom*) Inseparable, neceffarily connected, affixed, belonging to.

ملعون (*múlaoon*) Excommunicated, curfed, execrated, drove out from society.

ملفوف (*mulfoof*) Wrapped up, enclofed.

ملقب (*múlukkub*) Surnamed, a furname or nickname.

ملک (*múlk* or *mulk*) A kingdom, country: *Múlik*; a king: *Múluk*; an angel: *Milk*; poffeffion, property, eftate; alfo *Milkiyet*.

ملول (*múlool*) Fatigued, tired, languid, vexed, melancholy: *Múlool-hona*; to be melancholy, vexed, &c.

ملیح (*múleeh*) Agreeable, fweet, charming, beautiful.

ممالک (*múmálik*) Kingdoms, provinces, ftates, regions.

ممتاز (*múmtáz* or *moamtáz*) Chofen, diftinguifhed, eminent.

ممتد (*múmtudd*) Extended, prolonged: *Múmidd*; an extender or prolonger.

ممدوح (*mumdooh*) Praifed, celebrated, laudable.

ممر (*múmirr*) A pafs, paffage, ford, tranfit.

ممکن (*múmkin*) Poffible: *Múmkin-hona*; to be poffible: *Múmkinát*; poffibilities.

مملکت (*mumlúkut*) An empire, kingdom, realm; power, grandeur, magnificence.

ممنوع (*mumnooa*) Prohibited: *Mumnooát*; forbidden things.

ممنون (*mumnoon*) Obliged, receiving a favour.

من (*munn*) A maund, or weight equal to about 80lbs.

مناجات (*múnáját*) Prayers, recommendations.

منادی (*múnádi*) A proclamation: *Múnádi-kurna*; to proclaim, to publifh by a crier.

منار (*múnár* or *múnáreh*) A turret or minaret.

منازعت

منازعت (*mánázu-ut*) Conteſt, controverſy, litigation, altercation.

مناسب (*múnáſib*) Proper, right, fit, ſuitable, juſt : *Mún.iſúbut* ; ſuitableneſs, relation, connexion, compariſon.

منا‌بي (*múnábi*) Prohibited things, ſins, crimes.

منبر (*mimbur*) A pulpit, a reading-deſk.

منبسط (*múmbúſit*) Dilated, extended ; rejoicing, exulting.

منت (*minnut*) An obligation, favour ; ſupplicating with great humility and earneſtneſs : *Minnut-kurna* ; to ſupplicate with great humility.

منتخب (*múntúkhub*) Choſen, ſelected, a ſelection.

منتظر (*múntúzir*) Expecting, waiting for.

منتظم (*múntúzim*) Ordered, arranged.

منتقل (*múntúkil*) Tranſported, carried, paſſing (to another).

منتقم (*múntúkim*) Taking revenge ; (God) the avenger.

منتهي (*múntúhá*) The end, concluſion, boundary, extremity.

منجم (*múnujjim*) An aſtronomer or aſtrologer.

منجمد (*múnjúmid*) Congealed, concreted.

منحرف (*múnhúruf*) Changed, inverted, declining or turning from.

مند (*mund*) A poſſeſſive particle added to words, and ſignifying *poſſeſſed of*, or *endowed with* ; as *Khirud-mund*, poſſeſſed of underſtanding, judicious : *Dowlut-mund* ; poſſeſſed of riches, opulent, &c.

مندرج (*múndúrij*) Contained, inſerted, included ; comprehending, containing, &c.

منزل (*munzil*) A travelling ſtage, a day's journey, a manſion : *Munzil-gáh* ; a place where travellers ſtop to refreſh.

منزلت (*munzilut*) Dignity, ſtation, condition, rank.

منزول (*múnzúwil*) Periſhing, decaying, failing.

منسوب (*munſoob*) Relative, related, belonging to, depending upon.

منسوخ (*munſookh*) Cancelled, aboliſhed, obliterated, broken.

منش (*muniſh*) Nature, genius, diſpoſition ; greatneſs of ſoul, dignity of mind.

منشا

منشا (*munſhuá*) The principal, origin, ſource, beginning.

منشور (*munſhoor*) Diffuſed, ſpread abroad, divulged ; a royal mandate, a liberal diſpoſition.

منشي (*múnſhi*) A ſecretary, a writer (eſpecially of letters); a teacher of languages, particularly the Perſian ; a teacher of the Arabic being commonly called مولوي *Mowlúwi* or *Moulvi*.

منصب (*munſib*) Dignity, office, ſtation: *Munſib-dár*; a perſon holding any office or poſt, a nobleman, a man of rank.

منصف (*múnſif*) A diſtributor of juſtice, a judge ; juſt, equitable.

منصور (*munſoor*) Aided, defended, protected ; victorious, conquering.

مطلع (*múntúba*) Tame, trained, obedient.

منطق (*muntik*) Logick, reaſoning.

منظور (*munzoor*) Agreeable, pleaſing, acceptable, eligible ; ſeen, looked at, admired.

منظوم (*munzoom*) Arranged in order ; metrical, verſified, poetic.

منع (*múna*) Prohibition, inhibition, hindrance, obſtacle: *Múna-kurna* ; to prohibit, forbid, repulſe, hinder.

منعم (*múnim*) A benefactor ; beneficent, gracious, liberal.

منفرج (*múnfúruj*) Tranquil, contented, happy.

متفسد (*múnfúſud*) Corrupted.

منقار (*minkár*) The beak of a bird.

منقبض (*múnkúbiz*) Conſtipated, contracted.

منقتل (*múnkútil*) Slain, killed.

منقش (*múnukkuſh*) Painted, embroidered.

منقضي (*múnkúzi*) Finiſhed, compleated.

منقطع (*múnkúta*) Terminated, finiſhed, broken off, exterminated, disjoined.

منقي (*múnukka*) A ſpecies of raiſins.

منکر (*múnkir*) Denying, refuſing, not acknowledging, not believing in.

منکس (*múnukkus*) Inverſe, having the head inverted.

منکشف (*múnkúſhif*) Diſcovered, revealed, diſplayed.

منوال (*minwal*) Mode, manner, rule, form.

منهم

منهدم (*múnhúdim*) Demolished, destroyed.

منهزم (*múnhúzim*) Put to flight, discomfited, defeated, ruined.

منهي (*munbi*) Forbidden, prohibited.

مني (*múni*) Sperm.

منيت (*múniut*) A wish, desire, hope.

منير (*múneer*) Shining, splendid, illuminating, illustrious.

منيف (*múneef*) Eminent, exalted, noble, sublime.

مو or موي (*moo* or *mooe*) Hair.

مواجب (*múwájib*) Salary, pension, wages, hire, due.

مواجهت (*múwájubet*) Presence, appearance, meeting face to face :
Bil-múwájúbéh ; before, in presence of.

مواحنت (*múwáhúnit*) Hatred, dislike, enmity.

مواخزه (*múwákhúzah*) Taking satisfaction, retaliating, chastising,
calling to a severe account.

موازي (*múwázi*) Heads (of cattle); setts, pairs.

مواشي (*múwáshi*) Quadrupeds, cattle, especially sheep, cows, and
the like.

مواصلت (*múwáfúlit*) Meeting, interview, conjunction.

موافق (*múwáfik*) Conformable, consonant, congruous, apt, like,
agreeing, suiting ; favourable, propitious.

موافقت (*múwáfúkut*) Agreement, conformity, concordance, unanimity ; analogy ; propitiousness : *Múwáfúkut-kurna* ; to agree,
to enter into friendship, to be conformable, to conform.

موالات (*múwálát*) Friendship, affection ; pursuing a business steadily,
or without intermission.

موبد (*múbud*) A doctor, philosopher, a counsellor of state.

موت (*mowt* or *moat*) Death.

موثر (*mú-uffir*) Penetrating, making an impression, efficacious : *Mú-
uffur* ; penetrated, affected.

موج (*moaj*) A wave, surge, billow.

موجب (*mújib*) A cause, motive, reason : *Bé-mújib* ; without reason,
causelessly.

موجح (*mújid*) An author, caufer.

موجر (*mújir*) Hiring, letting to farm, renting.

موجود (*mowjood* or *mójood*) Exifting, prefent, ftanding before, at hand : *Mójood-hona*; to be prefent, at hand, to poffefs : *Mójood-kurna* : to produce, make appear, bring before.

موخخ (*mú-ukbkhuz*) Taken, feized ; retaliated upon, called to an account.

موخر (*mú-ukbkhur*) Pofterior, confequent ; the end.

مودت (*mú-wuddut*) Friendfhip, love.

مودي (*mú-uddi*) A caufe, a motive ; caufing ; paying, performing what is due.

مور (*moar*) An ant, a pifmire.

مورث (*múrus*) Hereditary poffeffion : *Móris*; a caufe, author: *Mowroos*; poffeffed by hereditary right.

موربچانه or مورچه (*moarcháneb* or *moorchab*) Ruft.

مورد (*mórid* or *mowrid*) A place of arriving, defcending, alighting, appearing.

موزون (*mowzoon*) Weighed, well adjufted ; verfe (juftly meafured).

موزه (*mózab*) A ftocking ; a boot ; ftockings, boots.

موسقي (*múfiki*) Mufic.

موسم (*mowfim* or *mófim*) Seafon, time.

موسوم (*mowfoom*) Marked, figned, impreffed, named, called.

موسي (*Múfá*) Mofes : *Múfuwi*; Mofaic.

موش (*moofb*) A moufe.

موصل (*múfil*) A carrier, bearer : *Múwufful*; happily arrived, joined.

موصوف (*mowfoof* or *mófoof*) Defcribed, celebrated, praifed ; before-mentioned ; a fubftantive noun.

موضع (*móza* or *mowza*) A village ; a place, a fituation.

موعد (*mow-id*) The time or place of a promife ; a promife ; *Mow-ood*; promifed, predicted, premifed.

موفور (*mowfoor*) Copious, full, numerous, abundant, many, plentiful.

موقر (*múwukkur*) Honoured, revered, refpected.

Z

موقع

موقع (*mowka*) A place where any thing falls, a contingency; proper.

موقوف (*mowkoof* or *mókoof*) Deferred, delayed, poftponed; laid afide, relinquifhed; dependant upon, belonging or reftricted to: *Mókoof-kurna*; to put off, delay, refer to, to relinquifh: *Mókoof-hona*; to be referred to, to depend upon (any particular event or circumftance).

موکب (*mowkib*) An army, forces; a choice body of troops.

موکد (*mú-ukkud*) Confirmed, corroborated; efficacious.

موکل (*múwukkil*) One who delegates power, a conftituent or principal.

مولا (*mowlí* or *múlla*) A judge, a lord: *Mowláná*; a title given frequently to perfons refpected for great wifdom and experience, and fometimes to poets.

مولد (*mowlid*) Nativity, birth: *Mowlood*; born, generated.

مولف (*mólif*) A compiler of a book.

مولوی (*mowlíwi* or *mowlvi*) A perfon poffeffing great judicial and theological knowledge, one fkilled in the Arabic, a teacher of the Arabic.

موم (*moam*) Wax: *Moam-butti*; a wax-candle.

مومن (*mómin*) Orthodox, faithful, believing.

مومیا (*momid*) A mummy.

مونث (*mú-unnus*) Feminine, effeminate.

مونس (*múnis*) A companion, intimate friend.

موهب (*mowhib*) A prefent or gift.

موید (*mú-iyud*) Strengthened, aided, fortified.

مهابت (*múbabut*) Majefty, greatnefs; reverence, fear, dread, awe.

مهاد (*mihád*) A throne, fopha, bed, chair.

مهال (*múhál*) Formidable, dreadful (place).

مهم (*múhúmm*) Affairs of importance; plural of *Móhimm*.

مهتدی (*múhtúdi*) Directed or guided (to the right road).

مهتر (*maibtur*) Greater; a chief, prince, lord; a fweeper, a goldfinder.

مجور

مهجور (múhjoor) Separated, cut off, left, forsaken.

مهد (méhd) A cradle, a couch.

مهدوم (múhdoom) Destroyed, totally ruined.

مهر (móhr or móhur) A seal; a gold coin; called, also, Ushurfi, and equal to sixteen rupees: Móhur-kurna; to seal: Méhr; love, affection: Méhr or Méhir; a marriage portion.

مهربان (méhr-bán) Kind, friendly, affectionate, loving; a friend: Méhrbáni or Méhrbángi; friendship, love, affection, kindness, favour: Méhrbáni-kurna; to befriend, to favour.

مهره (móhréh) A fort of stone used in giving a smoothness and glossiness to paper.

مهم (móhimm) An important affair or business; important, momentous, great; plural, Móhimmát.

مهمان (méhmán) A guest, a stranger: Méhmán-dári or Méhmáni; hospitality; Méhmáni; an entertainment, a feast, a banquet: Méhmáni-kurna; to entertain hospitably, to give an entertainment.

مهمل (móhmil) Negligent, careless; flow, slothful.

مهنت (méhnut) Service, labour; hardship, difficulty, misfortune: Méhnut-kurna; to labour, to work, to serve.

مهیا (múhiya) Prepared, ready, arranged.

مهیب (múhéeb) Awful, dreadful; a person whose appearance inspires dread or awe.

می (my) Wine: My-náb; pure wine: My-khwár; a wine-drinker: My-fúroash; a vintner or wine-merchant: My-kháneh; a tavern.

میان (mián or meeán) The waist, the loins, the middle: Mián or Miáneh; the middle or center of any thing, the scabbard of a sword: Miáneh; a fort of litter; also, middling: Miánji or Miánehi; a mediator, a procurator, a broker, a go-between: Miánúgi; mediation: Mián-bustah or Kúmur-bustah; ready, prepared (for action, or to engage in any enterprize): Dur-mián; between, amongst, in, into: Dur-miáni; the middle, the interior or internal part; mediation.

ح

میخ (*maikh*) A tent-pin; a hook, a tenter; a nail.

میدان (*mydán*) A plain, an open field.

میده (*mydah*) Fine flour.

میر (*meer*) A lord, chief, prince, head, leader, mafter (applied peculiarly, as a title, to the *Siyuds* or defcendants of Mahommed).

میراث (*mirás*) Heritage, patrimony, fucceffion.

میردها (*mirdúbá*) Properly a commander of ten men, but applied to a
fuperintendant of any fort, efpecially of the *Dawk* or poft.

میرزا or میرزا (*meerza* or *mirza*) A prince, a chief, a knight; applied
peculiarly to the race of Moghuls.

میزان (*mizán*) A balance, a pair of fcales; meafure, metre, rhyme,
profody.

میزبان (*maizbán* or *meezbán*) A landlord, one who hofpitably enter-
tains a ftranger, a hoft: *Maizbáni*; hofpitality.

میسر (*múiffir* or *móyuffir*) Attained, attainable, procurable, obtainable:
Móyuffir-bona; to be attainable or procurable.

میشوم (*myfhoom*) Unfortunate, unlucky, difagreeable.

میغ (*maigh*) A cloud; hence, figuratively, rain.

میکده (*my-kúdah*) A tavern.

میکون (*my-goon*) Wine-coloured.

میل (*mile*) Inclination, propenfity, affection, love, fondnefs, partiality,
prejudice in favour of: *Mile-kurna*; to love, to be inclined
towards, to have a partiality or fondnefs for: *Meel*; an inftrument with which they take away the fight.

میمنت (*mymúnut*) Fortune, profperity, happinefs.

میمون (*mymoon*) Fortunate, happy, profperous, auguft; a baboon,
ape, monkey.

میوس (*my-oos*) Defperate.

میوه (*maiwah* or *maiwéh*) Fruit: *Maiwah-dár*; fruitful.

ن

 نا (*ná*) A negative particle prefixed to nouns, and equivalent to *ir*, *un*, *in*, &c. in Englifh. —— We will infert under this article only the moft common of thefe compound adjectives, from which fubftantives are formed by the addition of the ufual termination ى or *i*.

ناامید (*ná-ómaid*, or, contractedly, *nómaid*) Hopelefs, defperate, defponding.

ناپاک (*ná-pák*) Impure, unclean, polluted, filthy.

ناپایدار (*ná-páedár*) Unfteady, not durable, inconftant, fickle, frail, momentary.

ناپدید (*ná-pideed*) Invifible, difappearing, not to be found.

ناپسند (*ná-púfund*) Difagreeable, difpleafing.

نابود (*ná-bood*) Annihilated, reduced to nothing, vanifhed.

ناپیدا (*ná-pyda*) Not appearing, not exifting, not to be found.

نابینا (*ná-beena*) Blind.

ناتمام (*ná-túmám*) Imperfect, unfinifhed, deficient, incomplete.

ناتوان (*ná-túwán*) Infirm, impotent, incapable.

ناچار (*ná-chár*) Helplefs, forlorn, wretched, miferable, without remedy; conftrained; by force, againft the inclination.

ناچیز (*ná-cheez*) Trifling, infignificant, contemptible, a nothing, a trifling, filly thing.

ناحق (*ná-buk*) Unjuft, injurious; unjuftly, wrongfully.

ناخن (*nákhún*) A nail, a claw, a talon.

ناخواه (*ná-khwáh* or *ná-kháh*) Unwilling, unwillingly.

ناخوش (*ná-khoofh*) Unpleafant; difpleafed, offended; indifpofed (ufed with *Mizáj*).

نادان

نادان (*nd-ddn*) Ignorant, unknowing, unlearned, illiterate ; a fool, a blockhead.

نادر (*nádir*) Rare, singular, uncommon ; precious, excellent : *Nádirah* ; a rarity, curiofity, wonder ; rare, curious.

ناوریست (*ná-dúrúft*) Not right or true, falſe, wrong.

نادم (*nádim*) A penitent, repenting, feeling ſhame or remorſe.

نار (*nár*) Fire: *Nári* ; fiery, full of fire.

ناراست (*ná-ráft*) Not ſtraight, crooked, not right, wrong, falſe.

نارنج or نارنک (*ndrunj, ndrung,* or *núrungi*) An orange : *Nárunji* or *Nárungi* ; of an orange colour.

ناروان (*ná-rúwán*) Not current, ſtagnant.

ناز (*nâz*) Blandiſhment, amorous or wanton playfulneſs or airs ; elegance, gracefulneſs : *Náz-kurna* ; to give one's ſelf affected airs, to play the coquet : *Náz o niáz* ; earneſt intreaty, ſoothing ſupplication : *Názneen* ; amiable, elegant, lovely.

نازک (*názik*) Delicate, tender, thin, neat, genteel, elegant : *Náziki* ; tenderneſs, delicateneſs.

نازل (*názil*) Deſcending, alighting ; happening : *Náziléh* ; a misfortune, diſaſter, calamity.

ناساز (*ná-fáz*) Diſſonant, diſcordant, not agreeing : *Náfázgári* ; diſcordance, diſſention.

ناسپاس (*ná-fipás*) Unthankful, ungrateful.

ناسزا (*ná-fúzá*) Unworthy, unmerited ; indecent, improper.

ناشایستة (*ná-fhdiftéh*) Unworthy, improper, unfit, indecent, unbecoming.

ناشتا (*náfhitá*) Hungry, faſting, having an empty ſtomach ſince morning.

ناشناس (*ná-fhinds*) Ignorant, unacquainted.

ناصب (*náfib*) Erecting, fixing, planting.

ناصح (*náfib*) A monitor, counſellor, adviſer.

ناصر (*náfir*) A defender, aſſiſtant.

ناصواب (*ná-fúwáb*) Not right, bad, unwholeſome, not ſalutary.

ناصور

ناسور or ناصور (*násoor*) A disease in the corner of the eye, a rheum; also, an old wound.

ناطق (*nátik*) Speaking, rational: *Nátikut*; the faculty of speech.

ناظر (*názir*) Seeing, observing; a keeper, a guardian, especially the superintendant or inspector of the Haram.

ناظم (*názim*) An arranger, an adjuster; hence, figuratively, a governor or ruler.

نافِ (*náf*) The navel.

نافذ (*náfiz*) Penetrating, passing, getting through; having effect; received or obeyed (an order).

نافع (*náffaa*) Beneficial, profitable, advantageous, useful.

نافَ (*náféh*) A bag or bladder of musk; musk.

نافهم (*ná-fehm*) Not understanding or comprehending.

ناقابل (*ná-kábil*) Unskilled, incapable, foolish.

ناقبول (*ná-kubool*) Disgusting, displeasing; loathing.

ناقص (*nákis*) Deficient, imperfect; worthless, useless.

ناگاه (*ná-gáh*) Suddenly, unexpectedly, all at once, unawares.

ناكس (*ná-kus*) Worthless, mean, base, sordid, unmanly; nobody.

ناگوار (*ná-gowár*) Indigested, indigestible; displeasing, disgusting.

نالان (*nálán*) Lamenting; lamentation.

نالايق (*ná-láik*) Improper, unworthy, unbecoming; unworthily.

نالش (*nálish*) A complaint, complaining: *Nálish-kurna*; to complain, to make or prefer a complaint.

نام (*nám*) Name; fame, reputation, renown; honour: *Bud-nám* or *Bud-námi*; a bad or ill name, or reputation, infamy, dishonour; abuse, detraction: *Bud-nám-kurna*; to abuse, defame, depreciate: *Námi*; famous, celebrated, illustrious.

نامبارك (*na-múbáruk*) Unfortunate, inauspicious.

نامدار (*námdár*) Illustrious, famous, glorious, having a name.

نامرد (*ná-murd*) A coward, an unmanly fellow; cowardly, unmanly, effeminate; impotent.

نامزد (*nám-zud*) Appointed, named, declared (for an office, &c.).

نامعلوم

نامعلوم (*ná-mãloom*) Unknown, uncertain.

نامقبول (*ná-mukbool*) Unacceptable, difagreeable, difpleafing.

نامناسب (*ná-múnáfib*) Improper, unfuitable, incongruous.

ناموافق (*ná-múwáfik*) Adverfe, contrary, differing, difagreeing.

نامور (*námwur*) Celebrated, famous.

ناموزون (*ná-mózoon*) Difcordant, unrhythmical; ill-made, deformed.

ناموس (*námoos*) Reputation, efteem, honour, glory.

نامه (*náméb*) A letter, epiftle; hiftory, work.

ناو (*náo* or *naw*) A boat.

ناوك (*náwuk*) A fmall arrow; properly, a tube from whence they difcharge fmall arrows.

ناہموار (*ná-humwár* or *ná-humwáireb*) Uneven, unequal, not level or fmooth, rough, rugged; unbecoming.

نای (*nái*) A reed, a pipe, a flute, a flagelet.

ناياب (*ná-yáb*) Undifcoverable, not procurable or obtainable, hard to be found, rare.

نايب (*náib*) A deputy, lieutenant, vicegerent.

نايچه (*náicheb*) A fmall reed (diminutive of نای *nái*), but efpecially that belonging to a *Hookah*, generally pronounced *Nychab*, and called by Europeans a fnake.

نايره (*náireb*) Fire; enmity, hatred.

نبات (*núbát*) An herb, a vegetable, grafs.

نبرد (*núburd*) A battle, engagement, war: *Núburd-gáb*; a field of battle.

نبض (*nubz*) The pulfe, the beating of an artery: *Nubz-daikhna*; to feel the pulfe.

نبی (*núbi*) A prophet.

نبيره (*núbeerah*) A grandfon, a fon's fon.

نتیجه (*nútijah* or *núteejah*) Refult, confequence, iffue, what neceffarily follows any action, reward, retribution (ufed both in a good and bad fenfe); properly, a fetus, offspring, birth.

نثار

نثار (*nifár*) Money thrown amongst the people on festive occasions: *Nifár-kurna* ; to scatter, disperse (money, &c. on such occasions).

نثر (*núfir*) Prose.

نجابت (*nújábut*) Generosity, nobleness, greatness.

نجات (*núját*) Liberation, freedom, salvation.

نجب or نجيب (*nujb* or *nújeeb*) Liberal, generous, noble.

نجف (*nújuf*) High ground to which water does not reach.

نجم (*nujm*) A star, a planet: *Nújoom* or *Ilm e nújoom* ; astronomy : *Ibl e nújoom* ; an astronomer or astrologer ; for the most part, however, used for the plural: *Nújoomi* ; belonging or relating to the stars.

نحس (*núbs* or *núhus*) Inauspicious, unfortunate, unlucky, bad.

نحو (*núbo* or *núbv*) Way, path, track ; manner, mode, grammar.

نحيف (*núbeef*) Lean, meagre ; wretched, miserable.

نخجير (*nukhcheer*) Hunting, the chace, prey.

نخست (*núkbúft*) The beginning, the first, at first.

نخوت (*nukbwut* or *nukbwéh*) Greatness, magnificence, pomp, parade, pride, haughtiness.

ندامت (*núdámut*) Contrition, repentance, penitence, shame.

نديم (*núdeem*) A companion, an intimate friend, a confidant, a privy counsellor ; plural, *Núdúmá*.

نذر (*nuzr*) A gift, an offering, a present (from an inferior to a superior) ; properly, a vow, or the performance of a vow.

نر (*nur*) Male, masculine, a male.

نرخ (*nirkh*) A tariff, the price or assize of provisions.

نرد (*nurd*) The game of draughts or backgammon.

نردبان (*nurdbán* or *nurdúbán*) A staircase, steps, a ladder, especially a scaling ladder.

نرگاو (*nurgáo*) A bull, a bullock.

نرگس (*nurgis*) A narcissus.

نرم

نرم (*nurm*) Soft to the touch, mild, gentle, tender: *Nurm-kurna*; to soften; to sooth, to mitigate, to pacify: *Nurmi*; softnefs, tendernefs.

نزا (*núzá*) Spreading or exciting diffention.

نزاد (*nú-zjád* or *ni-zjád*) Origin, root, feed; family, defcent, extraction.

نزاع (*nizá*) A difpute, contention, controverfy.

نزاکت (*núzákut*) Elegance, politenefs.

نزدیک (*nuzdeek*) ⎱ Near, about, with.

نزد (*nizd*) ⎰ Near, hard by, clofe to, neighbouring; almoft: *Nuzdeeki*; vicinity, neighbourhood, nearnefs, approach; corruptedly pronounced *Nuggeech* and *Nújeek*: — *Nuzdeek-úna* or *Nuzdeek-owna*; to approach, come near, come clofe: *Nuzdeek-hona*; to be at hand, to be nigh.

نزله (*nuzléh*) A cold (efpecially one of long duration), a catarrh.

نزول (*núzool*) A defcent, alighting: *Núzool-kurna*; to alight, defcend, fall (as rain), to fojourn; to happen, to befal.

نزهت (*nizhut*) Delight, joy, pleafure.

نسا (*nifá*) Woman, the female fex, a lady.

نسب (*núfub*) Lineage, race, ftock, family, houfe, genealogy.

نسبت (*nifbut*) Relation, reference, comparifon; relative, in refpect to, compared to; betrothed, contracted: *Nifbut-kurna*; to betroth.

نسخه (*núfkhah*) A copy or model, a phyfician's recipe, a medical draught; a writing, a book.

نسق (*nufk* or *núfuk*) Order, arrangement, regularity.

نسل (*nufl*) Offspring, progeny, defcendants, lineage, ftock, race.

نسیان (*nifián*) Oblivion, forgetfulnefs.

نسیم (*núfeem*) A gentle gale, the zephyr.

نشا (*núfha*) Crop-ficknefs, intoxication.

نشاط (*núfhát*) Gladnefs, joy, pleafure; improperly pronounced *Nifhát*.

نشان (*nifhán*) A fign, mark, a fignal; a ftandard, a pair of colours; a butt; a trace, a veftige; a fcar: *Khátir-nifhán*; a memorial, remembrance,

remembrance, something making an impression on the mind : *Khátir-nishán-kurna* ; to elucidate, to imprefs the mind with a juft conception of any thing : *Nishán-kurna* ; to make a mark, fign, or fignal.

نشيب (*núshaib*) A defcent, declivity : *Núshaib-gáh* ; a place lying low.

نصارى (*Núfári* and *Nufráni*) A Chriftian.

نصايح (*núfáyeb*) Counfels, advices, admonitions.

نصب (*nufb*) Fixing, erecting, planting : *Nufb-kurna* ; to fix, erect, plant, eftablifh.

نصر (*nufr*) Affiftance, victory ; alfo *Nufrut* : — *Núfeer* ; an affiftant, defender.

نصف (*niff*) Half, the half, the middle.

نصيب (*núfeeb*) Fortune, fate, lot, deftiny.

نصيحت (*núfeebut*) Counfel, advice, admonition ; alfo, reproof, chaf-tifement : *Núfeebut-kurna* or *déna* ; to advife, counfel, admo-nifh ; to reprove, chaftife.

نضارت (*núzarit* or *núzáreb*) Frefhnefs, beauty, pleafingnefs ; alfo *Nuzrut*.

نظارت (*núnárut* or *núzáreb*) Looking, viewing ; infpection, fuper-intendancy.

نظام (*nizám*) Order, difpofition, arrangement ; a compofer, arranger ; a governor (efpecially the Subah or Viceroy of the Decan) : *Nizámut* : government, arrangement, regulation : *Nizámut-kurna* ; to govern, regulate, &c.

نظر (*núzur*) The fight, vifion, look : *Núzur-kurna* ; to view, look, fee, behold, look at, regard.

نظرباز (*núzur-báz*) A juggler, playing with or deceiving the eyes.

نظم (*nuzm* or *núzim*) Order, arrangement ; poetry.

نظير (*núzeer*) Like, alike, refembling, equal to.

نعت (*núat* or *nát*) Praife, efpecially the praife of Mahommed.

نعره (*náréb*) Clamour, crying, noife.

A a 2

نعش

نعش (*ndfb*) A bier, a coffin (with a dead body).

نعل (*nál*) A horseshoe : *Nál-bund*; a farrier.

نعمت (*niámut*) Affluence, ease, wealth, the comforts or blessings of
life; benefit, favour, graciousness, beneficence; a blessing:
Nú-eem; pleasure, goods, comforts, blessings (of life); benefited, endowed.

نعوذبالله (*nú-úzúbilláh* or *nózúbilláh*) God defend or preserve us (from
any evil) ! God avert, or God forbid !

نغم or نغمه (*núgbum* or *nughméh*) Melody, song, modulation; a musical sound or tone; a soft, sweet voice.

نغاز (*núfáz*) Penetration; penetrating, passing, pervading, piercing;
obeyed (an order); escape (from an enemy).

نغط or نغاط (*nuffát* or *nuft*) Naptha (a bitumen).

نغاق (*nifák*) Hypocrisy, double-dealing, insincerity, enmity.

نغر (*núfur* or *nufr*) One person, one man : *Teen-núfur*; three persons, three men; used as far as ten: *Fee-núfur*; each man:
Chár seer fee-núfur; four seers (or 8 lbs.) each man.

نغرين (*nufreen*) An imprecation, curse; detestation, abhorrence.

نفس (*nufs*) The soul, spirit, body, blood, flesh, self; a person, individual, substance, essence; desire, lust: *Núfus*; the breath,
respiration : *Nufsáni*; carnal, sensual.

نفع (*núfa*) Gain, profit, utility, advantage, emolument: *Núfa-kurna*;
to profit, to gain : *Núfa-purrbna*; to prove or turn out profitable, to be emolumentary.

نفل (*nuft* or *núft*) A voluntary act of religion, the observance of which
is not prescribed; a charity or work of supererogation.

نفوذ (*núfooz*) Penetrating, piercing or passing through.

نفي (*núfi*) Annihilation, non-existence; prohibition; repulsed.

نغيس (*núfees*) Precious, valuable, coveted exceedingly, great riches.

نقا (*núká*) Purity, cleanness; pure, clean; also *Núkáwut*.

نقاب (*nikáb*) A veil.

نغاره (*aúkúreh*) A brazen or kettle drum.

نقاش

نقاش (*nukkásh*) A painter, a sculptor, an embroiderer.

نقب (*núkub* or *nukh*) A mine, a subterraneous excavation, a way through a mountain.

نتر (*nukd*) Ready money, cash.

نقره (*noakrab* or *nókrah*) Silver, coin.

نقش (*nukfh*) A picture, painting, drawing : *Nukfh-kurna*; to draw, delineate, paint.

نقصان (*noakfán* or *nukfán*) Lofs, injury, damage, detriment, diminution : *Nukfán-lugna* or *Nukfán-purrhna*; to suffer a lofs, to lofe, to fustain an injury or damage.

نقط (*núktáh*) A point, a dot, a fubftitute : *Núktah-dún*; a perfon of minute knowledge, one acquainted with fubtleties.

نقل (*nukl*) A relation, narrative, hiftory; imitating, copying, tranfcribing; a copy, tranfcript, an imitation : *Nukl-kurna*; to copy, tranfcribe; to imitate, to mimick; to move from one place to another; to relate, to narrate, to tell a ftory.

نقمت (*nikmut*) Punifhment; revenge, hatred.

نقي (*núki*) Pure, clean, excellent.

نقيب (*núkeeb*) A chief, leader; an intelligent perfon : *Núkeebut*; underftanding, penetration, intelligence.

نکاح (*nikáh*) Matrimony, conjunction (copulation) : — This fort of connexion is not the moft binding or honourable, nor is it confidered in India as a ftrict matrimonial engagement, although regarded as fuperior to a ftate of concubinage. Matrimony is properly exprefled by the Hindvi term *Beeá*, or, figuratively, by the Perfian word *Shádi* :—*Nikáh-kurna*; to marry, to take a wife : *Nikáhi*; matrimonial.

نکار (*nigár*) A picture, portrait, effigy; figuratively, a miftrefs or beautiful woman.

نکاه (*nigáh* or *nigéh*) A look; obfervation, beholding; cuftody, care : *Nigáh-kurna*; to look, view, obferve, behold : *Nigáh-rukhna*;

to

to take care of: *Nigáh-báni*; cuſtody, watching, or taking care of: *Nigáh-báni-kurna*; to guard, preſerve, watch: *Nigáh-bin*; a guard or keeper.

نکبت (*nukbut*) Adverſity, calamity, misfortune.

نکته (*núktah*) A point, a dot, a ſubtlety: See نقطه.

نکر (*núkir*) Sagacious, penetrating, ingenious; ſagacity.

نگران (*nigrún*) Looking, beholding, expecting.

نکو (*nikó*) Good, beautiful, excellent: *Nikói*; goodneſs, &c.

نکونسار (*nigoonſár*) Hanging the head through ſhame; inverted; turned upſide down, having the head downward and the feet upward.

نکهت (*núkhut*) Perfume, any thing odoriferous.

نگین (*núgeen* or *núgeenah*) A ring, a ſeal.

نم (*num*) Moiſt, humid, wet: *Num* or *Númi*; moiſtneſs: *Shub-num*; dew, night-dew: *Numgeen*; moiſt.

نما (*númd*) Showing, pointing out, a guide (uſed in compoſition): *Númayiſh*; appearance, form; viſion, ſight.

نماز (*númáz* or *nimáz*, and ſometimes *númáx*) Prayers: *Númáz-purrhna*; to ſay or repeat one's prayers.

نمد (*númud*) A ſort of rug, a kind of coarſe carpeting.

نمط (*númut*) A mode, manner, way.

نمک (*númuk*) Salt: *Númúkeen* or *Numkeen*; ſalted, ſalt: *Númuk-dún*; a ſaltcellar: *Númuk-húrám*; an ungrateful perſon: *Númuk-húlúl*; a grateful perſon: *Númuk-húrámi*; Ingratitude: *Númuk-húlúli*; gratitude: *Númuk-húrámi-kurna*; to act ungratefully.

نمونه (*nimoonah* or *númoonah*) An exemplar, model, mould, ſpecimen, proof.

ننگ (*nungg*) Honour, reputation, name; alſo, ignominy or diſgrace: *Nungg o nimoos*; honour and reputation (eſpecially as depending on one's female connections).

نو (*nó* or *now*) New, freſh, original.

نوا

نوای or نوا (*nírwá* or *nírwdi*) Voice, found, modulation, fong; opulence, the goods of the world, the means of fubfifting: *Bé-nírwá*; without the means of fubfifting, deftitute, indigent, ftarving.

نواب (*nírwáb* or *nírwáb*) A nabob, properly the plural of *Náib*, a deputy, vicegerent, lieutenant. In the fingular this term implies an office or ftation, but in the plural it is a title of honour; a nabob, therefore, not being neceffarily a governor or viceroy, we fhould rather fay the *foubab* or *foubahdár* of Oude than the *nabob* of Oude.

نواح (*nírwáh*) Complaining, bewailing, lamenting: نوح *Nooh*; the patriarch Noah, fo called (according to fome oriental writers) from the lamentations which his fituation in the ark drew from him.

نواحی (*nírwáhi*) Environs, borders, neighbourhood.

نوار (*nírwár*) A broad kind of tape.

نوازش or نواز (*nírwáz* and *nírwázifh*) Kindnefs, favour, courtefy: *Ghúreeb-nírwáz*; one kind to ftrangers; my kind or benevolent fir!

نواله or نوال (*nírwál*, *nírwáleh*, *nírwáleh*) A mouthful; a fingle handful; a pittance.

نوبت (*nóbut*) Period, juncture, conjuncture, occafion, opportunity, an accident, a time, turn; any thing happening or done periodically; a guard or watch, keeping watch, relieving guard; a fort of military mufic: *Nóbut-khdneh*; a watch-tower, a guard-room.

نوپیدا (*nó-pydi*) New, newly produced.

نوح (*nóhah* or *nowhah*) Lamentation: *Nóhah-kurna*; to moan, lament.

نور (*noor*) Light, fplendour: *Noor-bukhfh*; giving light (to the eyes): *Noor-jéhín*; the light of the world (names of women): *Nírani*; ferenity, brightnefs; bright, light.

نورد

نورد *(núwurd)* A ply or fold ; agreeable, acceptable ; worthy.

نورس *(nó-rus)* Young, fresh, tender, recent.

نوروز *(nó-roze)* The first day of the (Persian) year ; the day on which the sun enters Aries.

نوشتن *(núwishtah)* A writing.

نوع *(nóé or nó)* A sort, kind, species : *Noé-digur* ; another kind : plural, *Unwá.*

نوک *(noak)* A point : *Noak e kúlum*; the point or nib of a pen.

نوکر *(nókur)* A servant : *Nókúri* ; servitude, service : *Nókúri-kurna* ; to serve, to go into service.

نومید *(nómaid)* Hopeless : *Nómaidi* ; hopelessness.

نوید *(núwaid)* Happy tidings.

نه *(néh, núh)* No, not, neither, nor : *Núh hum, núh toom* ; neither I nor you.

نهاد *(nihád)* Nature, habit, quality : *Khátir-nihád*; inclination, will, determination, whatever the mind is fixed on.

نهار *(núhár)* The day : *Lyló-núhár* ; night and day.

نهال *(nihál)* A young plant, a shoot, a sucker.

نهان *(nihán)* Latent, hid, concealed : *Nihani* ; concealment, secretly.

نهایت *(núháyet or núháit)* The extreme, end, boundary ; excess ; excessively, extremely, exceedingly ; the utmost : *Bé-núháit* ; infinite, infinitely, without end, immense.

نهج *(núhj, naihj, or núhij)* Road, path ; manner, way.

نهر *(nubr)* A river, a stream.

نهضت *(núhzut or núhzut)* Departing, departure, rising up : *Núhzut-kurna* ; to depart, to march, to move.

نهنگ *(núhung or nihung)* A crocodile, a water monster, a sea-lion ; applied, figuratively, both to a sword and a pen.

نهی *(núhi)* Prohibition, an interdict.

نهیب *(niheeb, nihaib)* Fear, terror.

نی *(ny)* A pipe, a flute, a reed, a cane : *Ny-shúkur* ; a sugar-cane.

نیابت *(niábut)* The office of a deputy, vicegerency, lieutenancy.

نیار *(niár)* Fires ; plural of نار *nár.*

نیاز

نیاز (niáz) Supplication, prayer, interceding with great humility; necessity, want: Niáz-mund; a person in necessity, a supplicant; often applied to one's self, by way of humility, in addressing an equal, but more usually in addressing a superior: Niáz-kurna; to supplicate, to pray or beg submissively.

نیام (niám) A sheath, a scabbard.

نیت (niyut-neeut) Intention, purpose; will, wish, desire.

نیرنگ (nyrung) Deception, incantation, magic, sorcery.

نیرو (nyroo) Strength, power.

نیز (neez) Also, likewise, again.

نیزه (naizab) A spear, lance, javelin.

نیسان (nyfán) Spring rain; a fabulous sort of rain or dew, which, falling into shells, produces pearls, and, dropping into the mouths of serpents, poison. See *Ab e nyfán*.

نیستی (naifti) Nullity, non-existence, annihilation.

نیش (naifb or neefb) The sting (of a venomous animal).

نیک (naik) Good, beautiful, excellent: Naiki; goodness, excellence, &c.: Naik-bukht: fortunate, happy: Naik-núm; having a good name: Naik-nómi; reputation.

نیکو (naiko or neeko) Good, beautiful, elegant: Neeko-kár; a beneficent person, a performer of good actions.

نیل (neel) Blue, a blue, black, or dark colour; indigo, woad: Neel-goon; azure, blue, dark: Neel; the river Nile: Neeli; blue, azure, dark, black.

نیم (neem) Half, the middle: Neemah; half, a half: Neemah-áfteen; a garment with half sleeves: Neem-fúl or Neem-fáleh; a middle-aged person: Neem-roze; mid-day.

و

واپس *(wápus)* Returning: *Wápus-kurna* or *déna* ; to return, reſtore, give back.

وابسته *(wá-buſtah)* Bound, depending on: *Wábuſtagán* ; dependants, domeſtics, family.

واجب *(wájib)* Neceſſary, expedient, proper, worthy, deſerving: *Wá-jibi* ; propriety, juſtneſs, fitneſs: *Ghyre-wájibi* ; unfitneſs, in-juſtice: *Wájibi*, or, contractedly, *Wájbi* ; very juſt, very right !

واحد *(wáhid)* One, ſole, ſingle.

وادي *(wádi)* A deſert.

وارث *(wáris)* An heir, an inheritor.

وارد *(wárid)* Deſcending, alighting, arriving: *Wárid-bóna* ; to arrive, appear, happen, befal: *Wáridát* ; events, incidents.

واز *(wáz)* Open.

واسط *(wáſit)* The middle, a mediator: *Wáſitut* ; any thing interme-diate ; motive, cauſe, occaſion.

واسع *(wáſai)* Ample, capacious, wide ; God.

واصل *(wáſil)* Joined, connected, coupled ; arrived, met.

واضح *(wázih)* Evident, clear, manifeſt.

واضع *(wázai)* An eſtabliſher: *Wázai ul kánoon* ; a legiſlator.

واعظ *(wáiz)* A monitor, adviſer.

وافر *(wáfir)* Abundant, plentiful, copious, many, much.

وافي *(wáfi)* Compleat, entire ; plentiful, numerous ; ſincere, faithful.

واقع *(wákai)* Befalling, occurring, happening ; arriving, appearing ; figuratively, ſevere ; uſed with *Jung*, a battle or action: *Wákai* or *Fil-wákai* ; very true ! very right ! *Wákiát* ; acci-dents, events ; plural of *Wákiah* or *Wákiut*.

واقف

واتف (*wákif*) Intelligent, learned, skilled, expert, knowing: *Wá-kif-bína* ; to be acquainted with, to know, to be skilled in.

زوال (*wála*) Exalted, eminent, respectable, high, sublime: *Wála-jáb* ; of elevated or exalted dignity (one of the titles of the Nabob of Arcot).

والا (*wú-illá* or *willí*) Otherwise, if not.

والد (*wálid*) A parent, a father: *Wálidab* ; a mother.

والي (*wáli*) A prince, a chief, a superior or master, a governor.

واویلاه (*wáweeláb*)
وای وای (*wái-wái*) } An exclamation, loud cry, lamentation, moan.

واه (*wáb* or *wáb-wáb*) Oh! wonderful! excellent! admirable! (interjection of admiration or surprize).

وبا (*wúbá*) The plague, pestilence.

وتیره (*wúteerab*) A way, path, track; a mode, manner, habit: *Naik-wúteerab* ; a good disposition or habit.

وثوق (*wúsook*) Strength, firmness, steadfastness.

وثیق (*wúseek*) Firm, steady, strong: *Wúseekut* ; firmness, solidity, confidence, faith.

وجد (*wujd*) Ecstasy, excessive love; opulence.

وجود (*wújood*) Existence, substance, essence, body, person: *Bá-wú-jood* ; notwithstanding, for all that.

وجه (*wújéb*) Mode, manner, method, shape, form; appearance, aspect, countenance; substance, essence; plural *Wujoob*.

وجهه (*wujhab*) Allowance, pension.

وحدت (*wúhdut*) Unity; also *Wúhdániyut* : *Wúheed* ; alone, unique.

وحشت (*wúhshit*) A desert, a solitude; fear, dread; sadness.

وداد (*widád*) Love, friendship: *Wúdood* and *Wúdeed* ; a friend, a lover: God.

وداع (*widá* or *Ul-widá*) Adieu! farewell! God be with you: *Ul-widá-kurna* ; to bid adieu.

ودیعت (*wúdiut*) A deposit, trust: *Wúdiut-byát* ; death, depositing one's life.

ور

ور (*wur*) Added to nouns, implies poffeffion ; as, *Jánewur*, (having life) an animal, a living creature, &c.

ورد (*wurd*) Continual employment: *Wurd-zúbán*; fluency of fpeech: *Wurd* or *Wird*; a rofe; rofy or red.

ورزش or ورز (*wurz* or *wurzifh*) Cuftom, habit; gain, profit.

ورق (*wúruk*) A leaf (of a book).

ورود (*wúrood*) Arrival, coming; appearing, approaching, defcending, alighting.

وزارت (*wizárut*) The office or dignity of vizir.

وزر (*wuzr* or *wizr*) A crime, fin, fault; arms.

وزن (*wuzn*) Weight, meafure, metre, rhyme; honour, reputation, efteem: *Wuzn-kurna*; to weigh.

وزير (*wúzeer*) A vizir, a minifter.

وساطت (*wúsáfut*) Mediation, medium, channel, means.

وسط (*wúfut*) The middle or center; right, juft, proper, excellent, great, magnificent.

وسواس (*wufw.is* or *wifwás*) Temptation to evil; terror, diftraction of mind.

وسيله (*wúfeelah*) That which unites, connects, or effectuates any thing; a caufe, occafion (of bringing near or together); medium, means.

وصف (*wusf* or *wúff*) Defcription; praife: *Wúff-kurna*; to defcribe, to praife.

وصل (*wúfl* or *wúfil*) Conjunction: *Wufli*; conjunctive.

وصول (*wufool*) Arrival, conjunction, the enjoyment of a wifhed-for object.

وصيت (*wúfiut*) A laft will or teftament, a precept: *Wúfiut-kurna*; to bequeath (efpecially counfel); *Wúfiut-námeh*; a will or teftament.

وصيلت (*wúfeelut*) Society, company; meeting, interview.

وضع (*wúza*) Situation, pofition; difpofition, condition, conduct, mode of acting, operation, performance, procedure: *Wúza-kurna*; to deduct; to eftablifh.

وضو

وضو (wúzoo) Ablution : *Wúzoo-kurna* ; to perform one's ablutions.

وضوح (wúzooh) Evidence, proof : *Wúzooh-kurna* ; to make clear, to manifeſt, to prove : *Wúzooh-hona* ; to be evident.

وطد (wútid) Firm, ſolid, confirmed, corroborated.

وطر (wútur) A neceſſary thing ; neceſſity, uſe.

وطن (wútun) A country where one either reſides or was born, but uſually employed to denote the latter.

وظيفه (wúzeefah) A ſtipend, ſalary, allowance, a daily maintenance or allowance ; plural, *Wúzáif.*

وعده (wúdéh) A promiſe, an engagement : *Wádéh-kurna* ; to promiſe, to engage.

وعظا (wáz) Advice, admonition.

وفا (wúfá) Good faith, ſincerity, performance of a duty or promiſe, gratitude : *Wúfá-dár* ; faithful, grateful, a grateful perſon : *Wúfá-dári* ; fidelity, gratitude : *Bé-wúfá* ; faithleſs, ungrateful : *Bé-wúfái* ; faithleſſneſs, ingratitude.

وفات (wúfát) Death, deceaſe : *Wúfát-kurna* ; to die.

وفاق (wifák) Concord, harmony, good underſtanding.

وفرت (wúfirut) Plenty, abundance.

وفق (wufk or wúfik) A ſufficiency ; fit, ſuitable, agreeable.

وفور (wúfoor) Full, copious ; a multitude, abundance.

وقار (wúkár) Authority, dignity, honour, reputation.

وقت (wukt) Time, ſeaſon, opportunity : *Bé-wukt* ; untimely, unſeaſonable.

وقف (wukf) A bequeſt or legacy for pious uſes.

وقوع (wúkoo) A contingency, accident, event, occurrence.

وقوف (wúkoof) Experience, knowledge : *Bé-wúkoof* ; ignorant, a blockhead or ignorant perſon.

وكالت (wikálut or wúkálut) Deputation, the office or ſituation of a *vakeel* or ambaſſador.

وكيل (wúkeel) An ambaſſador, deputy, agent, a vakeel ; a counſellor or attorney at law.

والدت

ولادت *(wiládut* or *wildd)* Nativity, birth.

والایت *(wiláit)* A kingdom, region, dominion; corruptedly pronounced *Billát,* and uſed to ſignify Europe excluſively, both
by natives and Europeans. By *Wiláit* is alſo underſtood Tar-
tary, and the other regions lying to the northward of Hindoſtan. *Wiláiti* or *Billáiti*; belonging to Europe, European.

ولد *(wúlud)* A ſon, offspri g.

ولول *(wulwúleh)* Noiſe, murmur, clangour.

ولي *(wúli)* A friend; a prince, lord, preſident: *Wúli-ihd*; the heir
apparent, the appointed ſucceſſor: *Wúli-niámut*; a benefactor,
a lord or maſter, a patron.

وهب *(wúhb* or *wúhub)* Giving, beſtowing.

وهم *(wúhm* or *wúhum)* Suſpicion, diſtruſt, fear, conceiving a falſe
idea: *Wúhhám*; ſuſpicious, doubtful, fearful: *Wúhm-kurna*;
to ſuſpect, fear: *Wúhmi*; imaginary, conjectural; plural,
Wúhoom.

وي *(wy)* Oh! fy! alſo ويح *Wyh.*

ویران *(weerán* or *weeráneh)* Deſert, deſolate, laid waſte, depopulated,
ruined: *Weeráneh*; a deſolated place, ruins: *Weerán-kurna*;
to lay waſte, to deſtroy, &c.: *Weeráni*; deſolation, deſtruc-
tion, &c.

هاتف ‏ *(hátif)* Crying, exclaiming, but commonly fignifying an angel or aërial fpirit, who declares to mortals the will of Heaven, or fuggefts to them how they fhould act, in order to obtain their defires. The *Hátif* occurs frequently in poetry.

بادی ‏ *(bádi)* A leader, guide, director; the head or point of an arrow.

بار ‏ *(bár)* A ftring of pearls.

بای ‏ *(bái)* O! ah! alas! *Hái-bái!* alas! ah me! a noife.

بایل ‏ *(báil)* Terrible, horrible.

بیبب ‏ *(bibab)* A gift.

هجر ‏ *(bujr)* Separation, disjunction: *Hújr*; nonfenfe.

هجران ‏ *(bijrán)* Separation, disjunction, abfence, cut off (from one's friends or country).

هجرب ‏ *(bijrab)* The Higera, or Hejra, or Mahommedan era, computed from the flight of Mahommed from Mecca to Medina.

هجو ‏ *(bújó)* Satire; a fatire, a lampoon, a pafquinade; *Hújó-kurna*; to fatirize, to lampoon.

هجوم ‏ *(bújoom)* An affault, attack, impetuofity: *Hújoom-laowna*; to attack, affault, charge furioufly.

هدایت ‏ *(bidáyut)* Taking or fhowing the right way.

هدف ‏ *(bidif)* A butt or mark for archers; figuratively, any mark aimed at.

هدم ‏ *(bidim)* Ruin, deftruction: *Hádim*; a deftroyer.

هدهد ‏ *(búdbúd)* The lapwing.

هدیه ‏ *(búdiyéh)* A prefent, an offering of friendfhip.

هذر ‏ *(búzur)* Nonfenfe, frivolous talk or difcourfe.

هر (*bur*) All, every: *Hur-roze*; every day: *Hur-dum*; every moment: *Hur-wukt*; at all times, continually, &c.

هرا (*harrá*) Sound, voice, shout, a hurra: *Hurrá* or *Húrrá-kurna*; to shout; to put an end to any business in an abrupt and irregular manner.

هراس (*birás*) Terror, dread, fear; also *Hirásah*:—*Hirásán*; fearing, frightened.

هرج (*burj*) Tumult, sedition, confusion; also, *Hurj-murj*.

هرد (*burd*) Turmerick; corruptedly *Huldi*.

هرزه (*burzah*) Vain, futile, absurd, foolish; nonsense, trifles.

هرکاره (*burkáreh*) A sort of running footman; literally, a factotum.

هزار (*búzár*) A thousand: *Húzára* or *Húzár-dustan*; a nightingale.

هزل (*búzil*) A jest or joke: *Huzliát*; jests, pleasantries.

هزيمت (*húzeemut*) Flight, rout, defeat.

هستي (*husti*) Existence, being.

هشيار (*hóshiár*) Intelligent, prudent, wise, cautious: *Hóshiári*; prudence, caution, &c.: *Hóshiár-hona*; to be cautious, watchful, careful, prudent.

هضم (*huzm* or *búzim*) Digestion: *Huzm-kurna*; to digest.

هلاک (*húlik*) Ruin, slaughter, death, perdition, annihilation: *Húlik-kurna*; to drive to destruction, to annihilate, to ruin, kill, destroy.

هلال (*hilál*) The new moon, as far as the third day.

هلاهل (*húláhil*) A mortal poison that takes effect instantaneously.

هم (*hum*) With, together, along with; used in forming a variety of compounds, of which some examples follow.

همانا (*húmáná*) Like, resembling; the opinion, imagination; immediately, all of a sudden.

همايون (*húmáyoon*) Blessed, fortunate, august.

هما or همای (*húmái* or *húma*) A fabulous bird of happy omen.

همت (*himmut*) Resolution, determination, purpose, design.

همدم (*hum-dum*) An intimate friend or companion.

همراه

همراه (bum-ráb) With, along with: Humrábi; society, companion-ship.

همسایه (bum-sáyab) A neighbour, neighbouring: Hum-sáyegán; neigh-bours.

همعهد (hum-úbd) Coeval, contemporary.

همگی (bumgi) All, the whole.

همنشین (bum-núsheen) One who fits or converses with another.

هموار (bumwár or bumwáreb) Plain, even, level: Ná-humwár; im-proper, unworthy, unsuitable.

همو (húmoo or húmá) That, that very thing or person.

همه (búmab) All, the whole, every one.

همیشه (humaishah) Always, ever, continually, perpetually: Húmai-shagi; eternity, perpetuity.

هند (Hind) India: Hindi, Hindúi, Hindwi, Hindúwi, Hindvi, or Hindúvi; Indian, the Indian language.

هندو (Hindoo) An Indian, a Gentoo; plural, Húnood.

هندوستان (Hindoftan) India, Hindoftan, especially the provinces im-mediately joining to that of Dehli: Hindoftáni; a native of Hindoftan; any thing belonging to Hindoftan; the Hindvi or language of Hindoftan.

هندسه (bindúfab or bindfab) Generally pronounced Hindfab or Hin-dúfab; geometry; the Arabic figures or digits.

هنر (búnur or bónur) Virtue, knowledge, science, art: Hónur-mund; virtuous, learned, fkilful, &c.

هنگ (bung) The underftanding, wifdom.

هنگام (bungám) Time, feafon, period.

هنگامه (bung-ámeh) Difturbance, noife, confufion, riot, tumult: Hun-gámeh-kurna; to make a difturbance, &c.

هنوز (búnoaz) Yet, ftill.

هوا (bowá) The air, wind; atmofphere.

هاون (híwán or báwun) A peftle and mortar.

هودج (bowduj) Corruptedly, Howdah; a litter, alfo a canopy.

هودہ *(búdah)* Profit, advantage, ufe; truth: *Bé-hoodah*; unprofitable, ufelefs, idle, vain.

ہوس *(húwus)* Defire, luft: *Húwás*; libidinous.

ہوش *(hoafh)* Underftanding, judgement, fenfe: *Bé-hoafh*; foolifh, infane, infenfible: *Bé-hoafhi*; infanity, a trance, a fainting fit: *Hoafh-mund*; prudent, wife: *Hoafhiár*; fee ہشیار, prudence, watchfulnefs.

ہول *(howl)* Dread, terror, fright: *Howl-nák*; any thing terrible, dreadful.

ہوی *(húwá)* Defire, love, inclination, will, wifh.

ہویدا *(húwaida)* Clear, evident, manifeft, open.

ہیات *(hyát)* The face, afpect, countenance.

ہیبت *(hybit)* Fear, dread; awe, holding in reverence.

ہیچ *(haich)* Any, any thing; nothing.

ہیکل *(hykul)* A figure, form, image; the ftature or fhape of the body.

ہیمہ *(heemah)* Wood, fire-wood.

ی

ی *(yá)* Oh! ah! alfo—or, either.

یاد *(yád)* Remembrance, recollection, memory: *Yád-kurna*; to remember, to keep in memory; to recollect: *Yád-purrhna* or *Yád-lugna*; to come in mind, to think of (accidentally): *Yád-dáfht*; a memorial, a memorandum: *Yád-déna*; to remind: *Yád-kár* or *Yád-gár*; any thing given to a friend by way of memorial.

یار

یار (*yár*) A friend, a lover: *Yári*; friendſhip, love, intimacy; alſo, aſſiſtance, aid, defence, protection, ſupport: *Yár-wúfáddár*; a ſincere or faithful friend: *Yárán*; friends, intimates, companions.

بارا (*yárá*) Power, force, ſtrength.

یاس (*yúás*) Deſpair: *Yás*; fear, terror.

یاسمین (*yaſmeen*) Jaſmine or jeſſamine.

یاقوت (*yákoot*) A ruby.

یاور (*yáwur*) An aſſiſtant, a coadjutor, a friend, a companion: *Yáwúri*; aſſiſtance, victory.

یتیم (*yúteem* or *yúteemab*) An orphan, pupil, ward; a fatherleſs boy, a motherleſs kid or other animal; a valuable jewel, an incomparable pearl.

یخ (*yukb*) Ice.

یر (*yud*) The hand; power, vigour; benefit, ſervice.

یزدان (*yuzdán*) God: *Yuzdáni*; divine.

یسار (*yuſár*) The left: *Yuſár* or *Yuſárut*; opulence, affluence.

یعقوب (*Yákoob*) The patriarch Jacob.

یعنی (*yáni*) That is, that is to ſay, viz. to wit, otherwiſe.

یغما (*yughmá*) Plunder, booty, ſpoil.

یقین (*yúkeen*) For a certainty, unqueſtionable, without doubt; death, fate.

یک (*yuk* or *yek*) One, alſo the article *a* or *an*: *Yek-yek*; one by one; corruptedly *ek* and *ek-ek*. A few compounds are formed by prefixing this word to nouns, as *Yek-dil*, (of one heart) unanimous.

یکان (*yékán*, or *yégán*, or *yúgán*) Singly: *Yúgáneb*; ſingle, ſole, ſingular, incomparable, unequalled, having no parallel; alſo, agreed, unanimous: *Yúgánúgi*; concord, unanimity, union, conjunction; ſingularity, unity.

یکایک (*yúká-yuk* or *yek-iyek*) All at once, ſuddenly.

یکبارکی (*yuk-bárgi*) Once, alſo, all at once.

یلجهت

یکجہت (yuk-jibat) Of one accord : *Yuk-jibúti*; unanimity, friendſhip.

یکسان (yuksán) The ſame, alike, all one, equal to, of the ſame order or ſort : *Yuk-ſán-kurna* ; to make alike, to equal, to level : *Yukſáni*; uniformity, parity.

یمن (yúmun) The right hand or ſide ; Arabia Felix : *Yúmn* or *Yúmnut*; felicity, happineſs.

یمین (yúmeen) An oath ; the right hand or ſide ; ſtrength, power.

یوسف (Yúſúf) Joſeph the patriarch (the Adonis of the Eaſt).

یوم (yoam) A day (of twenty-four hours) : *Yómi*; daily, daily pay, proviſions, ſubſiſtence or allowance.

یونان (Yúnán) Greece ; *Yúnáni*; Greek, Grecian.

یونس (Yúnus) Jonas.

یہود (yúhood) A Hebrew, a Jew : *Yúhoodi*; Judaical, a Jew.

THE END OF THE SEVENTH PART.

AN
ACCOUNT

OF THE

PLAN AND CONTENTS

OF THE

NEW HINDVI GRAMMAR AND DICTIONARY,

PROPOSED TO BE PUBLISHED BY

WILLIAM KIRKPATRICK,

Captain in the Service of the Honourable the EAST-INDIA COMPANY,
and PERSIAN SECRETARY to the Commander in Chief in India.

THE work shall consist of EIGHT PARTS or General Divisions.

The first part shall treat very fully, under two distinct sections, of the characters and symbols used in the Hindvi, and of their various powers.

The second part shall treat copiously of the several parts of speech, under the following sections:

Sect. 1. Of Articles	Sect. 6. Of Participles
2. Of Nouns	7. Of Adverbs
3. Of Adjectives	8. Of Conjunctions
4. Of Pronouns	9. Of Prepositions
5. Of Verbs	10. Of Interjections

The third part shall treat largely of the etymology, or derivation and composition of words.

The

The fourth part fhall treat of the fyntax and idiom of the Hindvi, under three fections, viz.

Sect. 1. Of the arrangement, conftruction or pofition of words.

2. Of the agreement, government or regimen of words.

3. Of certain idiomatical forms, under the head of Mifcellaneous Remarks.

The fifth part will contain a copious collection of Hindvi Verbs, derivative and compound, as well as primitive ; of the latter of which alone there will be given near one thoufand, being feven hundred more than Captain Fergufon's Dictionary includes. — This table will confift of fix columns or divifions : in the firft column will be the Infinitive in Nagri characters ; next will follow the Infinitive expreffed, for the greater fatisfaction of the learner, in Roman characters ; in the third column will be given, in Englifh, its fenfe, or various fenfes ; in the fourth column, the fimple Imperative ; in the fifth, the Imperfect ; and in the fixth the Participle will be exhibited. —A great variety of compound Verbs will be alfo inferted in this table.

The fixth part fhall confift of a Vocabulary of pure Hindvi, and fhall contain (exclufive of primitive Verbs, of which none will be inferted in this divifion of the work, and of Compounds and Derivatives, which will be occafionally given) near two thoufand words. — To this part will be added, in Hindvi or Perfian, the names of thofe articles of the Materia Medica which are either produced or procurable in India ; and alfo (principally with a view to the convenience of the military fervants of the Company) a tranflation of certain parts of the articles of war into Perfian and Hindvi. — This abftract was prepared by the author, and firft publifhed at Calcutta in the year 1782, by order of the Governor General and Council.— Befides the profeffional purpofes which it is calculated to anfwer, it will ferve to exemplify, with the other exercifes, feveral of the rules laid down in the grammatical part of the work.

The feventh part will confift of a very copious collection of fuch Perfian and Arabic words as, having been adopted into the Hindvi, are in univerfal ufe.

N. B. All the words given in the two Vocabularies fhall, befides being printed in the characters proper to them, be expreffed, for the more entire fatisfaction of the learner, in the Roman character : in doing which, great care will be taken to convey the proper and precife found of every word.

The

The eighth part shall contain various exercises, or praxes, for the illustration of the rules given in the Grammar: to be divided into six sections, as follow:

Sect. 1. A large collection of familiar phrases ⎫
    2. Some dialogues ⎬ Hindvi and English.
    3. A collection of Hindvi proverbs ⎭
    4. Some tales.
    5. Some letters.
    6. Some poems, from Souda and Wulli.

Of the tales, letters, and poems, some will be accompanied by a translation, and others left for the learner to render into English, by way of lesson or exercise.

At the end will be given an alphabetical index, in Roman characters, of all the words contained in either of the vocabularies, or the table of Hindvi verbs, with references to the page, or part of the work, where every word, with its explanation, is to be found.

At his leisure the author purposes transposing the vocabularies and table of verbs, and forming a copious vocabulary or dictionary, English and Hindvi; wherein, after every English word, the corresponding word or words in Hindvi, Persian or Arabic, will be given in the characters proper to each. As this, however, will be a task of considerable labour, it must unavoidably form a separate publication.

PROPOSALS.

I. The work to be published in parts, and delivered to the subscribers in boards.

II. The price of the whole work (which will form a large quarto volume) to be, to subscribers, sixty sicca rupees.; or six pounds six shillings sterling.

III. The

III. The price of the feveral parts, as delivered feparately, to be regulated, as exactly as poffible, according to the total price of the entire work.

IV. No money to be received but upon delivery of the feveral parts of the work.

It was originally the intention of the author to have publifhed the work in an uniform and entire manner; but, to avoid lofing time, he, foon after his arrival in England, put the Perfian and Arabic vocabulary in the prefs, while the letter-founder was employed upon the Nagri type; which, owing to certain unforefeen, but unavoidable, accidents, is yet unfinifhed. Had it been prepared in time, he meant to have annexed the tranflation of the articles of war to the feventh part, which he now prefents to his fubfcribers, who, he trufts, will not think it very material in what order they receive the divifions of fuch a work as the one juft defcribed, which are not immediately or neceffarily dependant on each other.—The price fixed upon this part is twelve ficca rupees (being the fifth of the price of the entire work), and to fubfcribers in England one pound five fhillings.

JANUARY 20, 1785.

SUBSCRIPTIONS to this work will be received

In LONDON, by Mr. BECKET, BOOKSELLER, Pall-Mall;
At CALCUTTA, by PHILIP DELISLE, Esq. and
　　Mr. JOSEPH COOPER, PRINTER;
At MADRAS, by
And at BOMBAY, by GEORGE KIRKPATRICK, Esq.

Mr. BECKET will deliver the feveral parts of the work as foon after publication as poffible, to the fubfcribers in England; to which end, care will be taken to fupply him, by the earlieft opportunities, with a fufficient number of copies from India, where the work is intended to be completed.

9 783337 299538